INTRODUCTION TO PHONETICS

BY

L. F. BROSNAHAN

Professor of English
University of the South Pacific

AND

BERTIL MALMBERG

Professor of General Linguistics
University of Lund

CAMBRIDGE UNIVERSITY PRESS
Cambridge
London · New York · Melbourne

Published by the Syndics of the Cambridge University Press
The Pitt Building, Trumpington Street, Cambridge CB2 1RP
Bentley House, 200 Euston Road, London NW1 2DB
32 East 57th Street, New York, NY 10022, USA
296 Beaconsfield Parade, Middle Park, Melbourne 3206, Australia

Library of Congress catalogue card number: 75-26277

ISBN 0 521 21100 X hard covers
ISBN 0 521 29042 2 paperback

First published 1970
First paperback edition 1976

This book was originally published by W. Heffer & Sons Ltd, Cambridge.
It was first published by the Cambridge University Press in 1975.

First printed in Great Britain by W. Heffer & Sons Ltd, Cambridge

Reprinted in Great Britain
at the
University Printing House Cambridge
(Euan Phillips, University Printer)

INTRODUCTION TO PHONETICS

CONTENTS

v

FOREWORD

THIS is written as a first book in the study of general phonetics. The emphasis is on the basics, the organs of speech and of hearing, the methods of sound production in the vocal tract, the types of sound used in human languages, and the process of speech perception. The approach is humane and linguistic, with the focus of attention on the tongue and the ear of the phonetician as an investigator of speech rather than on his instruments or his experiments, and with due attention paid to the phoneme and the distinctive feature, the units in that border area where phonetics and the study of languages overlap.

The examples are mainly from the languages of Europe, with English clearly predominant, but we have tried to keep wider horizons in view, as in our simplifying and adapting fundamental ideas of K. L. Pike to set up a general framework for the description of all but the most exotic of human speech sounds, and in giving a more adequate coverage of tones and tone languages than is customary in books of this type.

We hope the book will be helpful, not only to beginning students in phonetics and linguistics, but also to teachers and students in modern languages, to speech therapists and audiologists, to all those, indeed, with an interest in the nature and working of the sound substance of human language.

Phonetics advances by the co-operative efforts of its workers, and often also of those in neighbouring disciplines, in the gathering and sifting of material and of ideas; our major debt for the contents of this introduction is therefore to our predecessors and colleagues, whose work we have built on and whose insights we have used—though perhaps not always in ways they would approve or agree with, and for this the responsibility is, of course, ours. To a few outside the field we are also indebted, to Dr R. A. Brown for saving us from some errors of interpretation of acoustics, and to our secretaries for their valiant assistance in the preparation of the manuscript and of the illustrations.

L. F. B.
B. M.

September 1969

CHAPTER 1

INTRODUCTION

1.1. The Linguistic Symbol

1.10. Human language is essentially a system of communication which depends on the distinctively human ability to form and use symbols. A comprehensive definition of a symbol is by no means easy, but for present purposes, we may describe a language symbol as a structure of two parts, one a stretch of sound or sounds perceptible to the ear, the other a meaning or idea stored in the brain, with these two parts linked or related to one another by what the psychologist calls a process of association. Thus in English, the stretch of sound [hɔːs],[1] a stretch which is traditionally represented in the written language by the sequence of letters *horse*, is one part, the meaning, "equine quadruped," is the other, and each is associated with the other to make up a symbol.[2]

Various names have been used to designate the two parts of the symbol: *signifiant*, form, expression, name, etc., for the perceptible part, and *signifié*, meaning, content, sense, concept, etc., for the intangible part. We shall use *expression* and *content*. Then the expression [hɔːs] is associated with the content "equine quadruped" to form a linguistic symbol in the English language. It may be represented in a diagram as

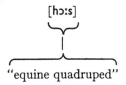

[hɔːs]

"equine quadruped"

in which the association between the expression and the content is represented by the vertical line.

---

[1] Symbols in this typeface are phonetic symbols, and represent sounds. Those used here represent the sounds of the standard British English pronunciation of the word *horse*.

[2] In modern linguistic theory the term *sign* is also used.

1

1.11. In languages in which a system of orthography is in use, the linguistic symbols may be represented by a series of characters or letters, which, by being imposed on paper, or wood, or stone, or by various other means may be given a form which is perceptible to the eye. Thus the English symbol we have been discussing may be represented by the sequence of letters *h o r s e*. The results of the use of such a system may be of rather different types. The spelling *horse* may in some circumstances or to some readers simply represent the expression [hɔːs]. In this case the nature of the symbol is not changed in any essential respect; the reader simply interprets the sequence of letters as the stretch of sound forming the expression, and to him the content is still associated with this expression. In diagrammatic form, this may be shown as

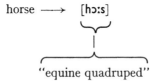

in which the arrow represents the interpretation of the reader.

In other circumstances, the spelling *horse* may, as a visual pattern, replace entirely the sound expression [hɔːs]: a practised reader may associate the spelling *horse* with the content "equine quadruped" directly, and not through the sound sequence. In this case, the spelling becomes the expression, and what is essentially a new symbol is formed. Diagrammatically, this may be shown as

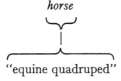

The stretch of sounds which constituted the original expression has now been by-passed, and no longer forms part of the symbol. The new symbol has what may be called a *graphic* rather than a sound expression, and as such its study falls outside the field of the phonetician.

1.12. The association between the expression and the content is in almost all cases in a language of an arbitrary and conventional nature. There is nothing in or about the expression [hɔːs] which renders it peculiarly or inherently suitable for association with the

2

1.1. THE LINGUISTIC SYMBOL

content "equine quadruped," nor is there anything in or about this content which renders it peculiarly or inherently suitable for association with the expression [hɔːs]. In fact, in another English symbol, an identical expression, [hɔːs], is associated with a very different content, "having a harsh or husky voice," and in other languages the same or very similar contents are associated with quite different expressions, in French [ʃval] or *cheval*, in German [pfeːrt] or *pferd*, and so on.

1.13. No upper limits to the length or extent of a linguistic symbol need be set. A stretch of sound such as occurs in an utterance by one speaker, or in a sermon, or in an American filibustering speech, even though it may be interrupted by pauses of the speaker, may be considered as forming, as a whole, a symbol. Such a symbol may clearly be very complex, but it is still a symbol formed by an association of an expression and a content. Or it may be viewed, just as validly, as being made up of sequences of other symbols. This reveals a characteristic feature of the organization of language: the symbols of a language are combined in one or other of a number of conventional patterns or structures to almost any extent or complexity required by the user.

Thus an English utterance such as, for example, *the boys are playing in the street* may be viewed as a single symbol or may be analysed into a considerable number of symbols. Thus *the boys* forms a symbol, as does *are playing in the street*, or *are playing*, or *are*, or *play*, or *ing*, and so on. Each of these units has an expression in the form of a stretch of sound and an associated content in the form of a concept or meaning, and thus falls within the description of a symbol above. These symbols have certain possibilities of occurrence relative to one another. Thus *the street* occurs as a symbol, but not *street the*, *-s* can occur with *boy* or with *street*, but not with *the* or *in*, *the boys are* and *are the boys* both occur, but not *the are boys*, and so on. Further, each of these symbols is a member of a class of symbols which can replace it in its particular position in the sentence. In this sentence, *boys* may be replaced by *girls, dogs, children I saw, giraffes from the zoo*, and numerous other symbols, but not by, for instance, the symbols *is, over, to read*, and a great many others.

1.14. The study of language is the province of the science of linguistics, and a great deal of the activity in this science has been

3

toward the investigation of the types of phenomena indicated in the preceding paragraph. This is the study of *grammar*, comprising both the study of the simple symbols, *morphology*, and of their combinations, *syntax*. In a very real sense grammar is the core of the subject: the symbolic nature of language is its most essential and characteristic feature. But the symbol is by definition a bipartite unit, and to some extent each of the parts of the symbol may be studied independently of the other. The branches of linguistics which concern themselves with these topics are *phonology* and *semantics*, phonology being the study of the expression, and semantics the study of the content.

1.2. The Study of the Expression

1.20.   The expression may be studied under two aspects. The first is that of the expression from the viewpoint of language, that is, the expression as the carrier of an associated meaning, and functioning as an integral part of language as a symbolic system. In this aspect, the interest of the scholar is in the nature and organization of the expression: the units into which it can be analysed, the relations between these units, the functions which they perform, and the patterns and hierarchies in which they occur.

This is the study of the *expression form*. The basic units here are the *phonemes*, the minimum distinctive units into which the expression chain can be segmented. The concept of the phoneme is a fundamental one in modern linguistics, and will be discussed in a later chapter (§ 10.1 f.). A general term for this study is *phonemics* (though occasionally *phonematics* is used); it is a humanistic study; and its methods, like those of morphology and syntax, have some affinity with the methods of such disciplines as logic, cultural anthropology, and sociology.

1.21.   The second part of the linguistic expression is that of the physical material or *substance* in which the expression form is realized. In a speech act, a linguistically ordered selection of phonemes, which constitutes the expression form, is realized or manifested in sound by articulatory processes in the speaker, transmitted to the hearer, and perceived by him. The expression substance, as it is termed, thus varies in nature with the stage in the process. It is convenient to distinguish five stages. Stage one is the innervation, the emission of patterns of nerve impulses from the brain through a network of nerve fibres to the vocal apparatus, i.e. the organs of the chest, throat and mouth concerned with speech. Stage two is the articulation, the series of movements of muscles and organs of the vocal apparatus which result in the production of audible sound. Stage three is the complex of continually varying sound waves which spread out through the air surrounding the speaker's head. Stage four is the hearing, the series of processes which take place in the ear and the organs just behind it, when the sound waves of stage three impinge on the eardrum. Stage five is again in the nervous system, but this time on the receptive side: the patterns of nerve impulses which convey to the brain information from the ear about the nature of the sound waves striking it.

The expression substance is the basic field of study of *phonetics*. Phonetics is accordingly concerned (1) with the operations which go on in the nerves and muscles of the speech mechanism of the speaker during the process of realization of the expression form, (2) with the nature and characteristics of the sound waves which are emitted by the speaker, (3) with the processes of hearing which go on in the auditory apparatus up to the point where the expression form is abstracted from the expression substance, and finally (4) with the relations between the data of each of these topics.

This is, it is true, a somewhat idealized description of the subject matter of phonetics; neither the beginning of stage one nor the end of stage five, which must both be closely connected with a centre or centres of the brain concerned with language, are able as yet to be delimited. And further, since both stage one and stage five take place entirely within the living human brain, they are peculiarly difficult to investigate; practically all the effort put into phonetic investigation has therefore been directed towards the understanding of the events of stages two, three and four.

1.22. Since the expression substance is made up of phenomena in the physical world—sound waves, muscular movements, nerve impulses—it is evident that many of the methods used to investigate this substance will be borrowed from the sciences which deal with acoustics on the one hand, and with anatomy and physiology on the other. This part of phonetics is thus in a certain sense a 'natural science,' though at the same time the phenomena examined are part of language, and consequently a humanistic study in that they relate to the behaviour of man in the community. For the analysis of sounds and of bodily processes in its investigation of speech phenomena, modern phonetics uses all existing methods and technical devices which seem appropriate, and sometimes invents new ones. It is in fact hardly possible to point to any special methods or instruments which are exclusively used in phonetics, though some are admittedly of little or no interest outside phonetics.

1.3. The Methods of Phonetics

1.30. It is useful to distinguish between phonetic studies carried out without other instruments of analysis[1] than the human senses, and such as are based upon the witness of registering or computing machines and technical analysing devices.

From the beginning of phonetics the phonetician has relied mainly on what he could feel of his own speech, and on what he could hear both of his own and of his subject's speech. By training and practice he gains a high degree of conscious control over the muscular functioning of his vocal apparatus, and by experience he acquires considerable skill in inferring from the qualities of the heard sound the nature of the articulations producing it. In so far as these skills are an integral part of it, phonetics is an art rather than a science, and an art which must be learnt, as any other, by a period of apprenticeship. Though there are today areas of phonetics in which useful work can and is being done without such skills, a competence in them is still essential for the bulk of ordinary work on the sounds of speech, the comparison of languages, dialect study, and so on.

1.31. Instrumental methods deriving from physiology and physics were introduced into phonetics in the second half of last century, in order to supplement and indeed to rectify the impressions deriving from the human senses, especially the auditory impressions, since these were held to be affected by the limitations of the perceptual mechanism, and in general, subjective. This is, of course, true, but the modern view is rather that the processes of speaking and of hearing, on which all language is ultimately based, are in practice controlled by the human sensory apparatus—the speaker both feels and hears proprioceptively what he is saying, and the listener hears

---

[1] The use of such devices as the gramophone or the tape-recorder does not, of course, imply in itself any instrumental analysis of the speech recorded, but simply serves the purpose of facilitating the speech analysis and conserving a replica of the speech specimens used.

ceteroceptively what is said—so that the limitations and characteristics of this apparatus are an integral given in phonetics. Phonetics, in other words, is not primarily the study of processes in the vocal apparatus or in the hearing apparatus or of sound waves as simple physical events, but the study of these phenomena as limited, modified, or distorted by the ways in which the human brain perceives and controls them. Hence the conception of rectifying the results of its operation is today rather regarded as based on a misunderstanding of the processes of speech.

The concept of supplementing the data available from sensory analysis by data available from instrumental analysis is, however, a perfectly legitimate one in the phonetician's investigation of the expression substance. And at the same time the use of instruments is valuable in ascertaining the nature of the limitations and characteristics of the human sensory apparatus by providing finer and more detailed analysis against which sensory analyses can be assessed. For these and similar purposes, instrumental methods are widely and justifiably used in modern phonetics. The "subjective" methods of analysis by sensory impression and the "objective" methods of analysis by instruments are complementary and not oppositive to one another.

1.32. In a general way, the introduction of machines, of measurements, and of instrumental analysis into phonetics has resulted in their use for detailed study of many of the phenomena which are present in the sound wave or in the articulatory process at any given moment, and in the changes in these phenomena from moment to moment. This is, strictly, an *instrumental* method of study, though it has often been called *experimental*. Until recently the two concepts have not been clearly distinguished, but phoneticians are now tending to refer to this type of investigation with the assistance of instruments as *instrumental phonetics*, and to restrict the use of the term *experimental phonetics*, to the type of investigation which has recently become popular as a result of the development of methods of reproducing the sounds of speech by artificial synthesis. By these methods, the phonetician has become able to experiment by adding, changing, or removing one or more features in a sound complex while keeping the rest of the features in it constant. The results of this sort of investigation have been very suggestive with regard to the mutual relations between various features of the sound wave and their role in the realization of the expression form. It is also quite obviously possible to experiment with various modes of functioning and operation of the vocal apparatus, and such work may also be properly termed experimental phonetics.

1.4. Phonetics and Linguistics

1.40. The above survey has shown that phonetics, both as an art and as a science, is primarily concerned with the expression level[1] of language. Because of the symbolic nature of language, however, it is hardly possible to consider this level without reference to the content level. Phonetics is obliged to take the content level into consideration, because, at any stage of the analysis, part of the phonetician's concern is with the effect which the expression unit he is examining and its different characteristics have on meaning. Only meaningful sound sequences are regarded as speech, and the science of phonetics, in principle at least, is concerned only with such sounds produced by a human vocal apparatus as are, or may be, carriers of organized information in language.

It follows from this that phonetics and phonetic analysis are very important in the study of language. An understanding of them is a prerequisite to any adequate understanding of the structure or working of language. No kind of linguistic study can be made without constant consideration of the material on the expression level. This is equally true of what has come to be called the traditional or 19th-century linguistics, with its historical or diachronic orientation and its concentration on language change and development—in which *sound-change* and the so-called *sound-laws*, the study of which might be termed *evolutive phonetics*, are central problems —and of the different modern schools or approaches which prefer to lay stress on language as a synchronic phenomenon and as a tool for communication. It is evident, indeed, that phonetics is a basic branch of the science of linguistics: neither linguistic theory nor linguistic practice can do without phonetics, and no language description is complete without phonetics.

---

[1] *Level* is here and frequently in linguistics used to refer to a layer in one or other conception of a language as a structure of layers in an abstract dimension. The two levels forming the layered structure of language here are those of expression and content.

1.5. Phonetics and other Fields

1.50. Apart from its key position in any kind of scientific analysis of language, whether synchronic or diachronic, phonetics plays an important part in numerous practical applications of linguistics. A few may be mentioned.

A knowledge of the structure of sound systems and of the acoustic properties and the production of speech is indispensable in the teaching of foreign languages. The teacher has to know the starting point, which is the sound system and the pronunciation of the pupil's mother tongue, as well as the aim of his teaching, which is a mastery of the sound system and the pronunciation of the language to be learnt. He must be able to point out the differences between these two, and to arrange adequate training exercises. Articulatory training and ear training are both equally important in modern language teaching. The introduction of technical equipment—gramophone records, tape-recorders, language laboratories, etc.—has brought about a revolution in the teaching of the pronunciation of foreign languages.

1.51. To the speech and voice therapist, a solid knowledge of phonetics is likewise essential. It is impossible to treat speech defects without a clear understanding of all the different aspects of normal speech and normal language. Phoniatrics and logopedics belong to phonetics and to linguistics just as much as, if not more than to medicine. All kinds of training of the voice and of articulation, whether the treatment of pathological defects or simply the development of better speech habits for public speakers, actors, broadcasters, etc., must be based on knowledge and experience gained in the study of the speech organs and of the acoustic and auditory characteristics of the sounds used in speech.

1.52. Another practical application of phonetics in medical and therapeutic work is within the field of audiology. For the development of adequate ear-training exercises and hearing tests for the hard of hearing, as well as for the construction of technical devices to facilitate the perception of speech by the defective ear, a thorough knowledge of the acoustic properties of speech sounds and of their auditory effect is essential. This is equally the case in the teaching of speech to the deaf, whether such therapy is directed at the training of residual hearing or at the teaching of the spoken language exclusively or mainly by articulatory training, the traditional method of teaching speech to the so-called deaf-mute children. With regard to the former, recent discoveries in the field of acoustic phonetics have established a firm basis for the practice of ear training with small children, in order to make such residual hearing as they may have (normally in the lower register of the tone scale) useful for language learning. The acoustic analysis of speech sounds has shown why, and to what extent, such training is possible and may be successful.

1.53. In recent years, phonetics and phonemics have become important in a number of technical fields connected with communications, those concerned, for example, with the development and improvement of sound-recording and reproducing apparatus, of telegraph and telephone systems, and so on. As a result, some work of considerable importance for phonetics, especially on the acoustic side, has been done by sound or communications engineers, often, of course, in collaboration with phoneticians. There are many indications of the directions of further development in this and closely related fields. Today a number of machines have been constructed which are able to synthesize with a high degree of intelligibility the sounds of human speech, and in the experimental stage are devices for "reading" the printed page, i.e. for converting the printed symbols or letters into synthetic speech. A little further away as yet, but apparently well within the bounds of possibility is the automatic or phonetic typewriter, which will convert speech directly into printed words on paper. Because of the obvious practical importance of advances in these fields, it is certain that further collaboration will develop between phonetics and sound engineering, to the mutual benefit of each.

1.54. The field of phonetics is thus becoming wider and tending to extend over the limits originally set by its purely linguistic applications. On the other hand, the growing interest in phonetics is doubtless partly due to increasing recognition of the central position of language in every kind of human activity. It is important, however, we believe, that the phonetician should remain a linguist and look upon his science primarily as a study of the spoken form of language. It is its application to linguistic phenomena, linguistic distinctions, and linguistic structures that makes phonetics a humanistic science in the proper sense of the word, notwithstanding its increasing use and increasing need of technical methods, and in spite of its developing practical applications.

CHAPTER 2

THE PHYSICS OF SOUND

2.1. Sound

2.10. Sound is, strictly speaking, the cortical interpretation of vibrations perceived through the sense of hearing, but by extension the term is used to refer to vibrations which might be so interpreted. Not all similar vibrations are perceived by the human hearing apparatus; such as do fall within its general range are called *sound waves*. The most common medium for transmission of such vibrations is air, but sound waves may be transmitted through other media, through any medium in fact which has mass and elasticity, i.e. the quality of inertia or resistance to movement and the tendency to return to its original condition if disturbed.

2.11. Sound waves in air usually emanate from a vibrating body, the source. As an example we shall consider a tuning fork and for simplicity assume that its prongs are vibrating continuously outward and inward in the simplest way possible in theory. When these prongs move outward they compress the neighbouring particles of air and this compression is transmitted outward through further neighbouring particles. When the prongs move inward the particles near them move back again causing a rarefaction and this rarefaction is transmitted outward over the same path as the preceding compression. A sound wave, thus, consists of a series of alternate compressions and rarefactions in the air spreading spherically from the source. It is termed a longitudinal progressive wave, *longitudinal* since the movement of the air particles is along the line of propagation of the wave, and *progressive* since the compressions and rarefactions travel outwards.

2.2. Sine and Complex Waves

2.20. To represent the sound wave so generated we may measure the variations of pressure in the air with the lapse of time as the compressions and rarefactions of our sound wave pass any point, and record our measurements in a diagram (Fig. 2.1).

11

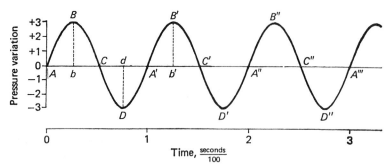

Fig. 2.1. The sine wave

The result is a smooth curve with alternate peaks and hollows. This curve is of exactly the same nature as that which a mathematician would obtain by plotting a graph of the values of the sine of an angle increasing indefinitely from 0°, and for this reason it is known as a sine curve, or a sinusoid. The dimensions of a sine curve may, of course, vary considerably, since these depend merely on the length selected for the units on the vertical and horizontal axes, but its nature remains constant in virtue of the fact that it is a sine curve. A sound wave in which the pressure variation with time is represented by a sine curve is called a *sine wave* or a *sinusoid*.

2.21. Our measuring instrument records that, as the sound wave passes, the pressure of the air rises from normal at point A to a peak or maximum at point B—the centre of the compression— then falls through normal, C, to a low point or minimum, D—the centre of the rarefaction—and rises again to normal, A'. From this point the process begins again, exactly repeating itself. The sequence of events represented by the line passing through $ABCDA'$ is known as a *cycle*, and the number of cycles in a given unit of time, usually a second, is the *frequency* of the wave. In our example we have three cycles in three-hundredths a second, equivalent to 100 cycles in one second, or a frequency of 100 c/s. The abbreviation c/s stands for 'cycles per second.'

The lapse of time at our measuring point between the arrival of any two successive maxima of pressure, i.e. between points A and B' or between B' and B'', is known as the *periodic time* or simply the *period*. The same time will elapse between the arrival of any two corresponding points in successive waves of the motion, e.g. between A and A', between C and C', etc. By inspection, this time

12

in our example is 1/100 second, or one centisecond. The period is the reciprocal of the frequency; if the frequency (F) of a wave is 256 c/s, the period (P) is 1/256 second, and so on. In formulae,

$$F = \frac{1}{P} \text{ and } P = \frac{1}{F}.$$

The maximum extent of the change of pressure from the normal in any cycle is the *pressure amplitude*, or simply the *amplitude*, of the wave. This is represented by the distances $B - b$, $B' - b'$, etc., or by the distances $D - d$, $D' - d'$, etc., since in our example as in any sine wave the extent of the rise in pressure above normal is the same as the extent of the fall in pressure below normal. The amplitude is a measure of the strength of the wave, the power of a progressive wave, i.e. the rate of flow of energy past a measuring point, being proportional to the square of the amplitude.[1]

Another measurement of importance is the *wavelength*, the distance between any two corresponding points in successive waves of the motion. To measure this we should need a device which would record the pressure variation at one given instant along the line of propagation of the wave. We could then represent the pressure variation with distance (not with time) on a graph. The resultant pressure-distance curve would be of the same nature as the pressure-time curve in Fig. 2.1, i.e. would be a sinusoid, but on it we could read the wavelength from the scale of values along the horizontal axis.

The wavelength can, however, easily be calculated. Since the speed of propagation of any sound wave in air may be considered to be 1,100 feet (330 metres) per second—it varies slightly with different temperature, pressure, etc.—and the wave in Fig. 2.1 has compressions 1/100 second apart, there must be 100 of them in 1,100 feet, so that they are 11 feet apart. The wavelength is thus 11 feet in this example. If the frequency were 256 c/s, the wavelength (λ) would be very nearly 4 feet 4 inches, and so on, according to the formula $\lambda = \frac{C}{F}$, where C is the speed of propagation of sound.

2.22. In Fig. 2.1 we have plotted pressure change against time. But if we had an instrument capable of recording the movement

---

[1] Following usual practice we distinguish *energy* as the ability to do work and *power* as the rate of work, i.e. the rate of use or flow of energy.

of a tiny particle of air while it was disturbed by the wave motion, we could diagram the position changes of this particle against time. Such a diagram is known as a displacement-time curve. If we had adopted the convention of representing a forward displacement by a point above, and a backward displacement by a point below, the time axis, it would have the same nature as the curve in Fig. 2.1, but if we had recorded it on the same time scale as Fig. 2.1, we would observe that the peaks and hollows of the displacement curve came at the points where the pressure was normal. The period and the frequency would be the same, but the amplitude in this case would be the maximum extent of displacement of our particle, quite a different thing from the maximum extent of pressure change, and occurring one quarter of a cycle after the latter.

From the displacement amplitude and the frequency—and a few other factors such as the pressure, temperature, etc.—we can calculate what the acoustician calls the *intensity* of the wave. With this term we must not confuse the popular use of the words 'intense' or 'intensity' with regard to sound, since these refer to the purely subjective impression of something similar to if not identical with loudness. (Cf. § 8.30 ff.) The acoustician's intensity is the power flowing through a unit of area at right angles to the direction of propagation of a progressive wave, and this quantity is proportional both to the square of the displacement amplitude times the square of the frequency and to the square of the pressure amplitude. Since the latter formula is simpler to work with, we shall normally use the term *amplitude* to refer to pressure amplitude.[1]

2.23. If near to our original perfect tuning fork emitting a sinusoidal wave with a frequency of 100 c/s we place another emitting a wave with a frequency of 300 c/s and, say, half the amplitude of the first wave, the compressions and rarefactions from the two

---

[1] In acoustics, measurements of intensity and of amplitude are often expressed in terms of decibels (db), the decibel scale being a logarithmic form of expression of the ratio of a given intensity to that of a specific reference intensity. An intensity ten times as great as another is 10 db above the latter, an intensity a hundred times as great is 20 db above, and so on. By extension, amplitudes are expressed in decibels in terms of their corresponding power of intensity values; an amplitude ten times greater than another (and thus equivalent to an intensity one hundred times greater) is also said to be 20 db above this other: and so on.

waves will mingle, and the pressure from moment to moment at our measuring point will be the resultant of the two pressures. We may diagram one case of this, a case in which a specific time relationship exists between the two waves, in Fig. 2.2, where A represents the pressure variation due to the wave from the first fork at the measuring point, B that from the second at the same point, and C that resulting from the addition of the two. The wave C is then a *complex* wave, that is, any wave which is not sinusoidal.

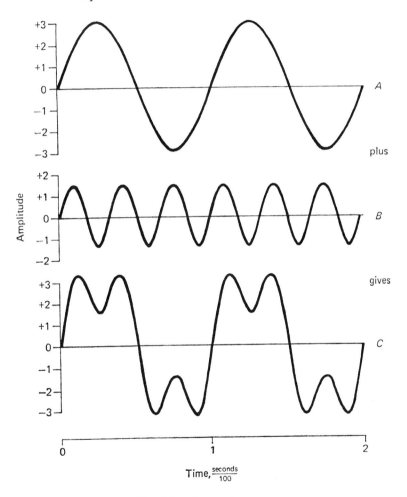

Fig. 2.2. A complex wave

15

2.3. Analysis of Sound Waves

2.30. We have now reached one of the bases of the science of acoustics, namely Fourier's theorem, which for our purposes may be interpreted as stating that any periodic wave consists exclusively of one or more component sine waves impressed on the medium of propagation. By the mathematical treatment usually known as Fourier or harmonic analysis any exactly repetitive wave can be resolved into a series of sinusoidal components. The frequencies of these components are always integral multiples of the frequency of repetition of the original complex wave, and this latter frequency, known as the *fundamental frequency*, is always the highest common factor of the frequencies of the component sinusoids. The sinusoidal components are known as *harmonics,* the frequency of the second, harmonic 2, being twice that of the fundamental, that of the third, harmonic 3, three times this, and so on. The term 'first harmonic' is nowadays not normally used.

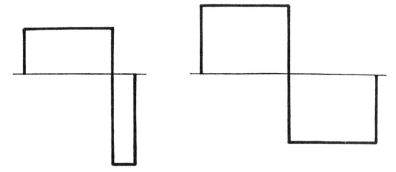

Fig. 2.3. Examples of square waves

In any case, not all the possible harmonics need be present. The wave A in Fig. 2.4 has by inspection a period of exact repetition of each cycle of 10 milliseconds, or a fundamental frequency of 100 c/s. By harmonic analysis this wave can be shown to consist of three sinusoidal components: harmonic 2 at 200 c/s, harmonic 3 at 300 c/s, and harmonic 5 at 500 c/s. Not only is harmonic 4 missing —there is no power at 400 c/s—but also there is no component with a frequency of 100 c/s. Nevertheless, a listener hearing the sound wave corresponding to A will hear a pitch of about 100 c/s. This is due to the properties of the ear, which in this case produces,

16

apparently in itself, a component—technically termed a *difference tone* (§ 9.21)—at approximately 100 c/s. It is convenient therefore to define *pitch* as the perceived impression of the frequency of repetition of a wave.

2.31. The possibility of analysis of a complex wave into a series of harmonic components is a fundamental mathematical concept which is used in acoustic phonetics, and it is worthwhile discussing it briefly. In the first place harmonic analysis can be applied only to waves which are periodic, i.e. in which the wave is exactly the same in every period, has been so, and will be so for all time—"nothing less than infinite time," as Joos (1948, 31) puts it, "will give perfect concentration of energy into discrete frequencies."

Secondly, any wave that is periodic, no matter how apparently complex in shape, is analysable into sinusoidal components, though in some cases the actual computation necessary may be too lengthy to be carried out: square waves such as in Fig. 2.3 are composed of an infinity of such components.

A third feature contributing to the importance of harmonic analysis is the fact that at any point the total variation of pressure with time in a complex wave is the algebraic sum of the variations produced by its individual components. At any stage from the generation to the reception of a complex wave, we can study each component separately and add up the results to give the total picture.

Lastly, as we shall note below (§ 2.50), perception in the sense of hearing seems to be very similar to harmonic analysis, so that the usefulness of this analysis may extend as far as the brain itself.

2.4. Phase

2.40. In Fig. 2.4, at the beginning of the cycle of the complex wave *A* each of the three component waves *B*, *C*, *D*, is at the same point in its own cycle: the air pressure is normal and about to increase as a compression passes the measuring point. Technically we say that at this instant the three waves are *in phase*, phase being defined as the stage of the cycle of vibration at a given instant. At a following instant, e.g. one millisecond later, in waves *C* and *D* the points of maximum pressure have passed, at different times in each case, while in wave *B* this point is not yet reached. The waves are then *out of phase*, or have *different phases*.

17

If we now alter the relative phases of our waves B, C, D, to those of B', C', D', the shape of the complex wave resulting as A' appears quite different. But a listener hearing the wave represented as A' will not distinguish it from that represented as A. The reason seems to be that the ear does not use the phases of components to distinguish between complex waves; in this case it analyses A' into B', C', D', with the same frequencies and amplitudes as B, C, D,

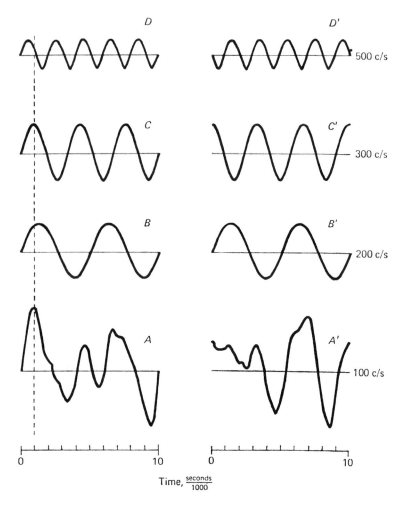

Fig. 2.4. Phase

18

and neglects their phase differences.[1] In phonetics, therefore, we may also neglect phase differences.

2.5. The Spectrum

2.50. The exclusion of phase leaves us with the frequency, or its reciprocal, the period, and the amplitude, or its derivate, the power, as the features of phonetic relevance. The ear appears to act as a practical harmonic analyzer (§ 9.2 f.): provided that they are not too numerous or too weak, the ear can distinguish the sinusoidal components of a complex wave, hearing each of them as a *pure tone*, and form an estimate of the relative strengths of each. On this assumption, known as Ohm's Acoustical Law, the harmonic analysis of a complex wave into components of varying frequency and amplitude gives us the information which is passed to the brain, and gives it to us in manipulable quantities. Thus if the sound wave corresponding to C in Fig. 2.2 strikes the eardrum, the information passed to the brain may be represented diagrammatically as Fig. 2.5*A*.

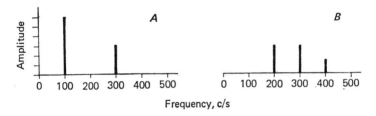

Fig. 2.5. Line spectra

Such a diagram we may call a *spectrum*. The frequency scale is along the horizontal, and the amplitude scale along the vertical axis. Similarly, Fig. 2.5*B* is the spectrum of wave *A* and also the spectrum of wave *A'* in Fig. 2.4 since the only difference between these two is in the relative phases of their components, and phase is not represented in the spectrum. Spectra such as these show that the power of the sound wave is exclusively present at certain definite positions in the frequency scale, i.e. there is no power at any point between these positions. This type of spectrum is known as a *line*

[1] There is good evidence, however, that the ear makes use of phase in locating the direction of a source of sound waves.

spectrum, and results only from a wave which is periodic, i.e. exactly repetitive (§ 2.31). Such waves, of course, do not exist, but in practice we assume that reasonable approximations to periodicity in the cycles of a wave do occur.

2.51.   When the power in a sound wave is not concentrated into certain discrete frequencies, we have what is called a *continuous spectrum*. As the term implies, such a spectrum indicates that some acoustic power is spread over an infinity of frequencies, though this may be an infinitesimal amount save at certain ranges of the frequency scale. A continuous spectrum always results from the analysis of a sound wave which is not periodic. Such an analysis cannot, of course, be done by means of Fourier's theorem, since to do so we must assume that the wave to be analysed is periodic. Analyses of non-periodic sound waves are made thus either by experimental means or by another mathematical treatment using a concept known as the Fourier Integral. Both of these methods give continuous, not line, spectra.

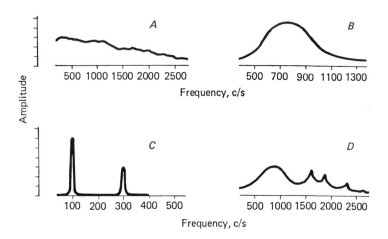

Fig. 2.6.   Examples of continuous spectra

In Fig. 2.6 examples of continuous spectra are depicted. *A* represents an apparently random distribution of power, *B* a common type of continuous spectrum in which most of the power is concentrated within a definite range, *C* the type of spectrum resulting from the experimental analysis of the sound of two ⋅ctual—and

20

very poor—tuning forks vibrating simultaneously at 100 c/s and 300 c/s—this spectrum may be compared with that of Fig. 2.5A which results from the theoretical analysis of the wave from two perfect tuning forks vibrating at the same frequencies—and D a mixture of a random distribution of power over a wide range of frequency and a few concentrations of it in small ranges of frequency.

2.52. We are now able to make a rough distinction between musical sounds and noises, the former having a "smooth, regular, and pleasing character with an assignable pitch . . ." and the latter "a rough, irregular, unpleasant character and no assignable pitch..." (Wood, 1940, 332). Pitch is dependent on an approximation to exact repetitiveness of the cycles of a sound wave (§ 2.30), and where a sound wave has this, its spectrum will show correspondingly an approximation to a line spectrum, for example, as spectrum C in Fig. 2.6. On the other hand, no assignable pitch indicates that the sound wave is not characterized by such repetitiveness, and its spectrum accordingly will not reveal concentration of power into discrete ranges of frequency but dispersion of power over wide regions of the frequency scale, as exemplified in spectra A and B of Fig. 2.6. The classification of the former as musical sound and the latter as noise is largely subjective, since in practice the two types of spectrum merge into one another through a sort of borderland, and since some spectra may be viewed as composed of both types, as D in Fig. 2.6.

In this case the impression will probably be of a musical sound with a background of random noise—or vice versa, according to the direction of the listener's attention.

2.6. The Source of Sound Waves

2.60. We may consider the processes in a body acting as a source of sound waves.

If, for example, a tuning fork is struck, a certain amount of energy is transmitted to it and stored in its vibration, in the motion and elastic deformation of its prongs. The vibrations of the fork set up sound waves in the surrounding air, and the fork is said to be radiating or emitting acoustic power. The rate of radiation of power at any moment is proportional to the amount of energy stored in the fork at that moment. In the case of a good tuning fork, the power output is practically all concentrated at one point in the frequency scale, and this frequency is called the *natural frequency* of the fork.

A tuning fork is, however, rather exceptional among sources of sound waves in that it can usually be considered to emit all its power in a simple sine wave at one frequency. Practically all other sources of sound waves emit complex waves. Two major types may be distinguished.

2.61. If a clarinet is blown on a steady note, energy is continually being transmitted from the breath through the reed to the air in the body of the instrument, and stored in the form of vibration of the air particles. It is this vibration that induces sound waves travelling outwards in the surrounding air.

The vibration of the air in a clarinet is, however, not so simple as the vibration in a tuning fork. The air tends to vibrate in several different ways and the sound wave emitted is a complex one. If we analyse this wave into a Fourier series we find that it is composed of a number of sine-wave components at differing frequencies, these being the harmonics of the complex wave (Fig. 2.7). Each harmonic component is the result of a *mode of vibration* of the air in the clarinet, a mode of vibration being any possible simple sinusoidal way in which that air can vibrate.

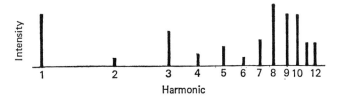

Fig. 2.7.   Spectrum of clarinet (after Miller)

These modes of vibration of a body are, save for their frequency relationship (§ 2.30), quite independent of one another. In any particular example some may be missing, and whether one is present or not has no effect on the presence or absence of another. In our example all harmonics up to the twelfth are present; further analysis would probably reveal higher ones. The amplitude of each harmonic may vary considerably; here the fundamental contains about 15 per cent of the power in the wave, harmonics 2 to 7 have each relatively little power, but harmonics 8, 9, and 10 quite a considerable amount between them, about 50 per cent of that in the whole wave. In general, the differences in the qualities of the sounds of various musical instruments arise from the different numbers and different relative amplitudes of the harmonics produced in each type of instrument.

2.62. The other major type of sound wave source is that emitting a sound wave which cannot be considered as approximating periodicity, i.e. one giving a noise spectrum (§ 2.52). Examples are the sound produced when a falling object such as a rock or a piece of wood strikes the ground, or when a jet of air impinges against a hard surface. In the former case the impact sets the object (and the ground) vibrating, but the vibrations are generally quite irregular (i.e. not repetitive), unstable, and occurring at an infinity of frequencies. The object has, in other words, an infinity of modes of vibration. In the second case we have likewise an impact of the jet of air and resulting vibrations in that jet of air but also turbulence and eddying in the area of the impact arising from friction between the air particles and the surface. The eddying results in pressure disturbances which are propagated in the surrounding air as sound waves (§ 2.11). Such sound waves are likewise spread over a very wide range of frequencies.

2.63. Any body allowed to vibrate at its natural frequency or frequencies is said to be in a state of free vibration. The characteristics of the free vibration of a body, and hence the type of spectrum of its output wave, depend on several factors. In the case of a tuning fork, the main factors are the size of the vibrating unit and its elasticity. Other factors being equal, an increase in the size or a decrease in the elasticity results in a lowering of the frequency of free vibration. In the case of a body of air, its size, shape, density, and the nature and extent of its connexions, if any, with other bodies of air are all important. The effects of these factors on the natural frequency of a body of air are complex and interrelated, but, in general, an increase in the size or volume of a body of air, or a decrease in the area of the orifice(s) to it, lowers the natural frequency of that body of air, and conversely.

The free vibrations of a body will gradually die away and the power output decrease as the energy stored in the body is radiated away in the form of sound waves and the body returns to its state of rest. The decay in the amplitude of the vibrations of the body and in the amplitude of the radiated sound waves is known as *damping*. A body in which the power output decreases rapidly when it is in a state of free vibration is said to be heavily damped—most sources of noise spectrums fall into this class—while a body in which the power output decreases relatively slowly while it is in a state of free vibration is said to be lightly damped—a tuning fork is a good example.

2.7. Response and Resonance

2.70. Any body which can act as a source of sound waves also has the property of absorbing energy from sound waves striking it—technically: *incident* sound waves—storing this energy by vibrating, and radiating it again in the form of sound waves set up in the surrounding air by this vibration. This reaction of a body to incident sound waves, i.e. the absorption, storage and radiation of energy, is known as *response*; it varies according to the characteristics of the body (and its surroundings) and according to the spectrum of the incident waves. To obviate the latter of these variables in the following we shall assume as a standard stimulus an incident wave with the same power at all frequencies.

2.71. Now the characteristics of a body responding to such a standard stimulus are similar to those it possesses when acting purely as a freely vibrating source of sound waves. This is basically due to the fact that in both cases the process of storage and emission of energy is the same; the only difference is in the manner in which the energy is transmitted to the body.

Thus a tuning fork which radiates practically all its energy at one frequency (its natural frequency, § 2.60), and radiates a negligible quantity at all other frequencies will also respond to incident acoustic power practically only at one frequency, and will respond negligibly to incident power at all other frequencies. The body of air in the clarinet discussed above (§ 2.61) will, on the other hand, respond to incident acoustic power at several frequencies, those corresponding to its several modes of vibration, and will hardly respond at all to acoustic power at other frequencies.

A frequency at which a maximum of energy is absorbed and radiated is known as a *resonant frequency*, and the responding body is said to *resonate*, or act as a *resonator* or have a *mode of resonance* at that frequency. Strictly speaking, the natural and resonant frequencies of a body do not coincide exactly, but for practical purposes we can neglect the difference between them.

2.72. As a result of the similarity of the two processes, the spectrum of the power output of a freely vibrating body when acting as a source of sound waves will also represent the response of that body to incident acoustic power. Each of the spectra in Fig. 2.6 may therefore be considered as the *response curve* of the source from which each is derived when this source is responding to our standard stimulus. Then curve A indicates that this source responds to some extent at any frequency but has no clearly marked resonant frequency; curve B that this source responds appreciably only within a range of roughly 500 to 1,100 c/s and resonates at a frequency of 750 c/s; and curve C that this source responds practically only at 100 and 300 c/s and resonates at both frequencies.

In the process of response the frequencies of the input sound waves are maintained in the output though changes in their phases occur as a result of the phenomenon of storage. If, therefore, the resonator whose response curve is represented by Fig. 2.6B is supplied with incident acoustic power in the range from 1,100 to 1,300 c/s and negligible power at other frequencies, the response of this resonator will be negligible, in the first place because the power of the input is mostly at frequencies to which it hardly responds at all, and in the second because in the range of frequencies where it does respond to an appreciable extent, there is negligible power for it to do so.

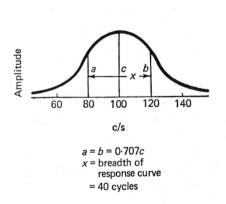

$a = b = 0.707c$
x = breadth of response curve
= 40 cycles

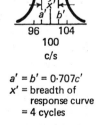

$a' = b' = 0.707c'$
x' = breadth of response curve
= 4 cycles

Fig. 2.8. Response curves

A response curve is thus a representation of the potential behaviour of a resonator; it shows how this body will respond to a specific power input at any frequency on the curve in comparison with how it will respond to the same power input at any other frequency on the same curve.

2.73. The range of frequency to which a resonator will respond —this being represented by the breadth of its response curve—is indefinite; strictly speaking a resonator will respond to at least some, even if infinitesimal, power at all frequencies. It is sometimes convenient, however, to use, as a measure of the breadth of a response curve, the difference in frequency between the two points on the response curve where the potential amplitude of the response is 0·707 times that of the response at the resonant frequency, i.e. where the potential power absorption and radiation is half that of the potential maximum (Fig. 2.8).

Now the characteristic damping of a body acting as a source of sound waves (§ 2.63) also applies when the body is acting as a resonator. Thus a resonator may be said to be heavily or lightly damped. But the damping of a body is also related to the breadth of its response curve in this way that a heavily damped resonator has a broad response curve, and a lightly damped resonator a narrow one.

2.74. In the process of absorption, storage and radiation of energy which is characteristic of response, a certain amount of the energy is dissipated in heat generated among the moving particles of the resonator. Because of this unavoidable loss the power radiated, even at the resonant frequency where the resonator's response is greatest, will be less than 100 per cent of the power absorbed. A resonator in other words, does not of itself provide power for re-emission— energy cannot be so simply created.

Yet if a vibrating tuning fork—the source—is held over the body of air in a vessel—the resonator—and the natural frequency of the former coincides with the resonant frequency of the latter, a listener perceives the resultant sound as much louder than that from the tuning fork alone. This is due to the fact that a resonator reacts upon the source of the sound waves, and increases its power output. It does this by facilitating the output of power from the source at the frequency or frequencies at which its response is large, i.e. those at which it resonates. If the rate of power output from a source is increased by such resonance, the duration of that output is of course shortened, for the same amount of energy at the source.

2.8. Filtering

2.80. If we construct a system with a source of sound waves and a resonator in such a way that the only power to reach a certain goal, a listener's ear for example, is that which has been passed

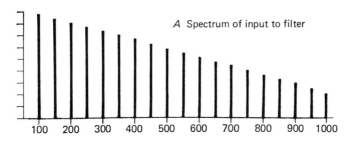

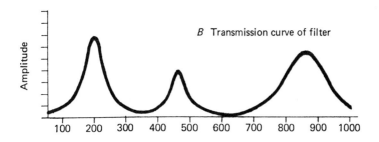

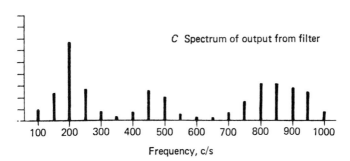

Fig. 2.9. Filtering

through the resonator, the resonator is then acting as a filter, and the process is known as filtering. The essential point is that a filter is merely a resonator integrated into a system in such a way that some or all of the power present at frequencies within the resonator's response curve is separated from power present at other frequencies.

2.81. The response curve of a filter is usually known as its *transmission curve* and the frequencies on this curve form the *pass-band* of the filter. The transmission curve of a filter then represents the potential behaviour of that filter; it shows the proportion of a specific power input which is transmitted at any frequency on the curve (cf. § 2.72 above). If the frequency of the input power is one at which the filter offers a good transmission, this power will be passed with little loss; if that frequency, on the other hand, is one at which the filter offers a poor transmission, the power will be passed with relatively large loss, and so on.

As an example, let us imagine a source of sound emitting acoustic power at 100 c/s, 150 c/s, 200 c/s, 250 c/s, etc., up to, say, 1,000 c/s. The line spectrum of this complex sound may be represented as Fig. 2.9A. If this source is enclosed in a box lined with vibration-absorbing material, and this insulation is effective, we shall hear no sound from the source. If we now insert in one of the walls of the box a filter, a hollow air-filled tube, for example, which has a transmission curve as represented in Fig. 2.9B, this filter will pass some of the power in the complex wave, and the sound we shall hear will have a line spectrum as Fig. 2.9C. The spectrum of the output power may therefore be considered as the spectrum of the input power, modified by the characteristics of the filter as represented in a diagram of its transmission curve.

CHAPTER 3

THE SPEECH APPARATUS

3.1. The Organs of Speech

3.10. Man had originally no special organ of speech. The different organs used for the production of speech sounds have been adapted to this purpose relatively late in the history of the human species. The lungs, the larynx, and the nasal cavity are parts of the respiratory mechanism. The tongue, the teeth, the epiglottis, etc., function in the process of chewing and swallowing the food. Yet, although, from a phylogenetic viewpoint, the human body does not possess any speaking apparatus and although not a single one of the organs involved in the speech mechanism is used only for speaking, we can, for practical purposes, use the term *organs of speech* in the sense of the organs which are active, directly or indirectly, in the process of speech sound production. It follows, however, from this, that the delimitation of these organs from others is to some extent arbitrary and that it is to a certain degree a question of taste which anatomical and physiological data should be included in a chapter on physiological phonetics. We shall confine ourselves here to a simple description of the main structures, and refer the reader for further information to any standard handbook of anatomy.

3.11. Taken in the sense proposed above, the organs of speech, which as a whole comprise the *vocal tract*, are essentially the following:

(1) *the respiratory mechanism*, which furnishes the flow of air needed for the majority of the sounds used in speech;

(2) the *larynx*, which is basically a valve regulating the flow of air in the respiratory mechanism and the main source of sound-wave energy;

(3) the *supraglottal tract*, from the glottis in the larynx to the lips, in which most of the noises of speech are produced and all speech sounds subjected to resonance.

3.2. The Respiratory Mechanism

3.20. *Respiration.* The *lungs* are spongy bodies composed basically of many small air sacs, the *alveoli*, where the blood is cleaned of its carbon dioxide and provided with fresh oxygen from the outer air. The alveoli receive their air from small tubes, the *bronchioles*, which come together into two large tubes, the *bronchi*, the right and the left. The bronchi in turn join in the *trachea* through which the air passes from the throat to the lungs. The lungs, enclosed in a large sac or *pleura*, are encased in the *thoracic cavity*, bounded above and laterally by the *rib cage*, and below by the *diaphragm*.

The act of respiration involves two phases, *inspiration* and *expiration*. When the thoracic volume is increased—by means of a downward movement of the diaphragm and an outward and upward movement of the ribs—the air pressure inside diminishes and air from outside flows into the lungs (inspiration). On the other hand, when the muscles initiating such movements of the diaphragm and the rib cage are relaxed, the diaphragm returns upward and the rib cage downward and inward, decreasing the volume of the lungs and forcing air out of the lungs (expiration). According to the role played by the diaphragmatic and the thoracic muscles respectively in the process, we sometimes speak of (1) *abdominal breathing* and (2) *thoracic breathing*. The choice between these two types is essentially dependent on posture, clothing, or individual habits. These different modes of realizing the respiratory process have no linguistic significance; the only phonetically important fact is the creation of an air stream to or from the lungs, the modification of which is at the base of most of the sounds used in speech.

3.21. It is important, too, to make a distinction between normal breathing, when no sound is being produced, and *speech-breathing*. The rate of the former, which is primarily determined by the amount of carbon dioxide in the blood, ranges normally from 10–20 inhalations per minute. It comprises a sequence of inspiration, expiration, and pause, the last being a phase of relative inertness which may disappear when the rate of breathing increases. Expiration and inspiration in normal breathing are of about the same duration, the ratio between them being about 1 to 1·1. In this type of breathing, the expulsion of the air in expiration is essentially due to the pressure exerted on the lungs by the weight and elasticity of the organs displaced during the inhalation. This type of expiration is thus relatively *passive*, although forced expiration is possible.

3.22. In speech-breathing, the inspiration phase is accelerated, the expiration phase, on the contrary, is prolonged, for the reason that the articulation of most speech sounds involves an obstruction offered to the air stream from the lungs at some point or points in the vocal tract. The ratio of the duration of intake to that of outgo ranges in normal conversation from 1:3 to 1:10 but occasionally amounts as far as 1:30. Speech expiration is an active process, the expired air being forced out of the lungs at a pressure regulated by the activity of several sets of muscles. Of these, the intercostal muscles, which raise and lower the rib cage, seem the most important.

3.23. The movement of respiration delimits the units of speech called *breath groups* (or *breath phrases*), a breath group being the stretch of an utterance produced between two intakes of air. In technically good speech, these breath groups correspond regularly to naturally delimited units of content. When this is not the case, the speaker is said to have a poor respiration technique.

3.3. The Larynx and the Glottis

3.30. *The larynx.* The trachea, or wind-pipe, is composed of a number of incomplete cartilaginous rings, open on the dorsal side, but enclosed and covered by tough, elastic tissue. Between the trachea and the vertebrae lies the *esophagus*. The cavity formed by the bronchi and the tube of the trachea probably acts as a resonator to vocal sounds of low frequency.

3.31. The uppermost ring of the trachea forms the base of the larynx. It is the *cricoid* (or *ring*) *cartilage*, which differs from the other cartilages of the trachea in its form—it is a complete circle resembling a seal-ring with its wider part at the back—and its large size.

The most important of the cartilages in the larynx is the *thyroid* (or *shield*) cartilage, which forms a shield-like structure (the "Adam's apple") on the front side of the larynx. It is open on the dorsal side. The extreme edges of this cartilage form two pairs of processes or horns, the *upper* and the *lower horns* (*cornua superiora* and *cornua inferiora*). The inferior horns are connected by a joint with the cricoid cartilage on either side, the superior horns with the *hyoid* or *tongue bone* by means of ligaments and muscles. The whole larynx can thus be said to be suspended on the hyoid bone which, in the form of a horse-shoe open on the back side, forms the upper boundary of the larynx structure and at the same time the point of attachment of some of the muscles of the tongue (Fig. 3.1).

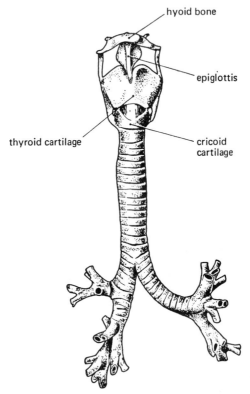

Fig. 3.1.   The trachea and larynx
Front view.   At the top is the hyoid or tongue bone resting on the superior horns of the thyroid cartilage and partly covering the epiglottis. The inferior horns of the thyroid cartilage are shown connected to the cricoid cartilage forming the top ring of the trachea.   At the bottom the trachea divides into two bronchi, and these in turn into the smaller bronchioles (after Rauber-Kopsch)

The *arytenoid cartilages* are two pyramid-shaped cartilages fastened to the upper surface of the back part of the cricoid cartilage by means of joints which permit them to move laterally on it. The anterior arms of the arytenoids (the *vocal processes*) are the points of origin of the two vocal cords, whose front ends are fastened to the anterior (inner) angle of the shield cartilage. The posterior arms of the arytenoids are the *muscular processes*, to which are fastened the two pairs of muscles which are mainly responsible for the movements of these cartilages—and hence for the positioning of the vocal cords. These are the *lateral crico-arytenoid muscles* and the *posterior crico-arytenoid muscles*, the former running forward and downward from the muscular processes of the arytenoid cartilages to attachments around each side of the cricoid cartilage, and the latter running backward and downward to attachments on the posterior surface of the same cartilage (Fig. 3.2).

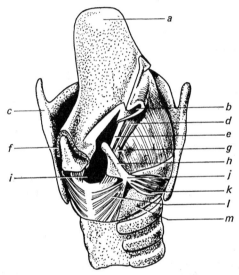

Fig. 3.2. The larynx, viewed from the rear
a, epiglottis; *b*, Morgagni's ventricle below the (cut-away) right ventricular band; *c*, thyroid cartilage; *d*, thyro-arytenoid muscle; *e*, (right-hand) vocal cord; *f* part of the ligament covering the inside surfaces of the larynx; *g*, vocal process of arytenoid cartilage; *h*, (right-hand) arytenoid cartilage; *i*, glottis; *j*, muscular process of arytenoid cartilage; *k*, lateral crico-arytenoid muscle; *l*, posterior crico-arytenoid muscle; *m*, cricoid cartilage (after Kahn)

The *epiglottis* is a spoon-shaped cartilage whose lower tip is fastened to the inner angle of the thyroid cartilage. It is connected to the hyoid bone by a ligament, and to the base of the tongue by the glosso-epiglottic fold. Since it has no direct muscular attachments, the epiglottis can be moved only by movement of the tongue and the hyoid bone. In this way, it can be pushed back and more or less cover the opening of the glottis, thus modifying the timbre of the laryngeal tone.

The whole of the larynx structure can be moved upward and downward. This mechanism can be used to vary slightly the volume of, and hence to increase or decrease the air pressure in, the supraglottal cavities (§ 4.21).

3.32. The vocal cords (which might more accurately, if less conventionally, be called vocal lips or bands, since they resemble these rather than cords) are two pairs of folds composed of ligament and muscle, the *thyro-arytenoid* muscle, in the ligament-covered inner wall of the larynx.

The upper pair, the *ventricular bands* or the so-called *false vocal cords*, have nothing to do with voice production in normal speech. When tightly closed, however, they can stop the outflow of air from the trachea. The small cavities between them and the lower pair of vocal cords are called *Morgagni's ventricles*; these probably have a certain resonatory effect on sound produced in the larynx.

The lower pair of folds, the *true vocal cords*, can be brought together by movement of the arytenoid cartilages following contraction of the lateral crico-arytenoid muscle, or drawn apart by movement of these cartilages following contraction of the posterior crico-arytenoid (Fig. 3.3). The opening between the vocal cords and

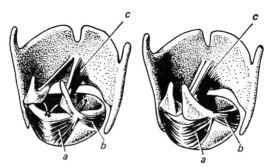

Fig. 3.3.   The arytenoid cartilages and the vocal cords
Rear view.   The arytenoid cartilages are turned around in their seating on the cricoid cartilage by the contraction of the posterior and lateral crico-arytenoid muscles, *a* and *b* respectively.   Contraction of the former opens the glottis (left-hand diagram) and contraction of the latter closes it (right-hand diagram).   *c* is the thyro-arytenoid muscle of the vocal cords (after Malmberg)

its continuation in the vocal processes of the arytenoids is called the *glottis* or *rima glottidis*. The anterior, *membranous*, part of the glottis has a length of about 15·5 mm in men and 11·5 mm in women; the dorsal, *cartilaginous*, part of it is about 7·5 mm in men and 5·5 mm in women, making average total lengths for the glottis of 23 mm and 17 mm, respectively.

3.33. The mechanism regulating the opening and closing of the glottis is very delicate and permits several possibilities (Fig. 3.4). The triangular form of the glottis, *A*, is that of normal respiration, the wider opening, *B*, that of deep respiration. In whispering, the membranous glottis is normally half or lightly closed and the cartilaginous glottis is open, *C*.[1] The hissing sound of whispering is due to the friction of the air stream against the vocal processes of the arytenoid cartilages. A fourth position, *D*, is that of phonation or voice, in which the whole glottis is closed by the action of the arytenoid cartilages closing the cartilaginous glottis and drawing the interior edges of the vocal cords together along the membranous glottis. Fifthly, the edges of the vocal cords may be brought together closely and firmly, often with one edge overlapping the other, so that the air flow is completely blocked at the glottis.

Besides these five positions, however, it would appear, from such results of glottal articulations as murmur, breathy voice, and vocal cord trills, that various other but rather obscure settings of the

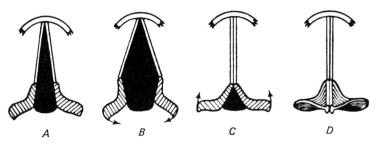

| A | B | C | D |

Fig. 3.4.   Glottal positions

Schematic diagram of some of the possible settings of the vocal cords (seen from above). *A* is for normal breathing, *B* for deep breathing, *C* for whisper, and *D* for voice (after Forchhammer)

[1] Photographic pictures taken by a high-speed camera now confirm both the triangular form of the cartilaginous glottis and that the membranous glottis is not completely closed as in the schematic design of Fig. 3.4*C*.

glottis are possible, some of them doubtless being intermediate between the voice and the whisper positions. No satisfactory treatment of these phenomena has yet appeared,[1] and we shall not consider them further.

3.34.   In the voice position, the vocal cords can be set into vibration, that is, into a steady repetition of opening and closing movements. The interaction of this vibration and the stream of expiratory air produces an approximately periodic sound which is known as the *glottal tone* or *voice*. The fundamental frequency of the glottal tone is determined by the rate of vibration of the vocal cords.

Among the factors influencing the rate of vocal cord vibration is the size or *mass* of these cords, or of those parts of them which are involved in the vibration (cf. § 2.63). The size of the vocal cords, as that of any other bodily organ, is related to age, sex, and general physical development. Individuals with large body form tend to have larger vocal cords than those with smaller physical development. Children and women tend to have shorter and smaller vocal cords than men. The larynx and the vocal cords grow considerably during puberty.

3.35.   The size of the vocal cords as vibrating units is to some extent under nervous control. By retaining the posterior part of the membranous glottis in the closed position, vibration may be confined to a small section of the vocal cords. This results in the so-called *falsetto* voice. Again, vibration may be confined to the edges of the vocal cords along the glottis, which results in the *head* voice. Or the vocal cords may vibrate as whole units, giving the *chest* voice. These different modes of vibration of the vocal cords are called *registers*; together they provide almost all the range of frequency available to the normal voice.

3.36.   The traditional conception of the mechanism of vibration in the larynx is briefly the following. The vocal cords, drawn into the voice position by the movement of the arytenoid cartilages and adjusted by the activity of a complex of muscles for a particular mode of vibration, close the glottis and prevent the flow of expiratory air from the lungs. The activity of the expiratory muscles continuing, the subglottal pressure of the expiratory air stream increases until the point is reached at which the muscular tension on the vocal

---

[1] See, however, Catford (1964).

cords is overcome. At this point, the cords are forced apart, from the underside upwards, and a puff or pulse of compressed air escapes through the glottis into the vocal tract above. The flow of air continues until the subglottal pressure has fallen to the point where the muscular tension of the vocal cords is able to reassert itself and force the cords together again, thus closing the glottis. The cycle then repeats itself, and continues to do so while the voice position of the vocal cords and sufficient subglottal pressure of expiratory air are maintained.

In this conception, thus, the opening and the closing of the glottis results from the action of the subglottal pressure and the reaction of the muscular tension in the vocal cords. The frequency of vibration is primarily determined, within the normal ranges of operation of the laryngeal apparatus, by the degree of tension of the vocal cords.

3.37.   In recent years, however, this simple theory of vocal cord vibration has not been free from criticism. The Danish phonetician, Svend Smith, likens the mechanism of vocal cord vibration in the low and normal ranges to the passage of an air bubble between two soft elastic pillows. The pressure of the subglottal air raises the closed and tensed vocal cords slightly and then forces them apart, from the subglottal lower surface upwards, but the puff or bubble of air

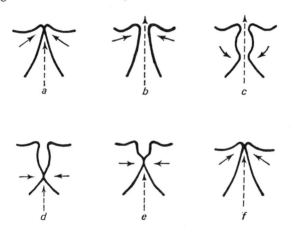

Fig. 3.5.   The vibration of the vocal cords
In *a* and *b* the pressure of the air in the trachea below forces the vocal cords apart.   In *c* and *d* the air flow through the glottis sucks the lower edges of the cords together.   In *e* and *f* the closure is rolled upward against the muscular tension to complete the cycle (after Svend Smith)

escaping through the open glottis has the aerodynamic effect of sucking the edges of the vocal cords together, again from the lower surface upward (Fig. 3.5).

3.38.   As to the vibration frequency, some French scholars (Husson, Garde) maintain that the opening and closing of the vocal cords (and not only their positioning and tension adjustment) is also to be regarded as under the control of the brain. Nerve impulses from the speech centre of the brain with a frequency corresponding to that of the glottal tone are reported to have been discovered during sound production. The vibration of the vocal cords must be considered, according to these new hypotheses, as a phenomenon of *rhythmic nervous activity* with the frequency of that vibration determined in the brain, not in the glottis. This quite revolutionary new conception, the neuro-chronaxic hypothesis, has yet to be confirmed; there are serious difficulties in accepting it from the viewpoint of neurophysiology. But in any case, even though it should eventually be substantiated, its validity seems likely to be confined within certain limits. If it is natural for a woman or a child to speak or sing one octave higher than a man, this is evidently because of differences in the length and thickness of the vocal cords and in the volume of the larynx and its resonators. The anatomical structure of the laryngeal and glottal mechanism determines the average register of the voice and the limits of frequency variation. The vibration of the vocal cords would thus have to be considered as the result of a combination of subglottal pressure and muscular tension on one side, and periodic nerve impulses and motor movements on the other. Further, some important instrumental evidence against the neuro-chronaxic hypothesis has been presented recently (Vallancien, van den Berg, Sonesson).

3.39.   The functioning of the larynx permits the important division of the sound material used in speech into *voiced* and *voiceless*, according to the presence or absence of this vibration of the vocal cords. During the production of most voiceless speech sounds, the glottis is open, though a certain type of voiceless consonant is produced with the glottis completely closed (§ 6.60 f.).

Recent discoveries seem to have proved that differences in the mode of vibration of the vocal cords are responsible for—or at least accompany—different vocalic qualities. How far these differences are determined by higher centres of speech control, and/or how far they result from the influence of the supraglottal system of resonators on the vibratory pattern of the vocal cords (§ 4.45) is difficult to determine. It appears, at any rate, that the acoustic type of the vowel being produced is at least partly laid down in the larynx itself. But the final and doubtless much the most important process in the determination of vowel quality is the filtering, in the vocal tract above the larynx, of the complex sound wave resulting from the vibration of the vocal cords.

3.4. The Supraglottal Cavities

3.40. The passage leading from the glottis to the outside air at the orifices of the mouth and nose is a tube which may be viewed as a series of connected cavities, namely, the *pharynx*, the *buccal* or *mouth cavity*, the *nasal cavity*, and, in some cases, the *lip cavity* (Fig. 3.6). The pharynx is the tube-shaped channel which leads from the larynx up to the mouth and through to the nasal cavities. It is customary to distinguish three parts, the *laryngeal pharynx* from the cricoid cartilage to the hyoid bone, the *oral pharynx* from the hyoid bone to the velum, and the *nasal pharynx* behind and above the velum in the posterior part of the nasal cavity. The volume of the laryngeal pharynx can be modified by the movements of the larynx, the tongue and the epiglottis. The volume of the oral pharynx depends essentially on the position of the tongue. If this is drawn back toward the rear wall of the throat—a position characteristic of the back or velar vowels—the volume of the oral pharynx may be reduced very considerably. The nasal pharynx together with the other cavities of the nose forms a voluminous and phonetically important resonator, usually referred to collectively as the "nasal cavity," because they function in speech sound production as a single unit. The participation of this nasal resonator in the filtering activity of the vocal tract is essentially regulated by the movements of the velum or soft palate (§ 3.43). Two pairs of muscles (the *tensores palati* and the *levatores palati*) flatten and raise the velum, closing the passage from the oral pharynx to the nasal cavity, and two more (the *pharyngopalatine* and the *glossopalatine* muscles) draw it downward, opening this passage. These possibilities permit an important division of articulations into *nasal* or *oral*, the former with the air passage through the nose open, the latter with this passage completely closed.

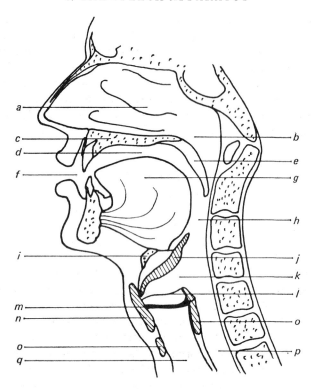

Fig. 3.6. The upper vocal tract
a, nasal cavity; *b*, nasal pharynx; *c*, hard palate; *d*, mouth cavity;
e, soft palate or velum; *f*, labial cavity; *g*, tongue; *h*, oral pharynx;
i, hyoid bone; *j*, epiglottis; *k*, laryngeal pharynx; *l*, ventricular bands;
m, vocal cords; *n*, thyroid cartilage; *o*, cricoid cartilage (front and rear);
p, oesophagus; *q*, trachea (after Heffner)

3.41. The different cavities which are to be found in the immediate neighbourhood of the nasal cavities, i.e. the *frontal*, the *sphenoidal*, and the *maxillary sinuses*, and the *ethmoidal cells* (opening into the nasal cavities by small ducts), are probably of little or no importance for the differentiation of speech sounds, though their form and volume may have some influence on individual voice qualities.

3.42. The oral pharynx opens into the mouth through the *oropharyngeal isthmus*, bounded above by the velum, below by the back part of the tongue, and on both sides by the *glossopalatine arch* (or anterior faucal pillars). This arch is formed by the bodies of the paired *glossopalatine muscles*, which arise in the central line of the velum and run downward and backward into the sides of the tongue. Another arch, behind the first is formed by the *pharyngopalatine muscles* and constitutes the edges of the opening from the oral pharynx. Between these two arches lie the palatine tonsils.

In swallowing, these two arches assist in driving the food downwards and keeping it from re-entering the mouth.

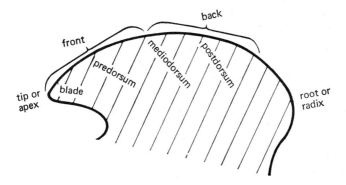

Fig. 3.7.   The main divisions of the tongue

3.43.   The *mouth cavity*, forward of the oro-pharyngeal isthmus, is bounded in the front by the teeth and lips, at the sides by the inner walls of the cheeks, above by the roof of the mouth and below by the tongue.

The front section of the roof of the mouth is formed of membranous covering over a bony structure. It is divided into the *dental area* at the teeth, the *alveolar area* at the alveolum, the ridge formed by the roots of the teeth in the upper jaw, and the *hard palate*, which may be subdivided into prepalatal, mediopalatal, and postpalatal areas. The rear section of the roof of the mouth lacks a bone framework. It is divided into the *soft palate* or *velum*, which in turn may be subdivided into pre- and postvelar areas, and the *uvula*, a pendulous projection into the oral pharynx from the end of the velum.

The part of the tongue which forms the floor of the mouth cavity can best be divided into sections by reference to points on the roof of the mouth. Thus, if the tongue is in the normal position of rest, there is, behind the *tip* or *apex*, the *blade* opposite the alveolar ridge

41

and the *dorsum* opposite the hard and soft palates. The dorsum may be further subdivided, from front to rear, into *predorsal, mediodorsal,* and *postdorsal* areas. Another frequently-used division of the tongue is into *front* and *back*, the front being that section opposite the hard palate, sometimes including the blade, and the back being that opposite the soft palate. Lastly there is the *root* or *radix*, that rear part of the tongue which forms the front wall of the oral pharynx (Fig. 3.7).

3.44. There are three principal directions of tongue movement, all mainly dependent on the action of a complex structure of muscles within the body of the tongue itself. First, the tongue can be moved upwards toward the roof of the mouth to narrow or completely block the air passage through the mouth—a closing articulation— or downwards from the roof of the mouth to widen this air passage —an opening articulation. Again the body of the tongue can be pushed forward or drawn back from its normal position of rest to extend in a lateral direction its range of articulation against the roof of the mouth. And finally the tip of the tongue can be moved independently and raised to approach or touch any point of the roof from the upper teeth to, approximately, the juncture between the hard and the soft palates. Two types of this movement need to be distinguished. The tip may be raised with retention of a more or less flat or convex surface to the dorsum, usually with some retraction of the body of the tongue. By this movement, contact can be made between the tongue tip and the roof of the mouth from the teeth to a point a little above the alveolar ridge. Alternatively, the tip may be raised with a concaving of the surface of the dorsum, a movement which enables contact to be made between the tongue tip, often on the underside, and the roof of the mouth from the teeth to the post-palatal or pre-velar limits. Articulations involving the latter type of movement are termed *retroflex*.

3.45. Besides the tongue, other organs can be viewed as articulating in the mouth cavity. The uvula has no power of independent muscular movement, but can be lowered into a groove formed by the back of the tongue and made to vibrate in a passing air-stream.

3.46. The vertical movements of the tongue which open and close the mouth passage are normally accompanied by a corresponding movement of the *lower jaw*, or *mandible*, the only movable bone of the face. This can be lowered so that the distance between the lower and upper incisors becomes about an inch and a half. It can also be swung a little from side to side, and slightly protruded, at least so much that the lower teeth can touch the upper lip. When the tongue position is low in the mouth in an open articulation the mandible is normally lowered, so that the angle between the two jaws is relatively wide. A high or close tongue position, on the contrary, is usually combined with a smaller jaw angle and consequently a smaller distance between the two sets of teeth. These jaw movements, which are normal concomitants of the essential movements of the tongue, are, however, not indispensable for the differentiation of the vowels since almost all vowel qualities can be produced with the jaws in the same position. This is easy to demonstrate with a pencil held between the teeth. Neither the protrusion of the jaw nor its sideward movements normally have any linguistic importance.

3.47. The lower teeth may be raised with the mandible to approach and make contact with the upper lip and with the upper teeth but neither of these articulations is known to be used in any speech sound. The upper teeth are fixed in the bony structure of the face and do not move independently; they may be articulated against, however, by the lower lip and by the apex, blade, and dorsum of the tongue.

3.48. The lips have a wide range of movement from the fully *closed* position to the widely *open*, and from the position *retracted* against the teeth to that *protruded* to their fullest extent. In some cases, it may be convenient to regard protrusion of the lips as resulting in the appearance of a small labial cavity forward of the teeth and bounded at the front by the inside surfaces of the lips (see Fig. 3.6). Generally, however, this labial cavity is included in the mouth cavity. The degree of opening of the lips then determines the cross-sectional area of the labial orifice to the mouth cavity, and the degree of protrusion affects its volume; both of these features, therefore, have considerable effect on the resonance and filtering properties of the upper vocal tract.

The shape of the labial opening varies from fully *spread* to fully *rounded*; intermediate stages where the shape is neither one nor the other are usually termed *neutral*. The construction and activity of the facial muscles controlling the movement of the lips favour the concomitance of the spread shape with the retracted position, and the rounded shape with the protruded position, but considerable variation is possible. When the mandible is lowered and the mouth widely open, the labial opening tends to a neutral shape. Besides these articulations, the lips can also function as a vibratile organ. In any position from fully retracted to fully protruded, the lips can be closed under muscular tension and set into vibration by an air stream passing between them.

3.5. Innervation of the Organs of Speech

3.50.   The organs of speech are innervated in very complex fashion by branches of a number of distinct nerves. Each nerve consists of a bundle of nerve fibres of two types, *motor* fibres which convey impulses from the brain to the muscles of the vocal tract, controlling their contraction and relaxation and thus all movement and activity of the organs of speech; and *sensory* fibres which convey impulses from the sensory receptors in these organs to the brain and thus keep the brain continually informed of the setting of the whole vocal tract.

The motor nerves controlling the process of respiration arise in various nuclei in the brain and pass to the muscles of the thorax and diaphragm via the spinal cord. These are termed *spinal* nerves. The nerves running to the other organs of the vocal tract arise also in various nuclei in the brain and pass through different routes in the head and neck to their end-points. These are *cranial* nerves. Of the more important organs of speech the larynx is innervated by branches from the vagus nerve, the tongue from the hypoglossal nerve, the lips from the facial nerve, and the mandible from the trigeminal nerve. Some of the muscles of speech, such as those controlling respiration, those of the uvula and the glossopalatine arches are innervated under the *autonomic* nervous system and are thus out of conscious control.

3.6. The Naming of Articulations

3.60.   The movements of the supraglottal organs sketched above are utilized in conjunction with the activities of the respiratory process and of the larynx in the production of speech sound. Such movements are known in phonetics as *articulations*, and the organs involved as *articulators*. In most cases, there is an articulator which moves, the *active* articulator, and an articulator toward or against which the articulation is made, the *passive* articulator. By joining the names of the active and the passive articulators in a compound adjective, we have a convenient means of describing or specifying any particular articulation, and also, since the passive articulator is usually stationary, of locating it in the supraglottal tract.

The number of possible articulations which may be described in this way will obviously depend, on the one hand, on the number and fineness of the divisions which are made of the organs of the vocal tract—if we divide the tongue into five divisions we shall have many more possible articulations than if we divide it into two. The number of articulations will also depend on an entirely different factor, namely, the range of movement which is anatomically possible to each of the movable named organs. This range of movement will vary slightly from speaker to speaker, but since the sounds of any language are, and must be able to be, produced by a wide range of individuals, we find in practice that no language requires articulations which are towards the limits of movement of the organs of speech.

In this situation, the writers of a textbook on phonetics must make their own decision as to what fineness of detail in description they will attempt, and, partly as a consequence, what range of sound-producing articulations they will include. In this book, intended as an introduction to the subject as a whole rather than to the sounds of any specific language, we have attempted to build up a terminology and a theoretical framework for speech sound production in which, without too much complication, a description can be found for practically all sounds known in the accumulated experience of phonetics to be used in any language, or likely ever to be found used in a language.

3.61. The main possibilities of articulation in the supraglottal tract may then be described as follows:

(a) radico-pharyngeal, in which the root of the tongue articulates toward the rear wall of the pharynx;

(b) dorso-uvular, in which the postdorsal area of the tongue articulates toward the uvula (and under this heading we subsume the special case of *uvular* articulation in which, though the postdorsum of the tongue articulates toward the uvula, it is the latter organ which vibrates in an air stream);

(c) dorso-velar, in which the dorsal area of the tongue articulates towards the soft palate;

(d) dorso-palatal, (e) lamino-palatal[1], (f) apico-palatal, in which the medio- or predorsum, the blade, or the tip of the tongue, respectively, articulates toward the hard palate;

(g) dorso-alveolar, (h) lamino-alveolar, (i) apico-alveolar, in which the predorsum, the blade, or the tip of the tongue, respectively, articulates toward the alveolum;

(j) lamino-dental, (k) apico-dental, in which the blade or the tip of the tongue, respectively, articulates toward the upper teeth;

(l) apico-labial, in which the tip of the tongue articulates toward the upper lip;

(m) labio-dental, in which the lower lip articulates toward the upper teeth;

(n) bilabial, in which the lower lip articulates toward the upper lip.

It is convenient to consider as a special class, (o) *retroflex*, those cases in which the articulation of the tip of the tongue against the hard palate, alveolum, or teeth is accomplished by concaving of the dorsum and blade (§ 3.44).

---

[1] Following Hockett (1955) we use *lamino-* with reference to the blade of the tongue.

CHAPTER 4

THE PRODUCTION OF SOUND IN THE VOCAL TRACT

4.1. The Functions of the Organs of Speech

4.10. The production of sound for speech in the human vocal tract presumably begins with nervous activity in the cortex of the brain. From such activity, trains of electro-chemical impulses stream along nerves through various routes in the lower brain to the muscles controlling and manipulating the vocal apparatus. Of the nature of the pattern of this innervation we know little, but we may reasonably infer, from our general knowledge of the intricate structure of the nervous system and our experience of the integrated working movements and adjustments of the vocal organs, that it must be extremely complex. This complexity will be both spatial, in that a large number of neurons and their affiliates will be involved over the vocal apparatus, and temporal, in that the neurons involved and the rate of discharge of impulses within those neurons will vary from moment to moment.

The result of these processes of innervation is a smooth, organized network of constantly changing activity in the muscles and organs throughout the vocal apparatus. By such activity vocal sound is produced.

It is convenient to regard this muscular and organic activity as performing three main functions in sound production. The first is the production of a movement of air, an *air stream*, in the vocal tract. The second is the conversion of some of the kinetic or potential energy of this air stream into acoustic energy in the form of sound waves. The third is the control over the resonatory transmission, the filtering, of these sound waves to the outer air, such control being exercised by modification of the physical characteristics of the various cavities between the glottis and the lips and nose.

4.11. All known sounds used in human speech depend essentially on an air stream. Sounds produced by other means, by percussion or scraping, for example, undoubtedly occur in the vocal tract, but

47

do not seem to be used by themselves, probably because the structure and plasticity of most of the organs in the vocal tract do not allow the production of sufficiently audible sound for speech purposes by percussion or scraping mechanisms. The two sets of teeth, it is true, can be struck or rubbed against one another to produce distinctly audible sounds, but no language appears to make use of these. Pike (1943, 103), however, stresses the fact that many sounds made by an air stream must also be accompanied by sounds produced concomitantly by the percussion or scraping of vocal organs while these are initiating or controlling air streams.

4.2. The Production of Air Streams

4.20.   The most commonly used source of an air stream is the respiratory activity of the lungs (§ 3.20 f.). Contraction of the peripheral muscles of the lungs expels previously inspired air through the trachea, larynx and supralaryngeal cavities to the outer air. The result is a stream of *egressive lung air*. Expansion of the lungs results in the reverse of this process, a stream of *ingressive lung air*. Following Pike we may call this the *pulmonic mechanism*.

4.21.   Other mechanisms may also be used for the production of an air stream. If a blockage can be formed anywhere in the vocal tract and moved, a flow of air will result in the same direction as the movement of the blockage. The air streams so produced are usually of small magnitude compared with that initiated by the pulmonic mechanism, but in some cases are usable for sound production.

The larynx has a certain range of movement upward or downward in the throat (§ 3.31). If the glottis is closed, upward movement of the larynx will result in a decrease in the volume of the pharynx and an egressive air stream flowing outward through the mouth and/or nose, while downward movement of the same organ, increasing the volume of the pharynx, will result in an ingressive air stream through the same passages. This may be termed the *pharyngeal mechanism*.

4.22.   The tongue likewise may initiate an air stream. If the tongue, raised to form a blockage at a point on the palate, is moved forward in the mouth while the blockage is maintained, an egressive air stream will result; if under similar circumstances the tongue is moved backward an ingressive air stream will result. Or if the tongue lying flat against the roof of the mouth is hollowed in the centre, a region of low pressure can be formed between its upper surface and the palate. If an orifice is now formed to give access to this low pressure region, an ingressive air stream will result. There are several places in the mouth where similar operations are possible; we shall term them all *oral mechanisms*.

4.3. The Conversion to Acoustic Energy

4.30. An air stream initiated by the action of any of the above mechanisms possesses kinetic energy by virtue of its motion, or, should actual motion be hindered, potential energy by virtue of its compression, and the next step in the production of audible sound waves in the vocal tract is the conversion of some at least of this energy into the acoustic energy of sound waves. This conversion is the second of the major functions of the organs of speech, and is accomplished in three main ways.

4.31. The first method is the interposition of some vibratile organ in the path of the moving air stream. Most commonly used for this purpose are the vocal cords, the uvula, the front and tip of the tongue, and the lips, and occasionally the ventricular bands or the epiglottis. The blockage so formed may be complete as is usually the case with the tip of the tongue against the alveolar ridge or incomplete as when the uvula is interposed, but in both cases the process is similar. Pressure is built up on that side of the interposed organ which faces the air stream until it is sufficient to overcome the resistance offered by the muscular tension of this organ and force an opening through which a pulse of compressed air escapes. With the resultant drop in the pressure of the opposing air, the muscular tension in the interposed organ reasserts itself and closes the opening again (cf. § 3.36).

This series of events is repetitive, the frequency of repetition depending on the resistance to movement of the interposed organ, this in turn depending on the mass of the organ and its muscular tension as controlled by innervation from the brain. It seems that the pressure of the air against the blockage may have some effect on this frequency. The consensus of opinion and the evidence from musical and physical analogues is, however, that this influence is not very important.

This type of vibration is essentially a passive, mechanical process in which cortical control is exercised only to the extent of determining the pressure and flow of the air stream and the muscular tension in the interposed vibratile organ. A somewhat different type of vibration of an interposed organ, but one which leads in practice to a very similar result, must, of course, be assumed for the operation of the vocal cords, if the neuro-chronaxic theory (§ 3.38) is valid, even to a limited extent.

The whole process is a method by which the action of an air stream mechanism combined with the action of an interposed vibratile or partly vibratile organ results in the compression of a body of air and its release in the form of discontinuous pulses of air travelling with relatively rapid motion through an intermittent opening.

There are several sources of sound waves in this process. The most important is the propagation of the compression in each pulse of air. As each pulse emerges from the opening it expands into the surrounding air, compressing neighbouring particles of air, and so setting up a sound wave (§ 2.11). Indistinguishably mixed with this will be a sound wave set up by compression of air at the point of collision between the rapidly moving air pulse and the relatively stationary air beyond the blockage.

The wave resulting from processes of this sort is usually of a complex nature, with acoustic power mainly concentrated into a fundamental component with a frequency equivalent to and depending upon the number of air pulses per second, and a large number of harmonics, generally of decreasing amplitude with increasing frequency. This is the sort of power distribution which may be considered to approximate a line-spectrum (§ 2.50). The total power in the wave, for a given muscular tension in the vibratile organ and a given pressure in the surrounding air, is dependent on the pressure and volume of the original air stream.

A second source of sound waves is the displacement of air in the repeated opening and closing movement of the vibratile organ itself. The process here is similar to that in the tuning fork: the outward, opening movement compresses neighbouring air particles and the return closing movement rarefies them. The resultant sound wave obviously has a fundamental frequency exactly the same as that produced by the air pulses through the opening formed during these movements, and its total power will be dependent on the amplitude of movement of the vibratile organ. This, on the same assumptions as before, will be dependent on the pressure and volume of the original air stream. It is very probable, from the behaviour of physical analogues, that in this wave there will also be a fundamental component and a series of harmonics of decreasing amplitude.

A third source of sound waves is the friction set up by the air pulses against the sides of the opening as they pass through. The general process of generation of sound waves from friction of air is common in the vocal organs. In the movement of air through any passage, provided a certain critical velocity is reached, the air particles close to the surface are set into turbulent eddying, whence result small variations of pressure which are transmitted through the surrounding air as sound waves (§ 2.62).

These waves are of numerous frequencies, and generally unstable, though under certain conditions they can approach periodicity. In the case of the intermittent openings provided by a vibratile organ, it seems very unlikely that this source of sound is of any importance, though an earlier theory considered the main function of the vocal cords to be the inducing of eddy formation in the air stream flowing through the glottis.

A fourth source of sound waves is percussion. The vibratile organ closing the opening under its own muscular tension may strike against part of itself, or against some other organ. Such an impact will set up vibrations both in the moving organ and the organ struck, and these vibrations will set up pressure waves in the surrounding air. But the softness and plasticity of the vocal organs concerned will damp rapidly the vibrations in them, so that any waves from this source will be of negligible magnitude and duration. In cases of percussion there is usually a second subsidiary source of sound waves, namely, the air expelled from between the striking surfaces before their impact. If the expulsion is sufficiently rapid, this air strikes against the surrounding air with sufficient force to set up pressure waves in a similar fashion to that outlined above. Again this seems to be a negligible source of sound waves in the vocal organs.

4.32. The second method of converting the energy of the air stream into acoustic energy is the interposition of some non-vibratile organ in the path of the moving air stream to form a blockage. Most commonly used for this purpose are the vocal cords, the tongue, the lips, and, rarely, the ventricular bands. The process is in many respects similar to that discussed above for a vibratile organ, save that it is not repetitive and we need consider only those cases in which the blockage is complete. Pressure is built up on that side of the interposed organ which faces the air stream, but the blockage is released not more or less automatically when a critical pressure is attained, but under direct innervatory control. At the release an explosive spurt of compressed air of very brief duration escapes and the pressure behind the blockage drops rapidly to normal. Thereafter, provided that the air stream mechanism is still operating, the unhindered flow of the air stream is resumed.

In some cases, however, the function of the blockage is not so much to restrain a flow of air towards a region of normal pressure as to restrain air at normal pressure from flowing to a region of reduced pressure. In these cases the flow may be potential rather than actual, but on the release of the blockage we have a similar brief explosive spurt of air flowing into the region of reduced pressure and a rapid rise of this pressure to normal.

The process is a method by which the action of an air stream mechanism combined with the action of an interposed non-vibratile organ results in the compression of a body of air and its release in the form of a single pulse of air travelling with relatively rapid motion through a small opening, small at any rate in the initial period of the release.

The sources of sound waves in this process are generally similar to those in the process of interposition of a vibratile organ, but the resultant sound waves differ considerably since there is but a single pulse, and not a series of pulses.

In the first place, the sound waves set up by the collision of the pulse with the opposing air and by the expansion of the air in the pulse (§ 4.31) die out rapidly since there is no succession of pulses. Such evidence as we have indicates that the wave from these sources is of very short duration with acoustic power spread over a large range of frequencies. The total power, for a given opening and given pressure in the surrounding air, will be dependent on the pressure and volume of the original air stream.

A second source of sound waves is the friction set up by the rapid movement of the air pulse through the opening provided by the release of the blockage. The process is as described above (§ 4.31), but in this case, since the opening is frequently effective as an opening for somewhat longer duration than the intermittent opening provided by the movement of a vibratile organ, the sound waves set up by friction, are probably often of more importance.

In the formation of the blockage, sound waves may be generated by percussion, and in the release of the blockage other sound waves may arise from compression of air particles in front of the moving organ. But as there is no repetition of these processes, it is probable that sounds arising from them are of small importance.

4.33. The third method of converting the kinetic energy of the air stream into acoustic energy is by the narrowing of the passage through which the air stream passes. The general construction of the organs of speech enables this to be done over a large extent of the vocal tract from the glottis to the lips, and the length and shape of the narrowed passage may be varied considerably. Other things being equal, the effect of the decrease of the cross-sectional area of a passage is to increase the velocity of the air flow through it.

The main source of acoustic power in this process is from the turbulent eddying set up by the rapid flow of air through the narrowed passage in the manner detailed above (§ 4.31). The greater the velocity of the air stream—over a critical velocity below which streamlined flow is obtained—the larger the pressure variations in these eddies and the more power in the sound waves from them. The distribution of this power along the frequency scale varies considerably from case to case, but in general there is a broad peak in the spectrum at a frequency dependent on the velocity of the air and the dimensions of the constriction.

4.34. The above survey has shown that in any method used in the vocal tract to convert the kinetic energy of an air stream into acoustic energy a number of distinct sources of sound exist. Each of the three main methods of conversion results in a mixture of sounds from more than one source, and the distinction of the power flowing from each source is as yet only possible in general terms.

The most useful distinction between the various mixtures of sound is that of periodicity as opposed to non-periodicity. As pointed out above (§ 2.50), true periodicity—exact repetitiveness of the cycles of a wave—exists only theoretically and certainly not in any sound produced in the vocal tract. Yet here, as is usually the case in the physical world, it is convenient to classify certain approximations to this state as periodic, and others, i.e. those not approximating a concentration of acoustic power into discrete frequencies, as non-periodic.

The main source of such periodic sound in the vocal tract is the process of vibration of some organ in the air stream. Some vibratile organs, however, the uvula for example, normally vibrate in such a low frequency range that the ear perceives the resultant sound not as a unity, but as a succession of single pulses. The fundamental sound wave from the vibration is still, however, approximately periodic.

The main sources of non-periodic sound are the blockage and release of an air stream by the interposition of a non-vibratile organ, and the turbulence and eddying in an air stream passing through a narrowed passage. Many simultaneous combinations of periodic and non-periodic sounds may occur, but it is usually convenient and possible to distinguish each type separately in terms of its source.

4.4. Theory of Resonance in the Vocal Tract: The Formants

4.40. Since the important methods of vocal sound production depend upon an air stream, and this in turn presupposes a passage of some sort, the vocal tract from the glottis to the lips, i.e. from the extreme points at which conversion of kinetic energy to acoustic energy is possible, must have, at least in part, the general form of a tube or passage during the production of sound. Any passage containing air will, if appropriately excited, act as a resonator, and its characteristics as such, i.e. the extent of its response to each differing frequency, will depend mainly on its total internal volume, the configuration of its various segments, and the size and nature of its orifices, including not only those at either end but also any internal narrowings of the passage which may act as orifices (§ 2.63). In addition, though we have no precise experimental evidence on the point, it is almost certain that the characteristics of a resonator are also, to some extent at least, affected by the nature of its inside surfaces.

From the above, two important conclusions may be drawn. The first is that a sound from any source in the vocal tract is subjected to the effects of resonance in at least part of that tract. Even in those cases where the acoustic power is generated at the lips with an egressive air stream, the passage behind the lips acts as a resonator to the sound waves so produced. And as a corollary, the complex of vocally-produced sound waves as propagated in the outer air is not the same as that produced at the source; this latter is never heard without the modifications imposed on it by resonance.

The second conclusion is that since the resonatory characteristics of any air cavity or air passage depend on its physical characteristics of volume, shape, and the sizes of its orifices, variation of these physical characteristics will result in modification of the resonatory characteristics of that passage. Such variation in the vocal tract is a function of muscular movement (§ 4.10).

In the following sections we shall consider these two conclusions in some detail.

4.41. There are two main methods of approach to a discussion of resonance in the vocal tract. The first is to consider the vocal cavities as a series of simple air cavity resonators—these are usually termed *Helmholtz resonators*—joined together, and to discuss the effect of variation in volume or orifice-area of each of these resonators on the total resonatory result. In a simple Helmholtz resonator, increase in the volume of the cavity lowers the resonant frequency and increase in the area of the orifice or orifices to the cavity raises it (cf. § 2.63).

This is a simple procedure, frequently used in previous work, and leading to suggestive conclusions with regard to the positions of the tongue and other organs and the resulting sound wave frequencies. But the simplicity is deceptive. The joining together of two or more Helmholtz resonators results in each affecting the mode of vibration of the air in all of the others—a phenomenon known as *coupling*. Hence the calculation of the resonance frequencies or of the effects of physical variation in a series of coupled Helmholtz resonators becomes rather complex. Besides this, however, the method is not, strictly speaking, applicable to the range of resonance phenomena in the vocal tract, since the dimensions of the main cavities are too large in comparison with the wave lengths of many of the sounds concerned. To give accurate results from the simple theory, the dimensions of a Helmholtz resonator must be smaller than a quarter wave length of the sound wave resonated. The main cavities in the vocal tract, the mouth and the pharynx, commonly range in length about 3 to 4 inches (8 to 10 cm), and thus function adequately as Helmholtz resonators only for sound waves below about 1,000 c/s (§ 2.21). In speech sound production, however, important resonance extends to frequencies up to at least 4,000 c/s, and this is difficult to treat in terms of cavity resonance theory.

4.42. The second method, that used in some of the more modern treatments, is to consider the vocal tract as approximating a resonant transmission line in the sense in which this term is used in communications engineering. This approach is very fruitful in phonetics since it enables a large body of established theory and of experimental results from apparatus more amenable to mathematical treatment to be applied to the processes of the vocal tract.

A transmission line is a system which transmits energy in the form of wave motion from one point to another, but one in which the length of that system is comparable to, or greater than, the wave length of the motion to be transmitted. This is in general a more valid treatment of the processes of resonance in the vocal tract, but it is also a much more complex procedure, and does not usually allow any simple conclusions to be drawn with regard to the relations between the configuration of the vocal tract and the resulting sound wave frequencies.

In the following sections we shall base our treatment on the consideration of the vocal tract as approximating a transmission line, but for clarity of explanation shall refer, where possible, to the implications of a configuration in terms of a network of coupled Helmholtz resonators.

4.43. In the vocal tract the spectrum of the input power is that of the complex of sound waves emanating from any source or combination of sources of such power, and the output spectrum is that of the complex of sound waves finally propagated in the outer air. The difference between these two spectra results from the particular transmission characteristics of the vocal tract—only in theory can a transmission line be free of distortion and loss.

The characteristics of the vocal tract as a resonant transmission line are those of a filter with a complicated transmission curve. Accordingly, sound waves within some ranges of frequency are given good transmission and those outside these ranges are offered poor transmission (§ 2.81).

The output from such a transmission line will clearly be characterized by a series of regions along the frequency scale in which any sound waves present have a relatively large proportion of their input amplitudes, and another series of regions, complementing the first, in which any sound waves present have a relatively small proportion of their input amplitudes. The former series of regions of the frequency scale constitute the *formants* of speech sounds. These are visible as peaks of acoustic power in a diagram of the output spectrum, and it has become conventional to number them as formant 1, formant 2, etc., according to their position on the frequency scale reading from the bottom. Thus, in Fig. 2.9 (p. 27), if the input power is as the spectrum A and the transmission curve of the vocal tract is as in B, the output would be as C, in which the formants 1, 2, and 3, are centred about 200 c/s, 450 c/s, and 850 c/s, respectively.

4.44. Since, as was shown above (§ 4.40), resonance or filtering occurs in the production of all sounds in the vocal tract, all speech sounds will have formants, but the actual distinguishing and the localization in frequency of the formants of many sounds is difficult. There are several reasons for this. For example, the source or sources of acoustic power in a particular vocal sound may not deliver input power at frequencies lying on the pass-band of the vocal tract, with the result that there will be no output power at formant frequencies (cf. § 2.72). Or the input power at a formant frequency may be very little in comparison with input power at other frequencies, and be overshadowed in the output. Or again the duration of the input power at a formant frequency may be too short to enable the formant to be detected in the output spectrum.

Clearly, also, different sources will produce sound waves of very different suitability for resonant transmission. The most suitable inputs come from sources initiating more or less periodic sound waves whose spectra show a concentration of the acoustic power into a number of discrete frequencies. Next most suitable come from sources initiating non-periodic sound waves whose spectra show acoustic power over a wide range of frequencies for an appreciable duration, and least suitable from those sources initiating non-periodic sound waves with acoustic power randomly distributed and/or in rapidly changing frequencies. Hence vocal sounds which have the more suitable sources of sound waves will usually have strong, well-defined formants, while those with less suitable sources will usually have weak, indistinct formants.

Such well-defined formants are typical of vowel sounds, and the existence of at least some formants in the vowels of human speech has been known since the work of Wheatstone in the early 19th century. It is only recently, however, that accurate knowledge has been obtained of their number, their frequencies, and their role in the determination of the perceptual qualities of those sounds in which they are well defined.

In such sounds two formants are almost always, and a third is usually present. Formant 1, in an average male voice, ranges between about 150 and 850 c/s, and formant 2 between about 500 and 2,500 c/s. The breadths of these formants measured in terms of the difference in frequency between the equivalents of the half-power points of a resonator (§ 2.73) vary from about 40 to 250 c/s, but average about 75 c/s. They also vary in intensity (§ 2.22). Information so far available suggests that at the lips formant 1 is frequently some five to twenty times as intense as formant 2. The frequency and intensity pattern of these two formants is now recognized to be the main determinant of vowel quality.

Formant 3 has a frequency ranging from 1,700 to 3,200 c/s. It tends to be high when formant 2 is high, and vice versa, and is normally less intense than formant 2. Though of significance in high front vowels, formant 3 is in other cases of much less importance in vowel determination than formants 1 and 2. Even higher bands of resonance, formants 4, 5, and 6, are commonly present in speech sounds, though their presence or absence seems to have little effect upon the intelligibility of the sounds. There is some evidence that they are more common and more clearly defined in sounds from voices which have been trained musically or which are considered to be of "good voice quality," but little experimental investigation of them has yet been made.

Female voices typically differ from male by higher frequencies of the formants produced. Fant gives 17 per cent as an average figure for this frequency difference.

4.45.   In this discussion of the resonatory origin of the formants in the vocal tract a few other points must be touched on. The first is the relationship of the source to the transmission line. If a transmission line is coupled to the source of sound waves to be passed through it, as is always the case in the vocal tract, the transmission line has a reactive effect upon the source. This effect is a rather complex phenomenon, but the net result is that the output of acoustic power from the source is facilitated at those frequencies which have a good transmission, while the output of acoustic power from the source at other frequencies may be hindered. Thus the source tends to deliver the greatest amount of its total acoustic power at the frequencies of the formants (cf. § 2.74).

A second point to be mentioned is that a transmission line can exhibit a phenomenon known as *negative resonance*, or *anti-resonance*, as a result of which the spectrum of its output is characterized by zero power, or at least minima of power, at certain frequencies. In some cases, negative resonances may be attributed to the resonance effects of added side cavities or bifurcations of the transmission line.

Further, we have so far made no mention of possible sources of loss of power during the process of vocal sound production. A certain amount of power is, of course, lost in friction during the process of transmission, since no actual filter is able to pass the theoretical maximum of 100 per cent of the power of the input (§ 2.74). The amount of this loss is, however, difficult to estimate and we know of no evidence bearing on it. Probably a much more important source of loss of power is parasitic vibrations in the surrounding flesh and bone structures of the head and throat. It seems likely that the soft fleshy surfaces in the vocal tract, and the air-filled bronchial tubes and lungs are responsible for absorbing a considerable amount of the power produced by any source, and parasitic vibrations of the bone structure of the upper part of the body must likewise account for some loss. Husson (1936) has calculated that of the energy expended at the glottis in producing normal vowel sounds about 80 per cent is lost in this manner.

4.46. The investigation of the resonatory characteristics and properties of the vocal tract has been pursued strongly in the last decade or so, notably by Chiba and Kajiyama, Dunn, Stevens, Fant, Ungeheuer, and their collaborators. The general procedure of much of this work is, while still maintaining as nearly as possible the volumes and relations of each of its parts, to so simplify the shape of the vocal tract that its resonatory characteristics can be worked out by the application of ordinary acoustical and transmission line procedures. For example, Dunn (1950) assumes the vocal tract to consist of a series of successive cylindrical resonators, larger in size for the main cavities and smaller for the orifices at the glottis, at the point of elevation of the tongue, and, as needed, at the lips. The dimensions of these resonators are based on measure-

4. THE PRODUCTION OF SOUND

ments taken from X-ray investigation of the vocal tract configurations. On this basis, the results of calculation of formant frequencies of the vowels approach closely their experimentally ascertained values, an indication that these assumptions may approximate the actual state of affairs.

More recently, considerably refined methods have been developed. Devices for producing synthetically formants and other components of speech to differing acoustic specifications have stimulated considerable experiment. Improved methods in radiography have permitted more accurate assessment of the volumes and shapes of the supraglottal tract during the production of speech sounds. The use of computers has enabled previously impracticable calculations of acoustic reactions and processes in the tract. The result has been steady progress in our understanding of the operation of the vocal apparatus, and Fant's book (1960), an outstanding survey of work with all these methods, leaves no real query as to the established validity of the formant theory of speech sound production.

4.5. The Modifications of Resonance

4.50. The second conclusion above, that variation of the physical characteristics of the vocal tract will result in modification of its resonatory and hence of its transmission characteristics (§ 4.40), may now be discussed. To do this it is most convenient to consider the vocal tract from the glottis to the lips as a tube-like body of air which can be differently formed or shaped by the activity of the articulatory organs. An elevation of the tongue toward the palate, for instance, forms two major cavities, one to the rear and one to the front of the raised tongue. Lowering of the velum opens an orifice to the nasal pharynx, thus extending the vocal tract to include the passage above the velum through the nasal pharynx and the nares to the outer air. There are other minor cavities also, which may be included or not, and which in some cases can be varied in shape: one between the teeth and the lips, another under the tip of the tongue, the laryngeal sinus, and so on. Not all these cavities, of course, need play a role in any one case of sound production; sound waves from some oral mechanisms, for example, may be affected only by resonance in the cavities of the front of the mouth.

In transmission line theory, the cavities forming that part of the vocal tract in use are all involved to some extent in the determination of the frequency and intensity of the formants, whereas in terms of the theory of Helmholtz resonators we would say that all the cavities are coupled through their common orifices with the result that each exerts some influence on the resonatory characteristics of all the others. The basic point is that in the process of resonatory filtering to which the sound-waves produced in the vocal tract are subjected, the whole body of air in that portion of the tract which is being used is excited into vibration, some parts responding more than others and at different frequencies from others. Hence, any formant resulting from such a process must be considered as the result of *a mode of resonance of the tract as a whole* or of that part of it which is in operation.

In this process, however, the amplitude and/or the frequency of any formant may be more dependent on the resonance in one part of the vocal tract than on resonance in other parts; when such is the case, it is possible—with a greater or less degree of validity according to the greater or less degree of dependence—to consider a formant as resulting from resonance in one specific part or cavity of the tract.

4.51. Of central importance to phonetics is the relationship between the configuration of the vocal tract and the frequencies of the formants associated with resonance in it. Though many problems remain, the main points are now fairly well understood. In the following sections we shall consider first the general conclusions by Stevens and House (1955) with regard to the trends discernible in the configuration—formant frequency relationship, and subsequently examine in more detail typical formant frequencies resulting from a few specific vocal tract settings. For evidence as to formant frequencies we have an increasing number of specialized studies, and a large amount of material in Potter, Kopp and Green, *Visible Speech* (1947). From the former we have fairly exact knowledge of the formant frequencies of a relatively small range of speech sounds, while from the latter the approximate frequencies of the formants of a large variety of speech sounds can be inferred.[1]

---

[1] The Acoustic Spectrograph, the instrument on which the records in Potter, Kopp & Green were made, is an instrument producing a visible graph of the frequencies in which acoustic power is present during a stretch of speech sound. The machine works by filtering to detect the power present in successive bands of frequency from 0–3,500 c/s in the sample, and then recording the results in visible form: frequency in the vertical dimension, time and thus

We shall simplify by classing the frequency of formant 1 as *low* if it falls in the range from 150 to about 500 c/s, and as *high* if above 500 c/s. Similarly, we may class formant 2 as *low* in the range 500 to about 1,200 c/s, medium in the range from 1,200 to about 1,800 c/s, and high if over 1,800 c/s. These values have been chosen simply for convenience.

4.52.   One of the most successful experimental investigations of the relationship between the configuration of the vocal tract and formant frequencies was carried out by Stevens and House in 1955. Their results suggested that a relatively small number of specific articulatory features could be isolated from the general contours and volumes of the vocal tract as exerting a disproportionate influence on the frequencies of the first three formants. The first of these articulatory features was the position of the constriction of the supraglottal tract, that part of the tract at which the tongue approaches most closely to the wall of the throat or the roof of the mouth. The second was the cross-sectional size of this constriction. The third was the size of the labial opening, calculated as the ratio of its cross-sectional area to its length.

The following are their conclusions on the general trends in the relationship of formant frequencies to these selected parameters.

Formant 1 is low when the opening at the lips is small or when the constriction formed by the tongue is toward the front of the mouth. It tends to be of high frequency when the labial opening is large and the constriction is near the glottis, that is, between the back or radix of the tongue and the wall of the throat.

Formant 2 is low when the labial opening is small and the constriction is near the glottis. It tends to rise in frequency as this constriction moves forward in the mouth or as the labial opening increases in size. The former seems more influential than the latter: with a small constriction between the tongue and the front of the palate or the alveolar ridge, formant 2 is high even with a quite small mouth opening.

Formant 3 tends to be low with a small labial opening and the constriction near the glottis. It rises in frequency, but over a much

duration in the horizontal, and intensity in the degree of blackness in the markings. Such recordings are known as *spectrograms*. (See Fig. 5.1.) The frequency scale on the spectrograms published by Potter, Kopp & Green is not, however, carefully calibrated, and the formant frequencies mentioned here have been determined by inspection.

smaller range than formant 2, as the constriction is moved forward and the size of the labial opening increased.

4.53. As a first typical setting of the vocal tract—position one—we may take that in which the front of the tongue is raised toward the hard palate or the alveolar ridge but with the tip pointing downward in the direction of the lower teeth (Fig. 4.1 *A*). Such a tongue position usually results in two main resonance cavities, connected by a short constricted passage of relatively small cross section between the dorsum of the tongue and the roof of the mouth. Of the two cavities, one is of considerable volume extending over the back of the mouth and the pharynx, the other of relatively small volume from the connecting orifice to the lips. The mandible is in a raised position, the labial opening is small, and the velum closes off the opening to the nasal pharynx.

This type of configuration is associated with a formant 1 of low frequency and formants 2 and 3 of high frequency. All result from modes of resonance of the air in the whole tract. If the vocal tract is considered to be formed of a pair of coupled Helmholtz resonators, there is some justification for regarding formants 1 and 3 as mainly dependent on the larger cavity to the rear of the constriction, and formant 2 as mainly dependent on the smaller front cavity. This should be looked on, however, as a pedagogical simplification.

Decrease in the extent of elevation of the front of the tongue has the effect of increasing the cross-sectional area of the constriction between the two cavities. This results in a rise in the frequency of formant 1 and a fall in the frequencies of formants 2 and 3. In terms of a network of Helmholtz resonators the relevant effects of such an articulatory change could be assumed to be the increase in the size of the opening to the rear cavity, and the increase in the volume of the front cavity. But the increase in the size of the connecting orifice increases the effect which each cavity has on the resonatory characteristics of the other—in other words, each formant becomes less dependent on a mode of resonance in one cavity and more dependent on a mode of resonance of the whole tract. Hence explanation of the changes in frequency in terms of changes in volumes or orifices of Helmholtz resonators becomes less valid.

There is a similar development if labialization in the form of lip-rounding is added to the typical articulation of position one. This addition is associated with a distinct fall in the frequencies of formants 2 and 3, the former usually into the medium range, but seems to have relatively little effect on the frequency of formant 1. The fall in formant 2 frequency may be viewed as partly a result of the increase in the volume of the front cavity with the protrusion of the lips and of the decrease in the area of the orifice there. But the effects of the addition of this articulation are acoustically not so simple; the decrease in the size of the labial opening increases the interaction of the two cavities in the vocal tract and hence the dependence of all formants on modes of resonance of the whole tract.

4.54. As a second typical setting of the vocal tract, position two, we may consider that in which the rear of the tongue is retracted and raised toward the soft palate or the upper part of the rear wall of the oral pharynx (Fig. 4.1 B). The velum is raised. Again two main cavities are formed, with a narrow connecting passage, one cavity extending forward over the mouth from the elevation of the tongue to the lips, the other extending downwards from the elevation of the tongue to the larynx.

This configuration, with the addition of the lip rounding with which it is usually but not necessarily accompanied, is associated with low frequencies of formants 1, 2, and 3. Since the constriction is neither near the front of the mouth nor near the glottis, these low frequencies are likely to be closely connected with the small size of the labial opening.

Decrease in the elevation of the tongue from position two can be accomplished in two distinguishable ways. The first is by lowering in an approximately vertical direction so that the constriction between the dorsum of the tongue and the rear wall of the oral pharynx is displaced downwards, and nearer to the glottis. As this happens, the frequency of formants 2 and 3 fall to even lower levels, bringing all three formants closer together on the frequency scale.

The other way of decreasing the elevation of the tongue from position two is by lowering so that the highest point of the tongue moves not only downward but also somewhat forward in the mouth. Such modification reduces the constriction between the dorsum of the tongue and the soft palate and at the same time moves it a little further away from the glottis. The former change tends to raise the frequency of formant 1 and to lower those of formants 2 and 3, while the latter tends to have the reverse effect. In theory the effects of the two might cancel each other out, but in actual examples of this modification the decrease in the elevation of the tongue is usually accompanied by an increase in the size of the labial opening, and the final result is an increase in the frequency of all three formants.

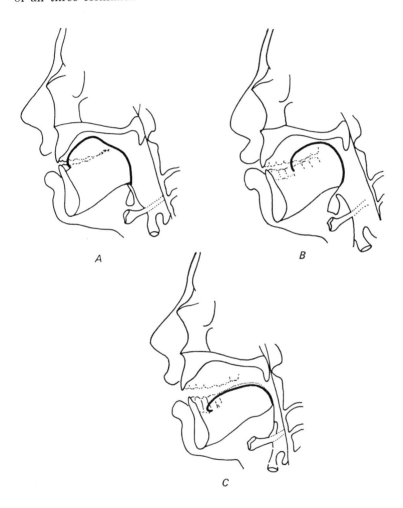

Fig. 4.1.   Typical settings of the upper vocal tract
A is the articulatory position in the English vowel [iː], *B* that in [uː] and *C* that in [ɑː].   The drawings are from x-ray photographs by F. Strenger, Stockholm (after Malmberg)

Position two of the vocal tract has been considered so far when accompanied by lip rounding. Unrounding of the lips increases the size of the labial orifice, and the effect again is a rise in the frequencies of all three formants.

In position two, however, the front of the tongue is able to vary its position quite considerably. As a subdivision of this position, therefore, those cases may be included in which the blade or tip of the tongue is brought close to the hard palate or the alveolar ridge. Retraction of the body of the tongue for such articulation is usually accomplished by bunching and elevating the rear of this organ in a fashion characteristic of position two. The resulting configuration of the vocal tract resembles a series of three connected cavities, the middle one taking the place of the former front cavity, and a new front cavity being formed forward of the palatal or alveolar constriction.

There is little theoretical evidence as to formant frequencies in such configurations, but the material available suggests that formants 1 and 3 are of low frequency and formant 2 of low or medium frequency.

4.55. As a third typical setting of the vocal tract, we select the case in which there is a large orifice at the lips but no pronounced elevation of either the front or the back of the tongue. In these cases, however, the root usually forms a constriction against the lower rear wall of the oral pharynx thus dividing the tract into a large buccal and a comparatively small pharyngeal cavity (Fig. 4.1 C). The velum is raised.

This configuration is associated with a formant 1 of high, and a formant 2 of low or medium frequency. Formant 3 is usually about the middle of its range.

The high frequency of formant 1 conforms to expectation from the nearness of the constriction to the glottis and from the large size of the labial opening. The frequencies of the other two formants are understandable as balances between articulatory features tending to exert opposing influences.

4.56. So far we have considered the transmission characteristics of the vocal tract as a whole, but at this point it may be helpful, in spite of the difficulty of a theoretical handling of the material, to consider the apparent acoustic effects of a number of articulations which are traditionally distinguished in phonetics, mainly from the fact that in the analysis of many languages it is possible to isolate them from the general articulatory setting of the vocal tract. We shall refer to the group of them as *minor articulations*.[1]

The first is *labialization*, the addition of lip-protrusion and rounding to the articulation of a sound. The effect of this addition to a configuration of the vocal tract is a lowering of the frequencies of all the formants. Formant 2 is especially affected. The extent of the lowering generally depends first on the degree of labialization —which seems to have relatively little effect until the reduction of the cross-sectional area of the labial orifice renders this comparable to or smaller than that of the constriction between the tongue and the roof of the mouth—and secondly on the frequencies of the un-labialized configuration: where these are high the effect is considerable, and conversely. Thus the addition of labialization to position one brings a lowering of several hundred cycles in formant 2 frequency but of only perhaps a few cycles in the already low frequency of formant 1.

The second of these minor articulations is *palatalization*, the raising of the front of the tongue toward the hard palate, with the tip turned downward. Such an articulation, which by itself is the most characteristic feature of position one, may also be added to any of a number of other articulatory settings of the vocal tract; it is then termed palatalization, and considered as a secondary articulation. The basic articulation to which it has been added is said to be palatalized. The acoustic effect of palatalization, the extent of which will depend, of course, on the degree of elevation of the tongue, is a small lowering in the frequency of formant 1, a considerable raising in that of formant 2, and a small raising in that of formant 3.

Thirdly, the elevation of the back of the tongue toward the soft palate or rear wall of the pharynx as in position two may be added to a number of other articulatory settings of the vocal tract, and in these cases is termed *velarization*. The effect of this articulation, which will vary with the extent of the elevation of the tongue to the rear, is to lower the frequency of formant 2 considerably, and that of formant 3 slightly, with little change in formant 1.

As a fourth articulation of this nature, we may consider *nasalization*, the addition of the nasal pharynx and passages to the resonating

[1] For the diacritics and modifications to symbols recommended for the representation of these minor articulations see Appendix I.

cavities of the vocal tract by the lowering of the velum (§ 3.40). The acoustic results of such addition are primarily an increase in the number of resonances and of negative resonances (§ 4.45) in the vocal tract. The intensities and frequencies of such additional resonances depend primarily on two factors, the characteristics of the various modes of resonance excited in the oral tract, and the closeness of the coupling of the nasal passages to the oral tract, this latter depending mainly on the size of the opening to the nasal tract. Since both these factors vary, the former in particular being different for each different sound, there is no simple feature of the spectrum which can be consistently associated with nasalization. What commonly occurs, however, in nasalized sounds, is a weakening of the intensity of formant 1 and the appearance of some extra formants, one about 200–300 c/s, another about 1,000 c/s.

The fifth articulatory modification of the transmission characteristics of the vocal tract is a contraction of the volume of the oral pharynx known as *pharyngealization* or, perhaps less commonly, *pharyngalization*. This has been discussed by Jakobson, Fant & Halle (1952), who point out that its acoustic results are perceptually similar to those of labialization. They publish a spectrogram of an Arabic pharyngealized consonant and its non-pharyngealized correspondent. Comparison shows that high frequency energy is slightly lowered, and suggests that the position of formant 2 is considerably lower on the frequency scale in the pharyngealized consonant.

The sixth minor articulation which may occur in phonetic systems is that producing a contrast between what is termed *tenseness* in vowels but *fortisness* in consonants on the one hand and *laxness* in vowels but *lenisness* in consonants on the other. Though the contrast between tense and lax vowels, and between fortis and lenis consonants has long been recognized in phonetics, it is only recently that the equivalence of tenseness and fortisness, and of laxness and lenisness has been understood.

Basically, tens or efortis articulations are characterized by higher air-stream pressure, a consequence of larger energy expenditure in the air-stream initiating mechanism, and by higher muscular tension in the organs articulating in the supraglottal tract. Associated with these features are normally also a greater precision of articulation, and a greater duration of the sound articulated.

Lax or lenis articulations on the other hand are characterized by lower air-stream pressure, and less muscular tension in the organs articulating, together with, normally, less precision and a shorter duration. Lax vowels, in addition, are characterized by a somewhat centralized articulation, i.e. one in which the highest point of the tongue is represented as close to the central area of the vowel quadrilateral (§ 5.42).

4.6. Coarticulation

4.60. We are now able to combine the information given in Chapter III about the organs of speech and their movement possibilities with the information we have just covered in Chapter IV, namely, the way in which sound waves can be set up in the vocal tract. As an example of the processes involved in the production of sound in speech, we shall attempt to describe the main articulatory movements in a speaker's pronunciation of the word *horse*. We shall assume that this is an isolated word, preceded and followed by silence, and we shall describe the activity of each of the articulatory organs in successive stages during its pronunciation. The main components of these activities are represented schematically in Figure 4.2.

4.61. Before any sound begins, the speaker is breathing normally. The glottis is open, with the vocal cords abducted into the position of normal breathing (§ 3.33), and the velum is lowered, opening the passage to the nasal pharynx (§ 3.40). The respiratory muscles are in a state of activity, producing alternately an ingressive and an egressive air stream through the trachea and the open glottis, the laryngeal, oral, and nasal pharynxes, and thence through the nares to the outside air.

The mandible is lowered smoothly, the lips part and begin to develop a rounded shape of the opening between them. The velum is raised, closing the orifice to the nasal cavities, and diverting an egressive air stream through the mouth cavity and lips to the outside air. The vocal cords are tensed and movement of the arytenoid cartilages begins to draw their edges across the glottis. The complex activity of the respiratory muscles initiating the air stream increases, not so much, probably, to increase the flow of the air stream as, by muscular balancing, to increase fine control over the rate of that flow. As the movement of the vocal cords limits the opening to the cartilaginous glottis, the velocity of the air stream through the narrowed opening increases, and sound waves

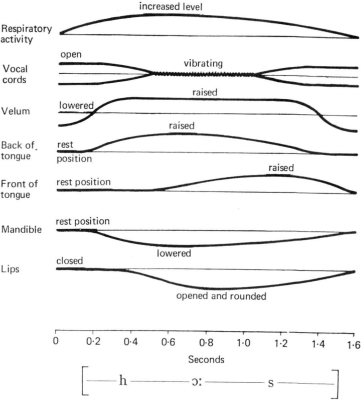

Fig. 4.2.   Coarticulation.   (See text p. 69 ff.)

begin to result from turbulence and eddying at that point, increasing
in intensity as the vocal cords draw together along the length of
the membranous glottis. These waves are then transmitted through
the supraglottal vocal tract to the outside air at the lips as [h], the
first part of this sound sequence.

While this activity is taking place in the larynx, the back of the
tongue moves backward from its position of rest and a little upward,
forming a gradually increasing constriction against the back wall
of the throat. The edges of the vocal cords along the membranous
glottis loosen and begin to flutter as some of the air stream pushes
through this glottis. Gradually, the flow of air through the cartilaginous glottis decreases, the turbulent eddying there becomes less,
and is replaced as the input to the vocal tract transmission line by

70

the sound waves generated from the periodic pulses of air through the vocal cords as regular cycles of vibration develop in the membranous glottis. The output at the lips, [ɔː], constitutes the second part of the sequence.

There is, however, no steady state: the lips attain and pass through the position of their maximum rounding and the back of the tongue moves smoothly through the point of maximum constriction. The blade of the tongue begins to move upward and forward. The body of the tongue follows, supporting and extending the movement of the blade. The mandible reaches the point of its maximum lowering and returns upwards towards its position of rest, the lips likewise begin to unround and close through a neutral position. The blade of the tongue approaches the alveolar ridge, and as it does so, turbulent eddying of the air stream begins in the narrowing constriction. The sound waves resulting are added to those from the vocal cords and filtered through the forward cavities to the outer air. The former increase in intensity as the constriction becomes greater, and the latter decrease as the vocal cords draw apart and their vibrations die out. The tongue blade moves smoothly through the point of maximum approach to the alveolar ridge. This marks the centre of [s], the third part of the sound sequence. Respiratory activity decreases, and the sound waves become weaker as the constriction at the alveolum lessens and the velocity of the air stream through it falls. The sound waves die out, the vocal cords relax into the open position, the body and blade of the tongue return to a position of rest, the velum opens, the mandible and the lips close. Normal breathing is resumed.

4.62. As appears even from this simplified description, the production of a stretch of sound involves a continually changing complex of movements of organs and muscles in the vocal apparatus. These movements are related to one another in various ways. Some, for example, presuppose the execution of previous movements, as the raising of the velum depends on the previous lowering of it; some depend largely on the more or less concomitant occurrence of another, as the opening of the lips depends on the lowering of the mandible; and some follow and form a smooth continuation of others, as the return movement of the body of the tongue during the release of the constriction against the back of the throat passes over into the succeeding movement forward to support the alveolar articulation of the blade, leaving no point at which the change from one articulation to the other can be precisely located.

Save for a point before any articulatory or breathing movement begins, and for one after all has ceased, there are no obvious or inherent breaks in the articulatory activity producing this stretch of sound, no points at which all the organs are motionless, or at which they are, so to speak, in phase—all at the same relative point along the cycles of their particular articulations. The stretch of sound [hɔːs] is produced by a continually changing, unbroken, complex of movements, often overlapping and interlocking with one another physically and temporally. The same description is valid for all stretches of human speech.

4.63. There is an important consequence of the overlapping and interlocking of articulatory movements: the nature of the articulation at any point or during any short segment of time is dependent on the nature of the articulation during a preceding period of time, and conversely, the articulation at any point or during any short segment of time will influence the articulation during the succeeding period of time. For example, the situation represented at and about time 0·6 in Figure 4.2 includes a raised level of respiratory activity resulting from the gradual increase in this activity during the period from time 0·0, and this raised level continues to be part of the articulation during the succeeding period. The articulation at the same time also shows the beginnings of vibration as the vocal cords are loosened along the previously closed membranous glottis and the air stream initiated earlier by the respiratory mechanism becomes diverted from the closing cartilaginous glottis. And again the vibration so beginning continues into the succeeding period of time.

It is usually not possible to be very precise as to the location or the duration of the period of time taken by a specific articulation in the stretch of articulatory activity. This will vary according to the particular articulation concerned and according to the nature of preceding and succeeding articulations in the stretch. In our diagram, the articulation of opening and rounding the lips begins about time 0·4, reaches its maximum just after time 0·8 and ends finally toward time 1·6; a total period of some three-quarters of the whole stretch. The opening of the lips is obviously a prerequisite to their rounding, but over what part of this period the lips can be said to be rounded is impossible to say. Similarly the movement of the front of the tongue, which begins about time 0·5, reaches a maximum about time 1·2 and ends toward time 1·6. But within this period, the points at which the raised front of the tongue begins and ceases to induce turbulent eddying of the air stream between itself and the alveolar ridge remain indistinct.

This state of affairs, the temporal overlapping, the physical interlocking and the consequential reciprocal influencing of articulations during adjacent periods of sound production is termed *coarticulation*, and the articulations are said to be coarticulated. Coarticulation is a fundamental and inescapable feature of the working of the whole mechanism of speech sound production.

CHAPTER 5

THE DESCRIPTION AND CLASSIFICATION OF SPEECH SOUNDS

5.1. Decomposition of the Expression Substance

5.10.   An important task in any science is the classification of the units of the material with which that science operates. This classification can be done in different ways and on different grounds according to the purpose which the scientist has in view, and the criteria of the success of a classification lie in its adequacy and usefulness in answering that purpose.

Classification presupposes first an analysis to isolate units to be classified and second a method of description of these units which enables some to be distinguished from others, and hence classes to be set up.

It will be recalled that in Chapter I we talked of the stretch of sound [hɔːs] as the expression of a symbol, but made no attempt to divide or segment this stretch into smaller pieces. Now it has almost always been assumed by phoneticians that such stretches are composed of smaller pieces, in differing selections and in differing orders, and that the smallest of these pieces are the basic units of study in phonetics. In spite of this assumption, and in spite of the fact that some segmentation is an obvious prerequisite to the study of those units, relatively little attention has been paid to the process of or procedures for segmentation of the stretch of sound.

In this chapter, then, we shall discuss first the procedure by which the phonetician decomposes and segments the raw material of his science as it comes to him from the mouths of the speakers, and second, the ways in which he may describe and classify the results of his procedure according to their characteristic features.

5.11.   As was pointed out in Chapter I, the material which is studied in phonetics, that is, the expression substance, is of different nature at each of the stages through which it passes. Up till the present, however, it is only at stages two and three, that is, as articulation and as sound waves, that this substance is really accessible to the phonetician. Hence stretches of articulation and stretches of sound form the basic material for him to work on. Let us assume then that a phonetician has collected on magnetic recording tape examples of the stretch of sound [hɔːs] as spoken by a number of speakers in various contexts and situations; and that, together with these, he has collected on motion-picture film X-ray recordings of the articulations used in producing those stretches of sound.

As the phonetician plays these sound recordings over, he is able to hear differences of various sorts between them. For example, if he is acquainted with the speakers, he will be able to recognize which speaker produced which examples in his material. This is clearly possible only because different speakers introduce different personal or individual qualities, partly of course depending on their sex and on their age, into the stretch of sound. If our phonetician is not studying these individual qualities of the sound, he abstracts them, in his mind—phonetics is partly an art (§ 1.3)—and concentrates his attention on what is left in each stretch.

He will then notice that these stretches are spoken with differing degrees of loudness, with differing inflections or pitches, and with differing speeds. Some of the differences of these features derive from the situations in which the stretches were articulated—one may be louder than another because the hearer was further away, or faster since the speaker was excited or had little time available and so on. These situationally induced differences are also abstracted from the material by the phonetician and, unless he is studying them, excluded from further consideration.

5.12. Some further differences, however, derive from patterns in the language itself. Thus, for example, the first [hɔːs] is clearly louder than the second in the sentence—*the horse was a black horse.* Again, the first [hɔːs] is pronounced with a falling or low pitch in the following piece of (imaginary) conversation and the second with a rising pitch—

"What's that at the door?"
"His horse."
"His horse?"

And thirdly, in the last piece of the conversation, the centre part of the word *his*, the vowel part, is shorter than the corresponding part in the word *horse*. These three features, being part of the language, are of interest to the phonetician. They are, it is obvious, ways in which this language makes a special use of three basic qualities of a sound wave, its intensity, its fundamental frequency, and its duration, for the purpose of carrying information from the speaker to the hearer.

Languages differ in their special uses of these qualities. In English, variations in two of them, the fundamental frequency and the intensity, are used to modify stretches of sound such as words, phrases, and sentences. It is customary for the phonetician to distinguish such modifications of stretches of sound as part of the suprasegmental or prosodic system of the language, a system which will be discussed in Chapter VIII. At this point, accordingly, our phonetician mentally removes them from his material.

Duration, however, is used in English as an integral feature of some of the shorter segments of the sound stretch, and our phonetician retains for consideration his observation of the difference in duration between the central parts of the words *his* and *horse*.

5.13. By these processes of abstraction, several *layers* have been removed from the original stretches of sound. What remains in each stretch is the basic substance of the signal; the individual characteristics, the situational differences, and the prosodic features have all been removed. This substance constitutes the *segmental layer*.

As outlined above, the segmental layer is an idealized abstraction which has its existence only as a concept in the mind of the phonetician. For the laboratory he must have material which he can store, observe, and work with in physical terms. For this there are two possibilities. The first is to use his original collection of tape-recorded stretches of sound, discounting at each observation or experiment the effects which he knows or takes to derive from the inclusion of the material of other layers. The second is to have new material produced with, as far as possible, standardized levels of pitch, loudness, and speed to eliminate or reduce the effects of differences in the situational and prosodic layers. And by the use of only one speaker, the individual layer, which cannot be excluded, can be kept constant.

5.14. Since the individual, situational, prosodic, and segmental layers exist in stage three, that is, as sound waves, there must be, in stage two, articulations and features of articulation which produce them. A similar process of decomposition into layers is therefore theoretically necessary with the material on articulation. The

76

methods of recording articulatory movements on X-ray film, however, do not yet result in recordings with sufficient material or in adequate detail, and techniques for analysing such records in a manner parallel to that which we have sketched for the sound have not yet been developed. The phonetician in practice is not able to distinguish layers in the articulation which correspond to the situational or prosodic features of the stretches of articulation. Nor is he able to do more than occasionally suspect features as due to individual differences in articulation. For working purposes, then, he has no other course than to operate with X-ray recordings corresponding to the sound recordings he is using, and to bear in mind the complex nature of the material on them.

5.2. Segmentation

5.20. In either articulatory or sound form, the segmental layer within the stretch [hɔːs] is continuous, with no obvious natural breaks or points of segmentation (§ 4.6). What the phonetician would like to devise is some means of segmenting this continuum from within, that is, by reference only to features observable in the continuum, and with no reference to anything outside it. Of the attempts to do this, we need mention only one, that of Pike, which up to the present is the nearest to successful.

Pike's segmentation is of the articulatory material. Each of the organs of the vocal apparatus is viewed as having fundamentally two possibilities of movement. One is a closing movement, leading to a closure or a narrowing at some point or relatively small section of the vocal tract. Such a closure or narrowing is termed a *stricture*. A *crest* of stricture is a point in a stricture-making movement where the stricture, or strictures if there are more than one being formed, approach more nearly a state of closure of the vocal tract than the stricture or strictures immediately preceding.

The other movement possible to the organs of the vocal tract is an opening one, that is, a movement in the reverse direction from a closing one, and leading towards a stricture of greater openness in the vocal tract. A *trough* of stricture is a point in a stricture-making movement where the stricture or strictures approach more nearly a state of openness of the vocal tract than the stricture or strictures immediately preceding.

Each crest or trough of stricture is then taken to be the centre of a segment in the articulatory continuum, the number of segments

77

in any stretch of articulation being equal to the number of crests and troughs in that stretch.

The addition of any stricture, to silence or to an existing stricture, adds a crest segment, and the subtraction of a stricture from an existing segment, adds a trough segment. The replacement of one stricture by another adds a crest segment if the replacing segment is of higher rank but a trough segment if of lower rank than the replaced segment. Strictures are ranked from high to low in the order: oral closure, oral fricative stricture, oral frictionless stricture (as in a vowel), nasal stricture (the raising of the velum to close the passage to the nasal pharynx), pharyngeal or glottal stricture.

5.21.   Let us, as an example, apply this procedure to the stretch of articulation necessary to produce the word [hɔːs] (§ 4.6). We start with silence and an open position of the vocal tract. The first stricture-making articulation is the smooth adduction and release of the vocal cords at the whisper glottis. The centre of this articulation, being added to silence, constitutes a crest of stricture. The second stricture-making articulation, which commences during, but soon replaces the first, is the upward and backward movement of the back of the tongue to form an oral frictionless stricture against the pharyngeal wall and its continuing forward movement releasing that stricture. The centre of this stricture, which is of higher rank than the replaced, is a second crest of stricture. The third stricture-making articulation is the forward and upward movement of the front of the tongue to form an oral fricative stricture against the alveolar ridge and the falling away, releasing movement. Again this stricture is of higher rank than the one it replaces, and its centre constitutes a further crest.

The whole stretch of sound is accordingly marked by three successive crests of strictures, and is hence taken to be formed of three successive segments.[1] The beginnings and ends of these segments are indefinite: no procedure has yet been evolved to establish the borders of segments in a continuous stretch of articulation.

5.22.   A procedure for the segmentation of a continuous stretch of sound has been outlined by Joos (1948). It is based on the recurrence

---

[1] No troughs of stricture occur in this stretch. If this is continued to include the plural inflexion, as [hɔːsɪz] *horses*, the following articulation is an oral frictionless stricture formed by the front of the tongue against the hard palate. Since this is of lower rank than its predecessor, its centre represents a trough of stricture.

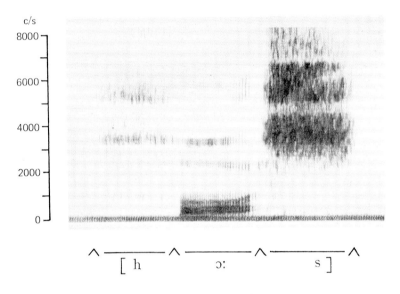

Fig. 5.1.   Spectrogram of [hɔːs] *horse*
The arrowheads mark the transitions and the lines extend along the
intervening segments (see p. 79)

facing p. 79

of recognizable features in the spectrographic recordings or spectrograms (§ 4.51) of such stretches. These are of two sorts. First there are periods within the sound stretch in which the acoustic structure —the frequencies and the intensities of the components—shows relatively little change. These may be termed *segments*. Secondly, there are periods, very much shorter than the former, in which the acoustic structure shows, in comparison, extremely rapid change. These are termed *transitions*. The segments and transitions alternate in the stretch of sound.

For example, in the spectrogram of [hɔːs] (Fig. 5.1), there is a very short period of rapid change from silence to a spread of acoustic energy over a wide range of frequencies—a transition; a period in which this spread is maintained—a segment; then another transition in which the diffuse acoustic energy is replaced by relatively strong clear formants[1]; a segment in which these formants continue; another transition in which the formants disappear and are replaced by considerable diffuse energy in the higher ranges of frequency; a final segment in which this is maintained; and a final transition to silence.

The location of these transitions and segments in the sound stretch is not always obvious or indisputable. The segments are not, as can be seen, clearly or definitely bounded, since their borders, the transitions, are somewhat blurred in time and also in frequency, but to the extent that they can be located, they provide a segmentation of the material in the acoustic layer from recurrent internal features.

5.23. The method of segmentation which is most generally used by phoneticians is based on a comparison and contrast of the stretch of sound or of articulation to be segmented with other stretches in the same language. Our phonetician, in other words, compares his abstracted stretch of sound with other similarly abstracted stretches to identify the parts or pieces in it which recur elsewhere. Thus, comparison with such stretches as those associated with the words *course, gorse, hearse, hoard, horn,* etc., suggests that [hɔːs] is composed of three parts, the first occurring also in first position in *hearse, hoard,* and *horn,* the second occurring also in middle position

---

[1] In our spectrogram, as in most of [h] followed by a vowel, outlines of the formant structure of the vowel may be discerned in the preceding [h]. (See §§ 4.6, 6.22.)

in *course, hoard, horn,* etc., and the third occurring in last position in *course, gorse,* etc.

This result, the recognition of parts of the stretch [hɔːs] as being the *same* as or *different* from parts of other stretches, is not reached through purely phonetic considerations. Phonetically, the middle part of the stretch of sound representing *hoard* is clearly longer, and the middle part of that representing *horn* clearly more nasalized, than the middle part of [hɔːs]. The classing of these three parts as the same cannot therefore be simply justified on the grounds of acoustic or articulatory sameness. It is, in fact, rather justified on the grounds of the similar functioning of these three parts in the general economy of English: all are representatives or manifestations of the same functional sound unit or *phoneme* of this language. The nature of phonemes and their functioning is discussed in Chapter X; at this point we must simply recognize that our phonetician's classification of parts of [hɔːs] as the same as or different from parts of other stretches in the language is the result of a judgment in which considerations both of physical nature and of linguistic functioning play a role.

The further step of locating the borders of these parts within the stretch of sound or of articulation, and thus segmenting it, is simple in practice since almost any user of the language can isolate the three segments of [hɔːs] as formal-functional units.

5.24. The three segments in the stretch of expression substance [hɔːs] are conventionally represented by the three characters we have used to refer to it, namely, [h], [ɔː], and [s]. They are the minimum units in the segmental layer. In the acoustic stage of the expression substance (§ 1.2) they are termed *sounds, speech sounds,* or *phones*. Since the first two of these terms are also used in other contexts with different referents, the last would seem the most satisfactory term, and we shall give it preference. But the student must be familiar with all three and their varying uses.

In the articulatory stage of the expression substance, the minimum units of the segmental layer have, surprisingly, no name in phonetics distinct from those of the acoustic stage, and are thus known also as *sounds, speech sounds,* or *phones*. A specific term is needed; we shall accordingly use *articule*. The term *(speech) sound* may thus be continued when reference is to a segment of the expression substance without distinction of phone and articule.

5.25. The articules themselves are often further segmented by the phonetician into three—a beginning or *approach*, a central portion or *hold* and an ending or *release*. Such segmentation seems to be done subjectively on the grounds of sensory impression of the articulatory movements or of the sound wave, and no more objective or explicit procedures exist for isolating these segments. The conception of an articule as consisting of an *approach, hold*, and *release* derives ultimately from, and reflects a now largely discarded theory of articulation, namely, that the vocal organs moved into position for the production of a phone, maintained this as a stationary position during that production, and then moved into the position for the following phone. For this reason, among others, the main one being that it is more applicable to some articules than others, the view of the articule as a tripartite segment is regarded with some reserve, and is less commonly met today. Nevertheless it is often helpful pedagogically and convenient descriptively to be able to refer, without any implication of stationariness, to differing portions of an articule, and for this the terms *approach, hold*, and *release* are useful. In a phone the segments corresponding to the approach and the release in an articule are frequently referred to as the *onset* and the *decay*, but no term seems to be in general use for the central portion.

5.3. Phonetic Alphabets

5.30. It may seem that we have followed a complicated and roundabout way to reach what is a perfectly obvious conclusion, namely, that the stretch of expression substance associated with the graphic symbol *horse* consists of three separate sounds [h], [ɔː], and [s]. We have seen, however, that the expression substance, acoustic and articulatory, is evidently continuous during this stretch; the obviousness of its segmentation into three derives mainly from our acquired experience and ability in manipulation of the segments as realizations of fundamental functioning units in the language. And the belief that the continuous stretch of speech consists of a succession of discrete units is further ingrained into us by the use of an alphabet. All alphabets—roman, cyrillic, semitic, devanagari, etc.—stem from a segmentation of the stream of speech on the basis of the form and function of linguistic units.

81

5.31. The symbols [h, ɔː, s] which we have used are from a phonetic alphabet, an alphabet which has been developed to assist in the representation of language sounds. The basic principle in such an alphabet is that one letter or character should represent one speech sound only and should represent it consistently. Phonetic alphabets have been proposed at least since the 17th century, but few early ones seem to have been used by other than their authors. With the great development of language study in 19th century Europe, interest increased and several such alphabets were developed. Some used the roman alphabet as a basis, supplementing it where necessary with extra characters or diacritics; others, the analphabetic ones, comprised entirely new characters, often partly symbolic of the positions of the organs of speech.

The most important survivor of these alphabets is that of the International Phonetic Association, the IPA, for short, and it is basically this alphabet we are using here. The IPA alphabet has been continually under the purview of the Association, and, from time to time, modified as seemed necessary. Its latest revision is reproduced below (p. 218).

Besides being the most widely used phonetic alphabet in the world, the IPA alphabet has also considerably influenced subsequent developments for more specific purposes or areas. Thus, during the twenties, a special orthography largely based on the IPA alphabet was developed for the spelling of African languages. In Scandinavia, a modified form of the IPA alphabet has been developed to cope with the special problems of the sound systems of the Nordic dialects. And the IPA alphabet has itself been subject to modification: the use of the typewriter has introduced changes, especially in the United States, to enable it to be handled more easily by the standard keyboard. A general convention in its use, however, is to include the symbols within square brackets [ ], or, in printed books, to reproduce them in a special typeface.[1]

5.32. One important development of more general interest should be mentioned. As phoneticians became more skilled, the number of distinct and distinguishable sounds continued to increase. Finer and finer differences between sounds were observed and duly incorporated

[1] An account of the principles and development of the IPA alphabet, together with an interesting survey of some of its more important precursors, is given by Albright (1958).

into phonetic analyses and descriptions. This led, eventually, to the conception of *broad* and *narrow* systems of phonetic transcription, the former incorporating only as much phonetic information as is necessary to distinguish the functioning sounds in a language—at this point phonetics approaches phonemics very closely—and the latter incorporating as much more phonetic information as the phonetician desires, or as he can distinguish.[1]

5.4. Articulatory Description

5.40. Given adequate samples, the comparison and contrast procedure sketched above enables the phonetician to isolate the sounds of the language he is investigating from its expression substance. His next task is the description of these sounds, that is, a description of the articulatory nature of the articules, and a description of the acoustic nature of the phones.

The description of articules is one of the oldest and commonest procedures in phonetics. To be adequate, a description must include the designation of the air stream involved, the specification of the organs of speech which articulate, the type of articulation performed, and, if this is not implied, the place of the articulation.

5.41. On the grounds of type of articulation, a major distinction is customarily made between two classes of articule, the classes being traditionally termed *vowels* and *consonants*. The tradition, however, is changing: there is a tendency today to limit these terms to classes of units distinguished on the basis of their functioning within a language, and to use *vocoid* and *contoid* as terms for classes of articules—or of phones—distinguished by features of expression substance. Then a contoid is characterized by a so-called *close* articulation, that is, a complete, partial, or intermittent blockage of the supraglottal air passage through the pharynx and mouth by an organ or organs in such a way that the air stream is blocked or hindered, or otherwise gives rise to audible friction (cf. § 4.3). A vocoid, on the other hand, is characterized by an *open* articulation, a lack of any such obstruction and consequent free passage to the air stream through this supraglottal passage.

Minor variations of this distinction, or of its interpretation, are found. Thus, though most phoneticians would agree that the blockage and release of the air stream at the glottis, as occurs

---

[1] For further discussion of this point see Appendix A to Jones (1962).

in [ʔ], characterizes this articule as a contoid, not all would agree that the narrowing of the air passage at the same place renders [h] a contoid, and many scholars view this particular articule as a voiceless vocoid. Again, in an articule like [l], the air passage is blocked in the centre of the mouth but the air stream is allowed to pass out round the sides of the tongue along the sides of the mouth. In many productions of [l] no audible friction is noticeable. Hence if the blockage in the centre of the mouth passage is viewed as the essential criterion, [l] would be classed as a contoid, but if the free passage to the sides, and the lack of audible friction are viewed as the essential criteria, [l] would be classed as a vocoid.

The problems here seem to arise essentially from the fact that close articulations which block the air stream completely—even if only momentarily—or intermittently are relatively easy to distinguish, articulatorily and acoustically, from other close or open articulations, but close articulations which are said to give a partial blockage are often difficult to distinguish from open articulations which give a free passage to the air stream. The criterion of the presence or absence of audible friction does not resolve all cases indubitably, since first the audibility of friction depends to some extent on the sensitivity of the individual ear, secondly the same articulation with an air stream of one velocity may give rise to distinctly audible friction and with one of a smaller velocity to inaudible friction (§ 4.33), and thirdly distinctly audible friction in a voiceless articulation may be completely masked if voice is added.

No satisfactory solution to these difficulties of a general articulatory description has yet been proposed. In any particular language or group of languages, of course, other criteria, for example of a functional nature, may be adduced to assist in cases of uncertainty. But without such additional helps, a certain arbitrariness is often unavoidable in the decision as to which articules have close articulation with partial blockage and which have open articulation with free passage of the air stream.

In most cases, however, the articulatory description is simple, unambiguous, and very satisfactory for pedagogical purposes. Thus if we describe articules formed on an egressive air stream from the lungs as *pulmonic* and *egressive*, those with conversion of kinetic energy to acoustic energy (§ 4.3) at the vocal cords *voiced*, those with conversion between the tongue and the alveolum or between the lips *linguo-alveolar* or *bilabial* respectively, those in which conversion is by means of blockage and release of the air stream *plosives*, and those in which it is by narrowing of the air passage *fricatives*, we can then describe [b] as a pulmonic, egressive, voiced, bilabial plosive contoid, and [s] as a pulmonic, egressive, voiceless, linguo-alveolar fricative contoid.

In this way a very accurate and detailed description of any articule can be built up. In lingual fricatives, for example, besides information on the air stream and the presence or absence of laryngeal voicing, the particular part of the tongue involved, the tip, blade, front, back, etc., the section of the roof of the mouth, and the type of narrowed passage, i.e. whether rounded or slit-like in cross-section, may all be specified. And lastly, if necessary, the position and shape of the lips may be indicated.

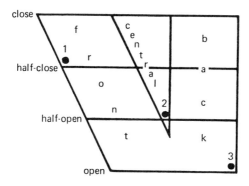

Fig. 5.2. The vowel quadrilateral

5.42. The vocoids are usually described with reference to the position of the highest point of the tongue during their production. This position is represented in a two-dimensional schematic diagram of the sagittal cross-section in the centre of the mouth cavity, the *vowel quadrilateral* (Fig. 5.2). The base line represents the physio-logical limit to downward movement of the upper surface of the tongue and the top line the limit to open articulation, above which obstruction or hindrance of the air stream and hence close articula-tion occurs. The vertical dimension then represents tongue elevation, and has four conventional reference points: *open, half-open, half-close close*, and reading from bottom to top. The lines at the side of the diagram represent similarly the limits to open articulation in a horizontal dimension, it being customary to represent the limits set by the alveolum and teeth to the left of the diagram and those set by the pharyngeal wall to the right. This dimension has three sections for reference, *front*, *central*, and *back*, reading from left to right.

Thus a vocoid in the production of which the position of the highest point of the tongue may be represented at the point marked 1 on Figure 5.2 or within a small region about 1 is termed a half-close front vowel. Similarly vocoids in which those positions may be represented at or about point 2 and point 3 are termed half-open central and open back vocoids, respectively.

To the specification of the position of the highest point of the tongue in terms of tongue elevation and tongue frontness or backness, may be added the details of lip-position, voicing, tenseness or laxness (§ 4.56), duration, etc., which are characteristic of the vocoid under analysis. Thus, for example, [e] may be specified as a pulmonic, egressive, voiced, half-close, front, unrounded, short, tense vocoid.

5.5. Acoustic Description

5.50.   The acoustic nature of the phones of a language may be described in several ways. The most obvious and the most complete is a description of the frequency, intensity, and duration of each of the sound waves composing that phone. The difficulty here is the acoustic analysis, a long and laborious calculation being necessary to determine the components of any complex sound wave (§ 2.3). In recent years a simplification has been introduced by the development of electronic devices such as the Acoustic Spectrograph (§ 4.51, note) which produces spectrograms.

A spectrogram represents the spectrum of the phone analysed. Differences in spectra may be described by, for example, such features as the presence or absence of energy at the fundamental frequency, the number and definiteness of the formants or their absence, the extent and positioning of randomly or diffusely distributed energy, and/or by the changes in these features within the duration of the phone. It is generally convenient to distinguish between phones with strongly defined formants and negligible power at other frequenices, the *resonants*, those with formants and power at other frequencies, the *semi-resonants*, and those with no distinguishable formants, the *non-resonants* (cf. § 4.44).

The resonants may be further described in terms of, for example, the positions of the formants on the frequency scale, whether the two lower formants are close together or wide apart, whether they are of similar intensity, etc. The non-resonants may be described by the range of frequency over which their acoustic power is spread, by the abruptness or smoothness of the onset and/or decay of the sound, by the presence or absence of periods of silence within the duration of the phone, etc. The semi-resonants may be described in terms of either or both of these sets of features.

5.51. A detailed systematic classification of segmental sounds with reference to describable features of their acoustic nature has been proposed by Jakobson, Fant & Halle (1952). To them each phone is a bundle of approximately simultaneous acoustic characteristics called *distinctive features*, which arise from the nature of the input source or sources used or from the effects of the resonatory transmission of the power from those sources. As the name *distinctive features* implies, however, this classification is not simply on the grounds of the acoustic nature of the segmental sounds but rather on the linguistic functioning of certain acoustic characteristics. A discussion will be found below (§ 10.6).

The acoustic structure of speech sounds may thus in theory be described in a fairly satisfactory way. In practice, however, there is considerable difficulty in evaluating the markings on spectrograms. For instance, the phonetician expects the apparatus producing such records to be sufficiently sensitive to react to components of quite weak intensity in the sound wave, so that he may be reasonably certain of not losing any relevant information in the process of analysis. One result of this is that in the typical spectrogram a large amount of information about the sound wave structure over a short period of time is displayed, and displayed within a small compass; and it is often by no means easy to discern in that information the features which are of importance for description. A further difficulty arises from the fact that repetitions of the "same" speech sound at different speeds of articulation, in different styles or contexts, or by different speakers, often reveal striking differences in acoustic structure. The features used for description must thus be broad enough and flexible enough to encompass variation of this nature, but at the same time be narrow enough to result in a useful description of types of speech sound.

5. SPEECH SOUNDS

5.6. Perceptual Description

5.60.   Since differences in the acoustic structure of incoming sound waves must be the means by which the mechanism of perception distinguishes different sounds, we should expect that the general types of speech sound which are identifiable on the grounds of acoustic structure should have corresponding general types of sound impression on the hearer's brain. Hence a description of speech sounds on the basis of their perceived qualities should be possible.

There is, however, a major problem in such work: we have no means of recording the impression which different sounds make on the apparatus of perception in the human brain. Without such recordings to serve as lasting material for study and experiment, investigators are practically limited to introspection of fleeting impressions or of memories. It is not surprising, therefore, that descriptions of sounds according to their impressions on the perceptual apparatus are as yet possible only in a very limited way.

The most obvious is the relatively easy description of speech sounds as those which are heard as musical sounds, those which are heard as noises, and those which are heard as a mixture of the two (§ 2.52). As we should expect, the membership of each of these groups correlates highly with that of each of the three types, resonants, non-resonants, and semi-resonants respectively, which are generally distinguished on features of acoustic structure (§ 5.50).

Difficulties arise, however, in the description of further differences of perceived quality. Differences in the pitch or in the loudness of musical sounds are broadly distinguishable, but differences in the pitch or in the loudness of components of such sounds—of formants, for example—are seldom discernible, even by the trained perception. And for description of the impressions of sounds as wholes, we are forced, by the poverty of language in this area, to rely on such synesthetic and subjective terms as *bright, piercing, dull, full, thin,* etc., which are quite unsatisfactory for scientific work. A method of description of speech sounds according to their perceived qualities is thus theoretically conceivable, and has been tried, but, up to the present, is not very advanced. There is no doubt, however, that the parameters proposed by Jakobson, Fant & Halle (cf. §§ 5.51, 10.6) are at least partly intended to be interpreted in terms of auditory distinctions (*acute* versus *grave, diffuse* versus *compact, strident* versus *mellow*) and that some of the terms used refer to subjective and perceptive experience rather than to objective, acoustic facts.

5.7. Discussion and Conclusions

5.70. It would appear from the foregoing that the most useful description for elementary purposes is upon an articulatory basis. A description of the movements involved in the articulation of a speech sound is simple to understand, unambiguous, involves no serious difficulty of terminology as does a description of any sound on a perceptual basis, and no complex equipment as is required for the analysis of the acoustic substance of any speech sound.

For so long as the acoustic structure of phones was not very well known to phoneticians, the primacy of articulation over acoustics in the description of speech was undisputed. This was the case in the so-called classical phonetics created during the second part of the last century by such men as Sweet, Jespersen, Sievers, Rousselot, and Passy, and became a tradition still strongly felt even in modern teaching of phonetics. The progress of physiological rather than of acoustic instruments and other technical resources contributed to the conservation of this tradition. Today, however, the acoustic data are numerous and detailed enough to permit, at least in principle, description and classification on this basis. The problem is, of course, not simply a question of cause and effect in the physical world—it is obvious that the articulatory movements precede and produce the sound waves of speech, just as the chains of nerve impulses from the brain in their turn precede and produce the articulatory movements. The point is rather with regard to the fundamental nature of speech: whether this is primarily an auditory phenomenon, to which all other features and stages are subservient, or whether it is primarily an articulatory and musculatory one.

For the former, the main argument is that speech is a method of communication between separate and separated individuals, and that its most characteristic and fundamental feature is the continually changing complex of sound waves linking speaker and hearer. In this view, the innervation and articulation in the speaker are operations directed toward the production of the sound complex, and, in the process, under continual control from the brain. This control is exerted in the form of modification of the articulatory movements as information about the nature of the sound complex being produced is continually fed back to the brain through the speaker's own auditory channels. Likewise, perception in the brain of the hearer is a process of hearing and of recognition of units of the sound complex directly from features of this sound complex, presumably by some process of matching the features being heard with stored patterns developed during previous experience with sound units (cf. § 9.82).

For the latter the view is that so succinctly put by Stetson, that "speech is a set of movements made audible." In this view, the articulation in the speaker is the central feature of speech, the sound complex being simply a medium by which information as to that articulation is conveyed to the hearer. Hearing and perception, then, are processes in which this information is extracted from the sound complex and interpreted by the hearer not with reference to stored sound patterns but with reference to the articulation patterns which he himself uses when he is acting as speaker.

This dispute is likely to continue for a long time—it is no pressing problem to the phonetician in practice. Currently, the tendency among phoneticians seems to be to favour articulation (Liberman, Fry, etc.; strongly opposed by one of the authors of this book). Joos's statement (1948, 113) is typical of this attitude: ". . . current theory is right in basing phonetic analysis upon articulation *primarily*, as the earliest overt aspect of speech, even though we may object to basing it on articulation *exclusively*." For the present book, the practical advantages and the overall simplicity render the choice of a description mainly in terms of the articulatory nature of speech sounds almost inevitable.

5.71. It is customary also, in introductory books on general phonetics, as opposed to works on the phonetics of specific languages or dialects, to describe a wide range of human speech sounds. The most effective way of doing this is not to describe a selection of rare or unusual sounds known to occur in some language or other but to devise a procedure for the description of a wide range of possible types of speech sound, to set up a framework, as it were, into which all sounds of human speech, save perhaps the most exotic, can be fitted.

The most successful attempt to devise such a general framework is undoubtedly that of Pike (*Phonetics*, 1943, *often reprinted*). Pike's approach is through a careful investigation of the potentialities of the human vocal apparatus. He attempts to uncover all the modes of functioning by means of which this apparatus can produce sound waves of sufficient audibility for use in speech, and at the same time to develop a terminology for the unambiguous description of each such mode of functioning. His framework, modified and much simplified, has been taken as a basis for the description of speech sounds in this book.

As already pointed out (§ 4.10), the organs of speech have three main functions in the process of speech: the production of an air stream; the conversion of kinetic energy of the moving air stream into acoustic energy; and the modification, by resonance, of the sounds so produced.

On this basis, it is possible to build up a framework for the description of speech sounds. The procedure followed here is firstly to take in turn each possible type of air stream, egressive and ingressive, through the mouth and through the nose separately, secondly, to consider each type of conversion feasible on an air stream, both singly and any combinations, and thirdly, to discuss the possible modifications of resonance of the sound waves produced by each of these conversions. Finally, the possibilities of combination of various air stream mechanisms are dealt with.

There would seem a place for every possible sound within this framework. The weakest point, theoretically, is probably the assumption that all the sounds in human speech are in fact based on an air stream. This appears to be supported by all evidence which is available up to the present, but for which there is no compelling necessity, save perhaps that most sounds produced by other means in the vocal tract are not sufficiently audible to serve the needs of vocal language (§ 4.11).

CHAPTER 6

THE SEGMENTAL SOUNDS

6.1. Introduction

6.10.   In the following pages we shall outline the main possibilities of sound production in the human vocal mechanism and give some indication of those most frequently used. The descriptions are based on the triple functioning of the organs of speech—the production of an air stream, the conversion of kinetic energy in this air stream to acoustic energy, and the resonance and modifications of resonance of the sound waves so produced.

From purely practical considerations, it has seemed desirable to make a few modifications of this schema. Firstly, the role of the larynx in speech is so fundamental and offers such possibilities of combination with other articulations that the methods which are used in this organ for conversion of kinetic energy in a pulmonic egressive air stream are better discussed together at the beginning (§§ 6.20–6.24) than separately at later points in the chapter.

Secondly, in the case of modifications of resonance, we have been forced to limit ourselves generally to the main types, since the theoretically possible modifications of any particular type of sound production as a result of the addition or one or more of what we have termed minor modifications (§ 4.56) are too numerous to mention singly. The limits to the use of these modifications seem to be those set either by the natural ranges of movement of the organs of the vocal tract or by the capacity of the nervous system to innervate and control a number of simultaneous muscular movements. There is a wide field here for personal experimentation. However, in a few cases where the use or non-use of some of these minor modifications is particularly common (as e.g. labialization in the vocoids (§ 6.21 f.) or where possible modifications seemed to have been somewhat neglected in previous work (as e.g. §§ 6.29, 6.40, etc.) we have gone into some detail.

Finally, we have confined ourselves in this chapter, to what may be called the basic type of sound production in any speech sound.

6.1. INTRODUCTION

Since the isolation of segmental sounds is almost always the result of operation with linguistic, and not with phonetic criteria (§ 5.23), there is no *a priori* reason why such segments should be phonetically homogeneous throughout their whole length. In practice we do, indeed, find that such segments may have approaches and releases which are perceptibly different from one another and from the central hold (§ 5.25). Save in a few cases where it seemed impossible to separate the approach and/or the release from the rest of the segmental sound, we have limited ourselves, perhaps somewhat arbitrarily in a few cases, to the type of sound production which seemed basic to or mainly characteristic of any segment.

6.11.   In this study, which treats a number of sounds which appear theoretically possible but which do not seem to have been observed in any language, difficulties of transcription have been considerable. We have used as far as possible the transcription of the International Phonetic Association (§ 5.31), supplementing it in a few cases, but we have not thought it necessary to create a large number of symbols for sounds which may never be found in use. In these cases we have left the description of the sound to speak for itself. For convenience, however, we print as Appendix II an index to all the symbols used in this chapter.

6.12.   An adequate description of a speech sound involves the specification of the source and type of the air stream involved. The pulmonic egressive air stream, however, is so overwhelmingly predominant in vocal sound production that it is simplest to regard it as being used in all cases except those in which another source or type is specified. Thus, in the following, such descriptions as *voiced vocoid* or *voiceless bilabial plosive* imply the use of the pulmonic egressive air stream.

Further, as noted above (§ 3.40), the pulmonic egressive air stream may be directed through the oral tract to the outside air, or, with the velum lowered, through the nasal tract. It is conventional in phonetics to specify the latter case with the term *nasal* in the description of an articulation, and to assume that, unless this is specified, the oral tract is in use. Hence such descriptions as *voiced vocoid* and *voiceless bilabial plosive* also imply the use of the oral tract. The term *oral* may then be reserved, in the description of sounds in this chapter, for the specification of an oral air stream mechanism (§ 4.22).

6.2. Pulmonic Mechanism: Egressive Air Stream Through Mouth

6.20. This is the commonest of all types of air stream and is used more frequently than any other in all known languages. With conversion of the kinetic energy of the air stream to acoustic energy only by the vibration of the vocal cords (§ 4.31), and with general resonance in the supraglottal tract, we have one of the commonest and most widespread of types of speech sound, the *voiced vocoids*. These are characterized by *open* articulation, that is, by a free, unobstructed passage of the air stream through the supraglottal tract (§ 5.41), and acoustically by the presence of strong, well-defined formants, normally at least three in number, and by the presence of very little acoustic power at frequencies outside the frequency bands of the formants.

6.21. The voiced vocoids may be subdivided into four subclasses according to the type of modification of resonance in the supraglottal tract used in their production.

(*a*) With the tongue fronted and elevated so that the highest point of the tongue is high in the front of the mouth: *close* and *half-close front vocoids*. Symbols: (unrounded) [i, ι, e]; (rounded) [y, ʏ, ø].

Typically, the front and blade of the tongue are curved to follow the surface of the hard palate with the tip pointed downward behind the lower teeth (Fig. 4.1A). The resonance system is as described above for position one (§ 4.53), and the resultant two lower formants are far apart on the frequency scale, formant 1 rising from about 250 c/s in [i, y] to about 400 c/s in [e, ø], and formant 2 dropping from about 2,500 c/s in [i] to about 2,000 c/s in [e] and from about 2,000 c/s in [y] to about 1,700 c/s in [ø].

No known language appears to lack at least one vocoid of this subclass, and a great many languages have two or more, differentiated either in the more basic characteristics of extent of tongue elevation or frontness, or in such accompanying features as length, or in minor resonatory modifications.

(*b*) With the tongue retracted and elevated so that the highest point of the tongue is high in the back of the mouth: *close* and *half-close back vocoids*. Symbols: (unrounded) [ɯ, ɤ]: (rounded) [u, ɵ, o].

Typically, the back of the tongue is curved to follow the line of the rear pharyngeal wall and the soft palate with the front and blade of the tongue sloping down to the floor of the mouth (Fig. 4.1B). The resonance system is as for position two (§ 4.54), and the resulting two lower formants are close together on the frequency scale. Evidence of formant frequencies in the unrounded types is scarce; in the others, formant 1 runs from about 250 c/s in [u] to about 500 c/s in [o], and formant 2 rises from about 600 c/s to about 800 c/s in the same cases.

Among members of this subclass labialization is extremely common, and its absence, giving a close or a half-close back vocoid with spread lips, very uncommon, though such does occur, for example, in Turkish and Rumanian.

This type of vocoid would seem to be almost as widespread among the languages of the world as the front type, though the rarity of the unrounded forms reduces the actual frequency of its occurrences.

(c) With the body of the tongue low in the mouth and a slight elevation to the front or to the back: *open* and *half-open, front* or *back vocoids*. Symbols: (front, unrounded) [a, æ, ɛ]; (front, rounded) [a, œ]; (back, unrounded) [ɑ, ʌ]; (back, rounded) [ɒ, ɔ].

The resonance and formant system discussed above for position three (§ 4.55) is typical of open and half-open back vocoids. Among these, the rounded forms have the two lower formants close together but in a higher frequency range than in the close back rounded vocoids, formant 1 rising from about 400 c/s in [ɔ] to about 500 c/s in [ɒ], and formant 2 from about 700 c/s to about 800 c/s. In the unrounded [ʌ, ɑ], both formants are somewhat higher in frequency, formant 1 being about 600–800 c/s and formant 2 being about 1,100–1,300 c/s.

The open and half-open front vocoids differ in that the slight elevation of the front of the tongue tends to draw the back of the tongue away from the pharyngeal wall, increasing the size of the orifice between the laryngeal pharynx and the buccal cavity and giving the whole supraglottal tract an approximation in shape to the mouth of a horn. Formant 1 falls from about 700 c/s in [a] to about 400 c/s in [ɛ] and formant 2 rises from about 1,300 c/s to about 2,000 c/s. In the rounded [a, œ], formant 1 has a very similar range of movement, while formant 2 rises over a lower frequency range, from about 1,300 c/s to about 1,600 c/s.

In the fully open articulation, the extent of front-to-back movement available to the tongue makes it more difficult to distinguish three positions for the highest point, as can easily be done when the tongue is raised near the roof of the mouth. In the case of the half-open articulation, however, it is just practicable to distinguish a central range of movement to the highest point of the tongue in addition to the front and back ranges. We shall consider the vocoids with this central type of articulation under subclass (d).

Though practically all languages seem to have at least one open articulation in the vocoids, relatively few use, as realizations of different phonemes (§ 10.1), two open vocoids differentiated only by frontness in contrast to backness. In most cases, features such as length or rounding accompany any such distinction at the fully open level. Half-open front and back vocoids are common, though as at the higher levels of close and half-close articulation, the rounded forms of back vocoids and the unrounded forms of front vocoids predominate.

(d) With the highest point of the tongue in a central position in the mouth: *close, half-close,* and *half-open central vocoids.* Symbols: (close, unrounded) [ɨ, ï]; (half-close, unrounded) [ɘ, ë]; (half-open, unrounded) [з, ɛ̈]; (close, rounded) [ʉ, ü]; (half-close, rounded) [ɵ, ö]; (half-open, rounded) [ɒ, ɔ̈]. In addition, [ə] is available for an unrounded half-close or half-open central vocoid.

The elevation of the body of the tongue to form a highest point in the centre of the mouth forms two resonance cavities in the supraglottal tract, one of considerable size extending over the laryngeal pharynx and the rear portion of the mouth cavity, the other smaller, comprising the front of the mouth cavity and extending to the lips. The orifice connecting these resonance cavities varies in size according to the extent of elevation of the tongue. When this orifice is relatively small, i.e. in the case of the close and half-close central vocoids, the system is of the same general plan, a larger rear and a smaller front cavity, as in the close and half-close front vocoids, and the formant picture is likewise similar with formants 1 and 2 at a distance from one another on the frequency scale (cf. § 4.53). On the other hand, when the orifice is relatively large, as in central, half-open vocoids, the resonance is of a more complex nature and these two formants come closer together on the frequency scale. In the rounded forms generally the two formants are closer together than in the corresponding unrounded ones. From [ɨ] to [з], formant 1 rises from about 200 c/s to about 500 c/s, and formant 2 falls from about 2,000 c/s to about 1,200 c/s, whereas in the rounded forms, from [ʉ] to [ɒ], the rise of formant 1 is from about 250 c/s to about 350 c/s and the fall of formant 2 from about 1,200 c/s to about 1,000 c/s.

Very many languages have one or two central vocoids, but relatively few seem to have more than this number, and even among those which have two such vocoids other minor features tend to support the basic characteristic of tongue elevation. By far the more common are half-close and half-open types, the fully close central vocoids being, in comparison, quite rare.

6.22. The second method of conversion of some of the kinetic energy of the air stream into acoustic energy in the larynx is by friction. In this process the edges of the vocal cords are brought close together to form a small opening which induces turbulent eddying in the air passing through. If there is no other blockage or obstruction to the outgoing air in the supraglottal tract, but merely general resonance of the sound waves so produced, we have *voiceless vocoids*. These are sometimes called *whispered*, since their glottal position appears to be in practice indistinguishable from the lightly closed position of the vocal cords in true whisper (§ 3.33).

The sound waves resulting from the eddying in the larynx are, in comparison with the case in which the vocal cords actually vibrate, very weak, and of numerous frequencies (§ 4.33). As a result of the transmission of these sound waves through the supraglottal tract, formants will arise, with frequencies depending on the physical characteristics of the tract (§ 4.40 f.), though, on account of the nature of the input spectrum, these formants will not be so well-defined in the output spectrum as in the case of the voiced vocoids (§ 4.44).

Voiceless vocoids therefore are characterized by an open articulation with a free, unobstructed passage for the air stream through the supraglottal tract and acoustically by a random distribution of sound waves of very low intensity over a wide range of frequencies with a few relatively weak formants in specific frequency bands.

Since the modifications of resonance possible in the supraglottal tract are the same for voiceless vocoids as for voiced vocoids, the same four subclasses as before (§ 6.21) may be distinguished. In each subclass, the positions of the articulating organs are the same as for the voiced vocoids so that we may distinguish (*a*) close and half-close front voiceless vocoids, (*b*) close and half-close back voiceless vocoids, (c) open and half-open front or back voiceless vocoids, and (d) close, half-close, and half-open central voiceless vocoids. As symbols for voiceless vocoids, the normal practice is to use the symbols for voiced vocoids with a small subscript circle, thus [i̥] represents a front close unrounded voiceless vocoid, [e̥] a front half-close unrounded voiceless vocoid, and so on.

The occurrence of voiceless vocoids as speech sounds in languages appears to be very restricted, doubtless as a result of their lack of audibility. They are, however, frequently to be observed in languages as personal or unstressed variants of voiced vocoids. Rumanian, for example, makes extensive use of them in unstressed, final positions.

In the voiceless vocoids which we have so far discussed, the frictional eddying in the larynx is, so to speak, not produced as an end in itself, but as a source of sound waves to be moulded into a particular acoustic form by specific transmission characteristics of the supraglottal tract. In the case of speech sound [h], which is also produced by friction in the narrowed glottis, it seems that the friction itself is the essential characteristic, and the supraglottal resonance of the resultant sound waves a concomitant feature of secondary importance. This is supported by the evidence of spectrograms, which show a distribution of energy up to, and often over, 5,000 c/s at considerably greater intensities than is normal in voiceless vocoids. This distribution is not completely random; the energy tends to show maxima about poorly defined formants at frequencies close to those of the formants of a following vocoid. On these grounds it may be maintained that [h] is a contoid, a voiceless glottal fricative. To some scholars, however, this distinction appears untenable, and [h] is then classed as a voiceless vocoid with the supraglottal articulation and hence the modification of resonance of the following vocoid.

The relative prominence of glottal friction and supraglottal resonance in the production of [h] varies from language to language, and it is perhaps to be expected that within certain ranges of this variation dispute as to its phonetic interpretation is possible. In all cases, of course, considerations of the functioning of [h] may be used to decide its classification as a contoid or vocoid.

As a simple speech sound [h] occurs both widely and frequently. It is rare, however, for a language to contrast phonemically two distinct forms of glottal fricative.

6.23.   The third method of conversion of some of the kinetic energy of the air stream into acoustic energy at the larynx is by blockage and release. In this case the vocal cords are brought together to check the flow of air and are opened suddenly to release the built-up pressure with the results detailed above (§ 4.32). The resulting sound waves are transmitted through the supraglottal tract. The result is a voiceless glottal plosive contoid [?], the so-called "glottal stop."

Acoustically this sound is characterized by an abrupt onset of acoustic power randomly distributed over a wide range of frequencies especially from about 500–2,000 c/s. The decay is likewise rapid as is characteristic of this type of conversion. The formants are very weak and usually indistinguishable in spectrograms (cf. § 4.44).

The frequency of the formants in [?] depends on the positioning of the supraglottal articulating organs. These may be effecting any of the minor modifications of resonance, labialization, nasalization, palatalization, etc., with their particular acoustic effects, or moving into position for the articulation of the following sound. In this case the frequencies of the formants of [?] will tend to approach those of the formants in that following sound.

The voiceless glottal plosive occurs in many languages. It is also not uncommon as a personal or stress variant of other voiceless plosive contoids. The sound is likewise occasionally used before word or syllable-initial vocoids either as a speech habit or to prevent vocoid hiatus.

6.24.   The fourth method of laryngeal conversion of kinetic energy of the air stream into acoustic energy is by a simultaneous combination of the methods of vocal cord vibration and of friction. This seems to be the method of production of [ɦ], which may be described as a voiced glottal fricative contoid, though the exact details of the laryngeal functioning are still obscure. There are two main possibilities. The first is that the membranous glottis is closed and the vocal cords vibrate, while at the same time the cartilaginous glottis is open and part of the air stream is allowed to escape through this with the development of frictional eddying. The second is that the vocal cords are brought close together, and set in vibration, but without completely closing the air passage. The former process would imply a combination of normal voicing and whisper, the latter rather the process of so-called breathy voice (§ 3.33). Neither of the

99

explanations is fully satisfactory, though the latter seems preferable. It is supported by the evidence of high speed films.

The acoustic picture of [ɦ] is, as expected, a random distribution of acoustic energy over a large range of frequency, as in [h], and weak but usually discernible formants. As in the case of [ʔ], the frequencies of these formants depend on the positioning of the supraglottal articulating organs, and hence as before wide variations of modification of resonance are possible.

As a variant of [h] in certain phonetic or other environments, [ɦ] is by no means uncommon in languages of the world. As the sole glottal fricative in a language, or in phonemic contrast to [h], it is, however, distinctly uncommon.

6.25. By interposition of a vibratile organ in the passage of the air stream, conversion of kinetic energy of that air stream to acoustic energy takes place in the manner detailed above (§ 4.31), and the sound complex is then selectively transmitted by resonance in the supraglottal tract. The contoids so produced have the general term *trills* and may be voiced, i.e. accompanied by the sound complex resulting from the vibration of the vocal cords, or voiceless, i.e. not so accompanied (§ 3.39).

There are four main groups: (*a*) the uvular trills [R̥, R] in which the uvula vibrates in a groove formed in the dorsum of the tongue; (*b*) lingual trills in which the tip or blade of the tongue vibrates against the alveolar ridge, the teeth, or the lips, giving apico- and lamino-alveolar trills, apico- and lamino-dental trills, for all of which the symbols [r̥] (voiceless) and [r] (voiced) are used, and an apico-labial trill, for which as yet no symbol has been allocated; (*c*) bilabial trills [ʙ̥, ʙ] in which the two lips vibrate against one another; and (*d*) retroflex apico-palatal trills [ɽ̥, ɽ] in which the tip of the tongue is bent up to vibrate against the hard palate.

The number of vibrations per second in trills varies somewhat in different speakers but is normally in the region of 16–20 per second. The number of vibrations in any particular occurrence of a trill sound varies from language to language, but is usually from two to four, rising to six or seven when deliberately stressed. Two vibrations is logically the minimum to which the term trill is applicable, but trills in practice are often shortened to one vibration. Such single vibrations are often termed *flaps*, and the resulting contoids *flapped*. In this direction, the trills approach the simple plosive (§ 6.28), but a dividing line can usually be drawn on the basis of the briefness or incompleteness of a flap articulation in comparison with a plosive articulation.

Acoustically the trills are characterized by rapid, successive fluctuations in their intensity, and an uneven, though not random distribution of energy over a wide band of frequency. Maximum energy comes in the range about 1,000–2,500 c/s for [R], and somewhat lower, about 500–2,000 c/s for [r], with weak but frequently distinguishable formants at frequencies about 300, 1,100, and 2,100 c/s in [R] and again somewhat lower in [r]. Evidence of the acoustic form of other trills is not available.

Trill articulations are widespread in languages. By far the commonest are the uvular trill and the lingual trills against the alveolum and the teeth, the retroflex trill is rare but does occur, for example in Herero, while the labial trills are not known to occur as speech sounds.

Two trill articulations are occasionally used as realizations of different phonemes in the same language. In Spanish, a flapped lingual *r* is phonemically opposed between vowels to a clear trill. Some languages (Portuguese, some Spanish and Southern French dialects) oppose phonemically lingual and uvular trills. In several languages, however, German, Dutch, Swedish, French, for example, both lingual and uvular trills are found as variant realizations of the same phoneme.

6.26.   By narrowing the passage of the air stream until turbulence of the air results, sound is produced in the manner detailed above (§§ 4.31, 4.33). This is subjected to resonatory supraglottal transmission, and voice may be added. The generic term for contoids of this type is *fricatives*.

It is usual to distinguish two groups of fricatives: *I Central Fricatives*, in which the constriction of the air passage is produced in the centre of the vocal tract, and *II Lateral Fricatives*, or commonly *Laterals*, in which the centre of the vocal tract is completely blocked but a narrowed passage is allowed the air stream at one or both sides.

Central fricatives can be articulated over almost the whole length of the vocal tract from the oral pharynx to the lips, and can conveniently be classified according to the organs involved in the formation of their constrictions (§ 3.61). The classes are as follows: (*a*) radico-pharyngeal; (*b*) dorso-uvular; (*c*) dorso-velar; (*d*) dorso-palatal; (*e*) lamino-palatal; (*f*) apico-palatal; (*g*) dorso-alveolar; (*h*) lamino-alveolar; (*i*) apico-alveolar; (*j*) lamino-dental; (*k*) apico-dental; (*l*) apico-labial; (*m*) labio-dental; (*n*) bilabial; and (*o*) retroflex, comprising apico-palatal, apico-alveolar, and apico-dental.

As symbols, the following are available, with that for the voiceless fricative preceding that for the voiced in each class: [ħ, ʕ] for the radico-pharyngeal; [χ, ʁ] for the dorso-uvular; [x, ɣ] for the dorso-velar; [ç, j] for the dorso-palatal; [ʃ, ʒ] for the lamino-palatal; [ɟ, ɹ] for the apico-palatal and one type of apico-alveolar; [ɕ, ʑ] for the dorso-alveolar; [s, z] for the lamino-alveolar and another type of apico-alveolar; [θ, ð] for the lamino- and apico-dental; [f, v] for the labio-dental; [ɸ, β] for the bilabial; [ʂ, ʐ] for one type of retroflex apico-palatal and apico-alveolar, and [ʈ, ʈ] for another. In general retroflex sounds can be indicated by adding a lowered, forward-pointing hook to the symbol for the corresponding non-retroflex sound.

The traditional classification of the central fricatives, especially those in the palatal, alveolar, and dental areas, and hence the allocation of symbols to them, is not solely based on the organs involved and the place of the constrictions, but is influenced by acoustic factors: clearly perceptible similarities between sounds produced at different places of articulation and clearly perceptible differences between sounds produced by the same organs. The latter arise mainly from variations in the shape of the articulating organs at or near the position of the constriction.

The most important of these variations is the cross-sectional shape of the constriction, which may be either groove-like or slit-like (Fig. 6.1), the former tending to result in a less widespread distribution of acoustic energy in the resultant spectrum. Other factors include the length of the constriction itself, and the position of other organs. For example, [ç, j] have a fairly short slit-like constriction, [ʃ, ʒ] a long groove-like constriction, and [s, z] a very short groove-like constriction.

The characteristic acoustic qualities associated with each of these articulatory variations are sufficiently prominent to dominate differences of resonance introduced by small changes in the position of the constriction. Thus the position of the groove-like constriction in [ʃ, ʒ] can be fronted into the alveolar area, that of the groove-like constriction in [s, z] can be backed into the prepalatal area or

Fig. 6.1.   Constriction shapes
Schematic design of the difference between groove-like (*A*) and slit-like
(*B*) constrictions with reference to lip types with movable articulators
(I) and to linguo-dental or linguo-palatal types where only one articulator
is movable (II)

fronted onto the inner surfaces of the upper teeth, and the slit-
like constriction of [θ, ð] moved from the inner surface to the lower
edges of the upper teeth, all with hardly perceptible differences in
the resultant sound complex. In [ɹ̟, ɹ] the constriction is also groove-
like, but runs down across the extreme apex of the tongue rather
than along its upper surface. This constriction can be formed over
a wide area from the palate to the teeth, but the articulation of
the edge of the apex instead of the surface of the blade or the
dorsum against the palate or the alveolum necessitates a concaving
of the upper surface of the front of the tongue instead of a convexing. The resulting difference in the resonatory characteristics of
the vocal tract is a major factor in the determination of the peculiar
acoustic quality of [ɹ̟, ɹ] as compared with fricatives formed on the
upper surface of the tongue.

As pointed out above (§ 5.41), fricatives merge gradually into
vocoids as the velocity of the air stream is lowered and the intensity
of the resulting frictional sounds reduced. Though all fricatives can
be weakened in this manner, a few seem particularly liable to it,
as is evidenced by their occurrence in various stages of vocoidization
in many languages. The commonest are [w] and [ɥ], voiced bilabial
fricatives with groove-like constriction to which are added velarization and palatalization (§ 4.56) respectively, [j, ɹ] and [ɻ].

Acoustically, the central fricatives are characterized by a distribution of power over a wide range of frequencies. This distribution
is very uneven—partly at any rate as a result of the random nature
of the source power—and varies considerably with the degree of
stress. Formants are usually indistinguishable in the spectrograms

103

of voiceless fricatives, and not always discernible in those of voiced ones. Frequencies of formants 1, 2, and 3 in some of the commoner fricatives are very approximately 200, 2,000, and 2,700 c/s in [ʃ, ʒ], 300, 1,600, and 2,500 c/s in [s, z], 400, 1,600, and 2,700 c/s in [θ, ð], and 400, 1,500, and 2,500 c/s in [f, v]. Much of the audibility and perceived impression of fricatives seems to come, however, from sound waves in higher ranges of frequency; all these fricatives, if sufficiently stressed, have perceptible acoustic energy at frequencies above 5,000 c/s, and a few much higher, [s] for example, at over 8,000 c/s (cf. Fig. 5.1). There also seem to be considerable differences of intensity and audibility between the different types. The [θ]- and [f]-types are, for instance, as a whole weaker than the [s]- and [ʃ]-types and the bilabial [ɸ] weakest of all.

Central fricatives, especially those formed against the hard palate or the alveolum, are very common and widespread sounds. Some, indeed, such as [s] and [j], seem to occur in almost all languages. The general impression gained from a survey of the occurrences of these fricatives is that the further the place of articulation of a class is away from the hard palate and alveolum, the less frequent is the occurrence of members of that class. Thus uvular fricatives seem to be less common than velar, and pharyngeal fricatives less common than either. Likewise the bilabial fricatives [ɸ, β] are apparently less common than, and only rarely phonemically opposed to, the labio- or linguo-dental varieties.

6.27. The lateral fricatives may be grouped into the same classes as the central fricatives, the only difference being that since the root of the tongue cannot be retracted sufficiently to touch the centre of the rear wall of the pharynx, there is no class of radico-pharyngeal laterals. All the other classes of central fricative (§ 6.26) have lateral correspondents in which the blockage is formed in the centre of the air passage, and these may as usual be voiceless or voiced

The symbol [ɬ] is often used for voiceless laterals articulated against the alveolum or teeth. Other symbols for laterals normally imply the voiced form; if necessary, voicelessness may be indicated by the diacritic [ₒ]. Those generally used are [ʟ] for dorso-uvular and dorso-velar; [ʎ] for dorso-palatal and lamino-palatal; [l] for apico-palatal, lamino- or apico-alveolar, lamino- or apico-dental; and [ɭ] for any retroflex lateral. The symbol [ɫ] is also often used, in transcriptions of English for example, for a velarized form of [l].

As with the central fricatives, the classification of the laterals formed on the palatal, alveolar, and dental areas, has been influenced by acoustic considerations. The formation of the dorso- and lamino-palatal laterals involves a convexing of the dorsum toward the hard palate, and the acoustic results of this articulation, which is not dissimilar to superimposed palatalization (§ 4.56), clearly differentiates them from the other classes of lateral.

The laterals are subject to considerable variation in the intensity of the frictional sounds produced in their characteristic articulation, though as a group they are produced with less friction than the central fricatives. Relatively strong friction occurs in the voiceless lamino-alveolar laterals of Welsh and Icelandic, and very strong friction in the voiced lamino-dental laterals of Zulu and Herero. For these last, a special symbol [ʆ] is often used. On the other hand, the commonest types of lateral, the voiced velar, palatal, alveolar and dental varieties of a large number of languages, have hardly perceptible and often imperceptible friction, and to the ear resemble voiced vocoids.

The formants are usually weak in voiceless laterals, but strong and well-defined in the voiced types. Frequencies in the alveolar class are about 350, 1,200 and 2,700 c/s for formants 1, 2, and 3, respectively, though in sequences formant 2 varies from about 700 to 1,600 c/s, doubtless as a result of the ease with which [l] is affected in the direction of velarization or palatalization by neighbouring articulations. Formant frequencies in the other classes of lateral are not available.

Lateral fricatives are commonly met with as speech sounds, especially in voiced forms, though it appears that only in relatively few languages are two or more phonemes realized by laterals. Among the classes, it is the alveolar and dental forms which are the most common, with the palatal and the velar classes becoming rarer in that order. None of the labial classes, i.e. apico-labial, labio-dental, or bilabial laterals, are known to be used at all.

6.28. By blockage and release of the flow of the air stream, sound is produced in the manner detailed above (§ 4.32). This is then subjected to resonatory transmission in the supraglottal tract, and voice may be added or not. The generic term for contoids of this type is *plosives*. Other terms in common use are *occlusives* and *stops*.

The release of the blockage in a plosive may be of two kinds; central release in which the blockage is released at its centre so that the resumed flow of the air stream is along the centre of the vocal tract; and lateral release, in which the blockage is released at one or both sides and the flow of air is, at least initially, along the side or sides of the vocal tract. Lateral release leads to a slight difference in acoustic effect; the flow of air along the inner wall of the vocal tract tends to result in somewhat more friction being generated during the release, and to the ear a plosive with lateral release gives the impression of being followed by an incipient homorganic lateral fricative. Of the two, central release of plosives is by far the more common.

A minor articulation commonly associated with plosives is *aspiration*. The release of the supraglottal blockage in any plosive allows a spurt of the air compressed behind that blockage to escape. The size and duration of this spurt of air is under articulatory control; it depends essentially on the pressure of the pulmonic egressive air stream behind the supraglottal blockage during and immediately after the release of this blockage, and on the relative phasing of this release and the next closure of the vocal tract. If the air stream pressure is low, and/or the next closure of the tract is simultaneous with the supraglottal release, the escape of air may be nil or negligible. On the other hand, if the pressure is high, and the next closure delayed, it may be very considerable, and clearly audible as a sound resembling [h] after a voiceless plosive and [ɦ] after a voiced. In these cases the plosive is said to be *aspirated*, or to have an *aspirated release*.

The symbol for aspiration is a raised inverted comma (or a superscript h) after the symbol for a plosive; thus [p'] or [pʰ]. The non-aspirated version of this plosive is symbolized by [p] or [p⁼].

A further minor articulation frequently associated with plosives is *affrication*. In the release of the blockage the movement of the active articulator or articulators tends to one or other of two polar types, a relatively rapid movement toward an open articulation or a relatively slow movement through (or even checked at) a stage in which the opening functions as a constriction in the air passage.

In the former type, the period during which turbulence and eddying in the released air stream occurs is brief, such turbulence being associated only with the relatively high velocity of the burst of air immediately subsequent to the release and decaying rapidly.

106

In the latter type, however, the stage of the narrowed passage is continued into the period after the release of the initial pulse of air and turbulence is induced in the subsequent, less rapidly flowing air stream to a sufficient degree and for a sufficient period for clearly audible friction to result. In these cases, the plosive is said to have an *affricated release* or to be an *affricate*.

In effect, an affricate may be regarded articulatorily, as combining the approach and hold of a plosive with the release of a homorganic fricative, the point of transjunction coming with the ending of the complete blockage of the air stream.

All plosives whether voiced or voiceless can be affricated, and affricates, as other plosives, may occur aspirated or not. The traditional symbol for an affricate is the combination of that for the plosive with that for the homorganic fricative, thus [pɸ, tθ, dz, gɣ], etc. Where it is necessary to distinguish affricates from sequences of a plosive plus a fricative, the two symbols may be linked as [t͡ʃ, t͡ʃ], or ligatures [tʃ, dʒ], employed.

The complete blockage of the supraglottal tract which is characteristic of a plosive can be formed at all the positions of articulation detailed above (§ 3.61) save between the radix of the tongue and the rear wall of the pharynx. The classes are accordingly as follows: (*a*) dorso-uvular; (*b*) dorso-velar; (*c*) dorso-palatal; (*d*) lamino-palatal; (*e*) apico-palatal; (*f*) dorso-alveolar; (*g*) lamino-alveolar; (*h*) apico-alveolar; (*i*) lamino-dental; (*j*) apico-dental; (*k*) apico-labial; (*l*) labio-dental; (*m*) bilabial; and (*n*) retroflex, comprising apico-palatal, apico-alveolar, and apico-dental plosives.

The symbols generally used are the following, voiceless preceding voiced: [q, G] for dorso-uvular; [k, g] for dorso-velar; [c, ɟ] for dorso- or lamino-palatal; [t, d] for apico-palatal, lamino- and apico-alveolar, lamino- and apico-dental; [p, b] for bilabial; and [ʈ, ɖ] for any retroflex plosive.

As with the fricatives, the traditional classification of the plosives in the palatal, alveolar, and dental regions and the assignation of symbols to them has been influenced by similarities and differences in the perceived impression of their sound complexes. The distinct differences between palatal plosives of the type [c, ɟ]; and those of the type [t, d] result largely from the convexing of the dorsum of the tongue toward the hard palate in the former, and the lack of such in the latter, and also from differences in the release. The relatively slow-moving dorsum does not release the blockage as cleanly as the more mobile and more precisely controlled apex, with the result that dorso- and lamino-palatal plosives have more distinct friction in their release than apico-palatals.

Acoustically, the plosives are characterized by a very abrupt onset with acoustic energy of considerable intensity spread over a wide range of frequencies and a rapid decay in which the energy distribution becomes limited to one or two very narrow ranges of frequency before ceasing. The formants of plosives are almost always impossible to distinguish, partly because of the short duration of the sound as a whole but more because of the changing sound complex of the input and the rapid variation in the physical characteristics of the vocal tract, which alters its transmission characteristics, as the blockage is released (see §§ 4.32 f., 4.40, 4.44). Such evidence as we have indicates that the velar, alveolar, dental, and labial plosives all have formants 1 in the low range about 200–400 c/s, and formants 3 in the high range of 2,000–2,800 c/s. Their formants 2 vary quite considerably, being about 900–1,100 c/s in [p, b], 1,800–2,000 c/s in [t, d], and varying from about 900 to 2,400 c/s in [k, g], which are very susceptible to modification from neighbouring vocoids. Experimental work on the acoustic form of plosives is briefly discussed below (§ 9.60 f.).

6.29. Simultaneous conversion of kinetic energy of the pulmonic egressive air stream to acoustic energy at two or more points in the vocal tract by similar or by different methods is in some cases possible. Generally the same method of conversion is used at each point—*compound* speech sounds—but some combinations of two methods, a fricative and a trill, for example, appear theoretically possible. These may be termed *complex* speech sounds. Under this definition, all voiced contoids save trills are complex sounds, but it is convenient to reserve the term for those sounds which have conversion by two methods other than voicing. All compound and complex sounds, then, may occur both voiceless and voiced. We shall not discuss here the possibilities of conversion at three or more points in the vocal tract; these have almost certainly only a theoretical interest.

The following main types of compound and complex speech sounds may be listed:

I. Compound Speech Sounds

(a) *Trills.* A uvular trill can easily be combined with a lingual trill, and either of these with a bilabial trill. None of these combinations is known to occur as a speech sound.

(b) *Fricatives.* A glottal fricative can be combined with any supraglottal fricative, and a large number of combinations of different supraglottal fricatives, e.g. dorso-velar plus apico-palatal, dorso-palatal plus lamino-alveolar, any pharyngeal or buccal fricative with a bilabial or labio-dental, etc., are possible. The major limiting factor to combination is the range of movement of the tongue. Spectrographic evidence of the acoustic characteristics of compound fricatives is lacking, but to the ear the impression is often difficult to distinguish from that of simple fricatives, as a result, doubtless, of the masking (§ 9.52) of the weaker sounds by the stronger.

The occurrence of such compound fricatives is rare, but some of the Bantu languages appear to have a compound apico-alveolar and labio-dental fricative (Meinhof, 1932, 11).

(c) *Plosives.* Within the limits set by its range of movement some combinations of plosives formed by the tongue are possible. Thus, for example, dorso-velar plus apico-palatal, or dorso-palatal plus lamino-alveolar. The examples of compound plosives which occur, in many African languages, are, however, apparently all the combination of a plosive articulated by the tongue and one articulated by the lips. Yoruba, for example, has the combination of a dorso-velar and a bilabial plosive, both voiceless and voiced [k͡p, g͡b]. To the ear the impression resembles a mixture of the two simple plosives, perhaps partly from the fact that the release of the two occlusions is seldom in practice exactly simultaneous, but more detailed evidence of the acoustic characteristics of such sounds is still lacking.

The combination of a glottal plosive with a supraglottal one, and more or less simultaneous release of the two is rather more common. This is thought to be the normal way in which the unaspirated voiceless plosives of a number of languages (Romance, Slavonic, etc.) are produced. During the supraglottal hold (§ 5.25) for [p, t, k], etc., the glottis is closed; it takes up the voice position (§ 3.33) for a following vowel simultaneously with or shortly before the supraglottal release, thus allowing the vocal cords to start vibrating at the moment of that release.

109

II. COMPLEX SPEECH SOUNDS

It is· possible to combine conversion by friction with conversion by a vibratile organ at a succeeding point in the vocal tract, but the reverse seems very difficult, if not impossible. Thus a bilabial trill can be added to any fricative formed between the dorsum, blade or tip of the tongue and the roof of the mouth or teeth. An apical trill can perhaps be added to a glottal fricative and to a dorso-velar fricative, but not, it seems, to a radico-pharyngeal or dorso-uvular fricative, since the retraction of the tongue in these last withdraws the apex from any area against which it can articulate. In a plosive, however, the blockage stops the flow of the air stream on which fricatives and trills depend, and no complex sound can include one. The occurrence of these possible complex sounds is unknown.

6.3. Pulmonic Mechanism: Ingressive Air Stream Through Mouth

6.30. An ingressive air stream, produced by the pulmonic mechanism (§ 4.20), can be used, in theory, as a basis for the production of all types of sound, both of laryngeal and supralaryngeal conversion, which have been surveyed in the preceding sections (§§ 6.20–6.29). In practice, however, such use of an ingressive air stream to produce simple speech sounds appears to occur only as a personal or occasional variant of the egressive air stream. Further, certain sounds are very difficult, if not impossible to produce on an ingressive air stream, a lamino-alveolar trill, for example, though on the other hand a few others, such as retroflex fricatives, are probably simplified.

There is no evidence available of the particular acoustic characteristics of ingressively produced sounds, though the use of the same methods of conversion of kinetic energy of the air stream to acoustic energy should result in the general characteristics of ingressive trills, plosives and fricatives being similar to those formed on a pulmonic egressive air stream.

6.4. Pulmonic Mechanism: Egressive Air Stream Through Nose

6.40. If the velum is lowered, free access to the nasal cavities and the passage to the outer air through the nose is permitted to an egressive air stream from the lungs (§ 3.40). If such access is added to a passage for the air through the mouth, we consider it a con-

110

comitant minor articulation and term the resulting sounds nasalized (§ 4.56), but if the passage through the nose is the only exit, because of blockage or closure in the buccal cavity, the resulting sounds are nasal contoids—contoids because the air stream has no free passage through the mouth (§ 5.41)—or simply nasals.

The supraglottal tract in nasals, the nasal tract, consists not only of the pharyngeal and nasal cavities but also of that part of the buccal cavity which is to the rear of the closure in the oral tract. The existence of this, as a side cavity coupled to the nasal tract, is important in the determination of the transmission characteristics of that tract (cf. § 4.45), and variation of its volume will affect those characteristics, and hence the output spectra of the various nasal contoids. This volume, it is evident, depends mainly on the position of the closure, being larger when the closure is toward the front of the mouth cavity and smaller when the closure is toward the rear. Each of the nasals, therefore, can be conveniently and appropriately classified according to the position and formation of the closure in the mouth cavity during its production.

The nasals are also classified according to the method of sound production used. With a few exceptions, each different closure can be combined with each possible method of conversion of kinetic energy of the air stream through the nasal tract. In the following sections we shall discuss these in the order: methods of laryngeal conversion, methods of supralaryngeal conversion, combinations of methods.

6.41.   The first method of conversion in the larynx is by the vibration of the vocal cords. With resonatory transmission in the supraglottal nasal tract we have *nasal voiced contoids* or simply, and traditionally, *voiced nasals*. According to the position of the closure in the mouth, we may distinguish the following classes: voiced nasals (*a*) with dorso-velar closure; (*b*) with dorso-palatal closure; (*c*) with lamino-palatal closure; (*d*) with apico-palatal closure; (*e*) with dorso-alveolar closure; (*f*) with lamino alveolar closure; (*g*) with apico-alveolar closure; (*h*) with lamino-dental closure; (*i*) with apico-dental closure; (*j*) with apico-labial closure; (*k*) with labio-dental closure; (*l*) with bilabial closure; and (*m*) retroflex, with apico-palatal, apico-alveolar, and apico-dental closures.

The symbols generally used are [ŋ] for the dorso-velar; [ɲ] for the dorso- or lamino-palatal; [n] for the apico-palatal, lamino- or apico-alveolar, lamino- or apico-dental; [ɱ] for the labio-dental; [m] for the bilabial; and [ɳ] for any retroflex nasal.

The traditional distinction between [ɲ] and [n] is due to the clearly perceptible acoustic differences which result, especially at the moment of release, from variations in the shape of the articulating organs at or near the point of articulation (cf. § 6.26). Dorso- or lamino-palatal closure involves a convexing of the dorsum of the tongue toward the roof of the mouth, a modification which tends to raise the frequencies of the formants in the resulting sound (cf. § 4.56).

Acoustically, the nasal voiced contoids resemble voiced vocoids with strong well-defined formants and little acoustic energy outside the frequency bands of those formants, but differ in the frequent occurrence of relatively abrupt onsets and decays and in the number of formants. Save when very unstressed, nasals usually have four distinct formants and frequently five.

The frequencies of the formants of [m] and [n] are very similar in spectrograms, [m] having formants at about 300, 1,000, 2,200, and 2,500 c/s, and [n] at about 400, 1,200, 2,200, and 2,700 c/s, though in many cases of these two sounds the formant frequencies of the first three formants overlap. In [ɲ] there is some evidence that formant 2 is considerably higher in frequency, about 1,600 c/s, and formants 3 and 4 slightly higher than in [m] and [n], while in [ŋ] formant 1 tends to be somewhat higher than in the other three, about 500 c/s, formant 2 varies over the range 1,000–1,200 c/s, formant 3 over the range 2,100–2,500 c/s, and formant 4 over the range 2,400–2,800 c/s. The variation of formant frequencies in [ŋ] may be due in part to the extent of the elevation of the tongue affecting the extent of the lowering of the velum—the greater the former, the less the latter—and hence the size of the orifice to the nasal pharynx.

6.42.   The second method of laryngeal conversion ·is by friction in the glottis. As in the case of the voiceless vocoids and the voiceless glottal fricative [h] (§ 6.22), it is necessary in theory to distinguish between relatively weak friction in the glottis which produces sound waves for subsequent moulding into a particular acoustic form in the supraglottal tract, and relatively strong friction which is taken to be in itself a primary component of the sound. Then with resonatory transmission through the nasal tract we have in the former case *nasal voiceless contoids* or simply *voiceless nasals* and in the latter *nasal voiceless glottal fricative contoids*.

The nasal voiceless contoids, as other nasal sounds, may be classified according to the positions of the articulatory closure in the buccal cavity, a procedure which gives the same set of classes as in the nasal voiced contoids (§ 6.41). Since no special symbols are current for the voiceless classes we may use those of their voiced correspondents with the addition of the usual diacritic of voiceless-ness. Thus [ŋ̊] represents a nasal voiceless contoid with dorso-velar closure, [m̥] a nasal voiceless contoid with libial closure, and so on.

When these sounds occur they are mostly contextual variants of the voiced types. No spectrographic evidence on their acoustic characteristics is available.

In the nasal voiceless glottal fricatives, the same classification according to the position of the closure in the mouth may be made. Hence we shall have nasal voiceless glottal fricatives (*a*) with dorso-velar closure, (*b*) with dorso-palatal closure, etc.

This type of sound, which is in effect a nasal [h], is not known to occur, and no symbols exist for its varieties.

6.43.   The third method of laryngeal conversion is by blockage and release of the air stream at the glottis. With resonatory transmission through the nasal tract, we have *nasal voiceless glottal plosives*.

These, as all nasal contoids, may be classified according to the positions of the articulatory closure in the buccal cavity. Thus we have nasal voiceless glottal plosives (*a*) with dorso-velar closure, (*b*) with dorso-palatal closure, etc.

This type of sound is not known to occur in any language.

6.44.   The fourth method of laryngeal conversion is by the simul-taneous combination of vibration and friction (§ 6.24). With resona-tory transmission through the nasal tract, we shall have *nasal voiced glottal fricatives*.

These fricatives, which are in effect varieties of a nasal [ɦ] (§ 6.24), may be classified in the usual manner of nasal contoids. Thus we have nasal voiced glottal fricatives (*a*) with dorso-velar closure, (*b*) with dorso-palatal closure, etc. There are no recognized symbols.

Whether a contoid of this type occurs in any language as a regular speech sound is unknown, but the form with bilabial closure is not

113

uncommon among speakers of English as a marginally linguistic interjection. It is represented in print as "h'm."

6.45. The conversion of kinetic energy of the air stream to acoustic energy can be carried out in the supraglottal nasal tract by various means, though these are fewer in number than in the case of the oral tract. On the same plan as before (§ 6.25 f.), we shall discuss the main methods and places of such conversion both with and without voicing from accompanying laryngeal conversion.

The first method is by the interposition of a vibratile organ. No such organ occurs in the supraglottal nasal tract, and there are therefore no nasal trills.

6.46. The second method of conversion, by friction, is possible in one place and perhaps also in a second. The root of the tongue can be retracted to approach the rear wall of the pharynx and form a narrowed passage in which turbulent eddying of the air stream may be produced. If this is combined with lowering of the velum, a *nasal radico-pharyngeal fricative* will result, and this can be voiced or voiceless. It is possible, further, to distinguish three classes of this sound, (*a*) with dorso-velar closure of the buccal cavity, (*b*) with labio-dental closure, and (*c*) with bilabial closure. The bunching and retraction of the tongue for the constriction in the oral pharynx seems to preclude the formation of other lingual closures used in nasal contoids.

The other conceivable place is a narrowed passage between the edge of the velum and the rear wall of the pharynx, where the velum is lowered to open the orifice to the nasal pharynx. It is doubtful, however, whether sufficient muscular control can be exercised over the movements of the velum to adjust the orifice to the size necessary for friction in the air stream to arise. If it can be done, a *nasal velo-pharyngeal fricative* will result and a number of classes, according to the position of the closure in the mouth, should be distinguishable.

The occurrence and acoustic nature of these sounds are unknown, and no symbols for them exist.

6.47. The third method of supralaryngeal conversion in the nasal tract is by blockage and release. This can be done only by the velum, which can be raised to block the nasal tract at the orifice to the nasal pharynx and lowered to release the air pressure built up in the oral pharynx and the part of the buccal cavity to the rear of the closure in the mouth. This articulation results in a *nasal velo-pharyngeal plosive* to which voice can be added or not. The usual classes can be distinguished according to the position of the closure of the oral tract. We have thus a nasal velo-pharyngeal plosive (*a*) with dorso-velar closure, (*b*) with dorso- or lamino-palatal closure, and so on.

None of these plosives are known to be used as speech sounds and their acoustic characteristics are obscure.

6.48. The possibilities of compound and complex conversion (§ 6.29) in the nasal tract are very limited. A few compound fricatives may be hypothesized, a voiceless or voiced glottal fricative (§§ 6.42, 6.44) combined with a nasal radico-pharyngeal or a nasal velo-pharyngeal fricative (§ 6.46), for example, but the occurrence and acoustic characteristics of such combinations are unknown.

The same holds for what seems the only possible complex sound in the nasal tract, the combination of a voiceless nasal (§ 6.42) with a nasal radico-pharyngeal or velo-pharyngeal fricative.

6.5. Pulmonic Mechanism: Ingressive Air Stream Through Nose

6.50. An ingressive air stream through the nose can be initiated by the pulmonic mechanism and may be used as a basis for the production of all the types of nasal sound, both of laryngeal and supralaryngeal conversion, which have been surveyed in the previous sections (§§ 6.40–6.48). In practice, however, the use of such an ingressive air stream to produce normally occurring speech sounds is very rare, if, indeed, it occurs at all, and ingressive nasals seem to be confined to personal or occasional variants of the egressive nasals.

There is no evidence available of the particular acoustic characteristics of ingressive nasals.

6.6. Pharyngeal Mechanism

6.60. By the use of the possibilities of movement of the whole larynx, an egressive or ingressive air stream can be produced (§ 4.21). This air stream is of limited duration, and weak in comparison with that initiated by the pulmonic mechanism, but it can be used to produce speech sounds. In phonetic works, the egressive types of such sounds are usually termed 'ejective,' or 'glottalized' and the ingressive 'injective' or 'implosive.' The former term in each case appears to be gaining currency, and will be used here. Thus *ejective* and *injective* may be taken as convenient replacements for 'pharyngeal egressive (air stream)' and 'pharyngeal ingressive (air stream)' respectively.

The pharyngeal air stream, like the pulmonic, is able to flow out through either the oral or the nasal supraglottal tracts, and the methods of conversion of its kinetic energy into acoustic energy and the various modifications of resonance possible in these passages are likewise the same as in the case of the pulmonic air stream.

In the operation of the larynx, however, a difference is possible. The pharyngeal mechanism requires normally a closed glottis[1] for the production of an air stream, and therefore none of the usual methods of laryngeal conversion, which require some opening of the larynx, are possible. But if as a result of closures at the velum and in the buccal cavity, there is no free exit through the supraglottal passages for the pharyngeal air stream, the movement of the larynx creates an air stream with potential flow (§ 4.30). The release of the blockage at the glottis converts this potential flow to actual, and kinetic energy in the air stream should be convertible to acoustic energy at the glottis. We thus have the possibility of reverse ejectives and injectives, in which the air stream flows into and from the trachea and lungs. Such sounds, however, are unlikely to be of more than theoretical interest, and need not be further discussed.

6.61. *Pharyngeal Mechanism: Egressive Air Stream through Mouth.*

Since laryngeal conversion is not normally used with an air stream initiated by the pharyngeal mechanism, ejective sounds are voiceless only. The methods of supralaryngeal conversion of the kinetic energy of pharyngeal egressive air in the oral tract are the interposition of a vibratile organ, the constriction of the air passage, and the blockage and release of the air stream.

Thus by the use of a vibratile organ with a pharyngeal egressive air stream through the mouth, we have *ejective voiceless trills*, and these may be grouped, according to the particular organ used, into the same classes as the pulmonic egressive trills (§ 6.25).

By the formation of a narrowed passage with a pharyngeal egressive air stream through the mouth, we have *ejective voiceless fricatives*, both of the central and the lateral type, and these may

---

[1] See § 6.80 for exceptions.

be grouped, according to the position and formation of their constrictions, into the same classes as the pulmonic egressive central and lateral fricatives (§§ 6.26, 6.27).

By blockage and release of the pharyngeal egressive air stream, *ejective voiceless plosives* result, and these may be classified, according to the organs involved in their blockages, into the same classes as the pulmonic egressive plosives (§ 6.28).

There is no special set of symbols for these ejective sounds, the most frequent way of representing them being by the use of the symbols for the corresponding pulmonic sounds, with the addition of a superscript comma as a diacritic to indicate their ejective nature. Thus [r'] may be used to symbolize an ejective voiceless apico- or lamino-alveolar trill, [ç'] an ejective voiceless dorso-palatal central fricative, [p'] an ejective voiceless bilabial plosive, and so on.

Acoustically, the ejective sounds are of similar basic structure as the corresponding pulmonic egressive sounds, though they tend to be weaker in intensity and of shorter duration. In this last respect particularly ejectives stand out: the relatively small volume of air in the oral tract is soon expended in the egressive air flow, and very rapid decay of the resulting sounds is characteristic.

Ejective sounds can hardly be considered common in the world, but they do occur in languages of North America, the Far East and Africa. The plosives are by far the most frequent, the fricatives are, in comparison much rarer, and ejective trills, so far as known, do not seem to occur at all.

Since laryngeal conversion is not possible with an egressive air stream initiated by the pharyngeal mechanism, all compound and complex sounds with such an air stream must result from conversion of its kinetic energy to acoustic energy in the supraglottal tract, and none of these sounds can occur voiced. With these limitations, all the types of compound and complex sound which are possible with a pulmonic egressive air stream can in theory be produced with a pharyngeal egressive air stream.

Hence we have (*a*) ejective compound trills, formed by simultaneous production of any two of the simple trills, (*b*) ejective compound fricatives, formed by simultaneous production of any two of the simple fricatives, and (*c*) ejective compound plosives, formed by simultaneous production of any two of the simple plosives.

A few complex sounds resembling those possible with the pulmonic egressive air stream (§ 6.29) are perhaps just possible. Thus, an ejective bilabial or apical trill might be added to an ejective dorso-velar fricative.

None of these ejective compound or complex sounds are known to occur in languages.

6.62. *Pharyngeal Mechanism: Ingressive Air Stream through Mouth.*

An ingressive air stream produced by the pharyngeal mechanism can be used, in theory, as a basis for the production of all the types of sounds, which have been surveyed in the preceding section (§ 6.61). In practice, however, such use of the pharyngeal ingressive air stream to produce simple sounds is very rare indeed, and both the acoustic characteristics and occurrences of these injective sounds are unknown. Injective plosives, however, occur not infrequently in certain combinations of sounds, the implosives (§ 6.80).

6.63. *Pharyngeal Mechanism: Egressive Air Stream through Nose.*

As in the case of the pulmonic mechanism, the supraglottal nasal tract can be opened to the egressive air stream from the pharyngeal mechanism by the lowering of the velum, and again a major factor in the determination of the transmission characteristics of this tract is the position of the closure formed by the organs in the buccal cavity (§ 6.40). Like other ejective sounds, those produced in the nasal tract result from conversion of kinetic energy at points above the larynx, and hence only voiceless types occur.

The first method of supralaryngeal conversion, by the interposition of a vibratile organ in the air stream is again impossible (§ 6.45).

The second method, by friction, is in theory possible in a narrowed passage for the pharyngeal air between the root of the tongue and the rear wall of the pharynx, giving an ejective nasal radico-pharyngeal fricative, but in practice this is very difficult to articulate with audible results. The possibility of friction between the velum and the rear wall of the pharynx, to give an ejective nasal velo-pharyngeal fricative, is also remote. The occurrence and acoustic characteristics of these sounds are unknown.

The third method, blockage and release of the air stream, is possible at the velum (§ 6.47), and gives an ejective nasal velo-pharyngeal plosive. All the six classes of the position of the closure in the buccal cavity can be distinguished. We have thus an ejective nasal velo-pharyngeal plosive (*a*) with dorso-velar closure, (*b*) with dorso-palatal closure, and so on (§ 6.41). The occurrence and acoustic characteristics of these sounds are unknown.

Among the ejective nasals, no complex conversions seem possible, and the only hypothetically possible compound conversion would seem to be the combination of the two ejective nasal fricatives, one or even both of which may be non-existent.

6.64. *Pharyngeal Mechanism: Ingressive Air Stream through Nose.*

In theory an ingressive air stream initiated by the pharyngeal mechanism can be used as a basis for all the sounds discussed in the above section, but in practice the use of such an air stream appears very rare, and injective nasals are unknown.

6.7. Oral Mechanisms

6.70. By the forward movement of a dorso-velar or dorso-palatal blockage of the oral tract an egressive air stream results in the mouth, and by movement backward an ingressive air stream (§ 4.22). These oral air streams are of very limited duration and much weaker than those produced by the pharyngeal mechanism. A generic term for sounds produced from oral air streams, seems to be lacking, though the term *clicks* is used to refer to oral ingressive sounds. Pike uses also the term *egressive-click* for oral egressive sounds.

As is suggested by these terms, sounds produced from an oral air stream frequently have an abrupt onset resulting from the conversion of a potential air stream to an actual flow. Such abrupt onset does not necessarily occur in sounds produced with the oral mechanism—though it doubtless leads to increased audibility—and sounds with gradual onset from an actually flowing air stream are quite possible.

The flow of the oral air stream is normally limited to the forward part of the oral tract, and the methods of conversion of its kinetic energy to acoustic energy are limited to those possible in this part. As in the pharyngeal mechanism, however, reverse air streams can be produced in which the flow is towards or from the rear of the mouth.

The use of the tongue as the initiator of the air stream has a limiting effect on its range of articulation in oral egressive sounds. Thus, for example, the retraction and raising of the dorsum against the velum to form the movable blockage limits the forward extension of the front of the tongue, and the formation of an air cavity in front of this movable blockage limits considerably the range of possible linguo-palatal articulations.

Since the larynx is not connected with the flow of air from the oral mechanism it cannot be used to vibrate in that flow, and hence sounds from the oral mechanism are normally voiceless. Voicing from the pulmonic mechanism can, however, be added to oral sounds (§ 6.80).

There are a few recognized symbols for oral ingressive sounds but none for oral egressive. If necessary, a diacritic, perhaps a superscript inverted comma placed before the symbol for the corresponding pulmonic egressive sound, could be used to indicate an oral egressive air stream.

6.71. *Oral Mechanism: Egressive Air Stream through Mouth.*

The methods of conversion possible in the forward part of the oral tract are the interposition of a vibratile organ, the constriction of the air passage, and the blockage and release of the air stream.

Vibratile organs interposable in an oral egressive air stream are the tongue-tip and the lips. The muscular tension and control of the body of the tongue in its forward movement during the initiation of the air stream, however, seems to inhibit tongue tip vibration, so that oral egressive apico- and lamino-alveolar and apico- and lamino-dental trills hardly exist. The oral egressive bilabial trill [$'\rho$] is easily articulated, and the resultant sound is quite audible but of limited duration.

A constriction of the passage of the oral air stream can be formed in several places from the palate to the lips, and oral egressive central or lateral fricatives produced. Both types include the classes: (*a*) apico-palatal; (*b*) lamino-alveolar; (*c*) apico-alveolar; (*d*) lamino-dental; (*e*) apico-dental; (*f*) apico-labial; (*g*) labio-dental; (*h*) bilabial; and (*i*) retroflex, comprising apico-palatal, apico-alveolar, and apico-dental.

The oral egressive central fricatives are weakly but distinctly audible, the lateral fricatives mostly less so. None are known to be used.

Blockage and release of the oral air stream results in oral egressive plosives. These occur in the same classes as the oral egressive central fricatives above, but none are known to be used as regular speech sounds in a language.

6.7. ORAL MECHANISMS

It appears very difficult to produce a compound oral egressive trill by the simultaneous articulation of tongue-tip and bilabial trills. Compound fricatives on an oral egressive air stream, with an apico- or lamino-alveolar or dental constriction combined with a labio-dental or bilabial constriction are not difficult to produce. Whether a compound plosive is possible, with one blockage between the tongue as articulator and the alveolum or the teeth, and a second at the lips, for example, is doubtful. The sole complex sound which seems to be possible on an oral egressive air stream is that of a fricative formed between the front of the tongue and the alveolum or teeth plus a simultaneous bilabial trill. The above sounds are weakly audible; none are known to occur in any language.

6.72. *Oral Mechanism: Ingressive Air Stream through Mouth.*

Unlike the case with the pulmonic or the pharyngeal air stream mechanism, it is the ingressive air stream from the oral mechanism which is more commonly used in languages than the egressive. All oral ingressive sounds actually occurring seem to be based on an air stream initiated by the release of a rarefaction of the air in the forward part of the oral cavity. The common abrupt onset of sounds produced with such release is doubtless responsible for the generic term *clicks* for oral ingressive sounds. The prior production of a potential air stream is not of course necessary; if there is no further blockage in the oral tract, the backward movement of the closure formed by the tongue against the roof of the mouth will initiate an ingressive air stream with normal flow. This flow of air, however, is so weak that the theoretically possible oral ingressive trills and fricatives with gradual onset hardly exist. In practice, it seems that the only type of oral ingressive sound used in any known language is the plosive formed by the release of a cavity of rarefied air.

The following classes are possible: (*a*) dorso-palatal; (*b*) lamino-palatal; (*c*) apico-palatal; (*d*) dorso-alveolar; (*e*) lamino-alveolar; (*f*) apico-alveolar; (*g*) lamino-dental; (*h*) apico-dental; (*i*) apico-labial; (*j*) bilabial; and (*k*) retroflex, comprising apico-palatal, apico-alveolar, and apico-dental varieties. The point of release of the potential air stream in each case, however, may be either in the medial line of the mouth, giving oral ingressive plosives with central release, or at one or both sides, giving oral ingressive plosives with lateral release.

A bilabial click, with central release—which is the articulation of a kiss—occurs in Bushman. An apico-dental click with central release [ɿ]—which is similar to the sound used in English-speaking countries as an exclamation of annoyance and conventionally represented by *tut tut*—and apico- or lamino-palatal clicks with central release [C] occur in Zulu, Hottentot, Bushman, and Suto. A retroflex apico-palatal click, also with central release, occurs in Bushman dialects. In Xhosa or Khosa, a lamino-palatal click with lateral release [ʖ] occurs, as the first sound of this name, for example.

The symbols used here are those recognized by the I.P.A. In earlier works the letters [c, q] were used for the linguo-dental and linguo-palatal clicks with central release, and [x] for the linguo-palatal click with lateral release. Other writers have abandoned letters entirely and used [/] for the dental click, [≠] for the alveolar, [/] for the retroflex, all with central release, and [//] for the palatal click with lateral release.

No spectrographic evidence as to the acoustic structure of these sounds has yet become available.

6.73.   *Oral Mechanism: Reverse Egressive and Ingressive Sounds.*

As in the case of the pharyngeal mechanism (§ 6.60), it is possible with the oral mechanism to generate a potential air stream if the forward end of the oral tract is closed. In this case, forward movement of the dorso-velar closure will compress the air in the forward part of the oral tract, and release of this closure will result in an egressive air stream flowing to the rear into the pharyngeal and, if the velum is open, nasal cavities. Similarly, backward movement of the dorso-velar closure will rarefy the air in the oral tract, and release of this closure will result in an ingressive air stream flowing forward from the pharyngeal and, if the velum is open, nasal cavities. As before, the initial spurt of air at the release might be used itself as a plosive, or as an abrupt onset to frictional conversion of the subsequent flow of air through a narrowed dorso-velar passage.

From this mechanism we have reverse oral egressive and ingressive dorso-velar plosives and fricatives. No trills seem to be possible. These sounds are very muffled and barely audible, and as far as known, not used in any language.

6.8. Combinations of Mechanisms

6.80. ⸰ Certain possibilities of simultaneous combination of air stream mechanisms exist. By converting kinetic energy in each of these air streams into acoustic energy a number of combinations of sounds can be produced. Thus, for example, an air stream may be initiated by the oral mechanism quite separately from another initiated by the pulmonic mechanism. On the former air stream, an oral egressive bilabial trill may be articulated, and on the latter, a pulmonic egressive nasal voiced contoid, with dorso-velar closure. The total result, whether from an acoustic or articulatory viewpoint, is a combination of the two sounds ['ρ] (§ 6.71) and [ŋ] (§ 6.41). The addition of [ŋ] in this way to oral ingressive plosives results in the so-called 'nasal' or 'nasalized' clicks of Hottentot, Zulu and Xhosa.

In this and similar cases the two sound-producing mechanisms are operating quite separately. A more complex case is that of the combination of voicing from the pulmonic mechanism with pharyngeal ingressive, i.e. injective, sounds (§ 6.62). As Pike (*Phonetics*, 95) explains it, the production of an ingressive air stream by downward movement of the larynx (§ 4.21) may be accompanied by a slight leak of air through the glottis from the lungs. Such a small pulmonic egressive air stream may be set into vibration by the vocal cords without being of sufficient volume to destroy the partial vacuum caused by the laryngeal movement and thus prevent the occurrence of an ingressive air stream. In this case both the pharyngeal ingressive and the pulmonic egressive air streams flow toward the pharyngeal cavity, and are clearly in nice balance with one another.

By this combination, laryngeal voicing from the pulmonic mechanism may be added to all pharyngeal ingressive sounds, but, as far as known, only the plosives are affected in actual languages. These are traditionally known as *implosives* and have been allocated the symbols [ɓ, ɗ, ɠ]. Thus [ɓ] is an injective bilabial plosive with pulmonic egressive voicing, [ɗ] an injective apico- or lamino-alveolar plosive with pulmonic egressive voicing, and [ɠ] an injective dorso-velar plosive with pulmonic egressive voicing. Retroflex articulations may also occur; an injective retroflex apico-palatal or apico-alveolar plosive may be produced and voiced by combination of the same mechanisms.

These implosive consonants are common in a number of languages of central and southern Africa. In West Africa, in at least some dialects of Idoma and Yoruba and probably more widely, the compound stop [ɠ͡ɓ] is also implosive.

Besides the above cases, a few other ways of combining simultaneously sound-producing articulations using different mechanisms of air stream production may be possible, but practically nothing seems to be known about them. The only discussion in the literature is that of Pike (*Phonetics*, 94 ff.).

CHAPTER 7

COMBINATIONS OF SOUNDS

7.1. Transitions between Sounds

7.10. The segmental sounds as described in Chapter VI are abstractions, acoustic or articulatory types or classes. In actual speech any such sound occurs in combination with others in chains of varying length and with different prosodic or suprasegmental phenomena (§ 5.12). This is true even if in some cases a single speech sound may seem to function alone as an utterance, as English [aː] *are*, or Latin [iː] *go!*, for instance. Such single speech sounds are necessarily accompanied by phenomena such as intonation, intensity variation, and length, and consequently do not appear in real isolation.

7.11. We have already stressed that the speech wave is physically a continuum. The methods of its segmentation described above (§ 5.20 f.) all result in a general similarity in one respect: a sequence of segments whose central portions are comparatively easily located, but whose margins or borders are somewhat indistinct. Even in the language-influenced segmentation accepted as a general basis for this discussion, the borders are taken to be located subjectively by native speakers and not objectively by the phonetician. In ordinary language use, these borders are seldom isolated or noticed in any conscious way by the native speaker of a language, but evidence is accumulating that features occurring at and about them contribute in important ways to the identification of the neighbouring segments. In any case, these borders and the features associated with them belong to the sound substance of language, and their analysis and description consequently forms part of phonetics.

The borders between segments are also important from a very different point of view. The study of evolutive phonetics suggests that borders between segmental sounds are frequently the starting points of sound changes, those events which lead to observable differences in the phonetic substance of a language at points separated in time. In this and the following chapters we have permitted ourselves to digress a little from the central theme of description to add pertinent illustration of this phenomenon from historical phonetics.

7.12. On the acoustic level, the borders between successive phones are termed *transitions*. These transitions vary, both with respect to the features constituting them, and with respect to their spread or extension in time. We shall discuss examples of the three main types of such transitions, those between vocoid and vocoid, those between vocoid and contoid, and those between contoid and vocoid.

7.13. The oscillographic recordings made in the thirties by Gemelli (1950), Borel-Maisonny, and others showed that vocoids were far from being steady-state phenomena physically, and that hardly any two adjacent periods of a vocoidal sound wave had exactly the same curve-form. But if the auditory impression of the "same" sound (cf. §§ 5.23, 10.1) is conserved, these slight variations of sound structure have no real importance in communication. The term *monophthong* refers to a perceptively uniform vocoid. But a vocoid sequence may also be characterized by a perceptible gradual change or glide in a given direction, e.g. from a more diffuse ([i]- or [u]-like) to a more compact ([ɑ]-like) spectrum. (For the terms *compact* and *diffuse* see below, § 10.61.) If this glide is not divided by a syllabic boundary into two parts (or interrupted by a pause or other intersection, noise, glottal stop, etc.), it may be called a *diphthong*. Consequently any such perceived glide may be classified on the acoustic level as a diphthong, quite independently of any functional classification of it either as a sequence of two vowels or, as is sometimes convenient, a combination of a vowel and a consonant. In all these cases, spectrograms show a constantly and smoothly changing formant pattern.

Not all cases of striking formant changes can, however, be interpreted as representing phonetic diphthongs. The reaction of the perceptual mechanism is, for instance, very much influenced by the rapidity of the change. Only if the change is slow and smooth, does the auditory impression become that of a diphthong. If the change is rapid, and, so to speak, cuts off the steady-state formant structure by a sudden modification, the ear may hear a contoid. Now it has been well known for a long time that a plosive contoid can be perceived and distinguished without the presence of any explosion phase (the only really audible part of a plosive), as, for instance, when it is followed by another stop. An example is English [ækt] with an unexploded [k]. This was an indication that the transitional phase of the vocoid could function as a cue to the contoid. From Potter, Kopp & Green's work (1947) and later spectrographic evidence we know now that these transitions do exist. We can see them very clearly on spectrograms and also observe that any combination of a given vocoid with a given contoid has its own characteristic transition in the spectrum (e.g. Green, 1959).

The nature of this transition in any particular case will reflect the change in the modes of resonance of the supraglottal tube which takes place when the organs move from the contoid setting to the vocoid or vice versa, and will be therefore dependent on the specific articulation of the two units which are combined. Let us take as an example the sequence [pi]. The lips have to pass from the closed position for [p] to the open (spread) position for [i] at the same time as the glottis has to adjust itself for the production of voice. If the lip-opening is not completed—and in fact it is normally not —when the formant structure of the vocoid begins to appear, this structure will be modified. The first portion of the vowel will be formed with reduced lip opening and the frequencies of the formants (particularly of formant 2) will be somewhat lowered (§ 4.52). The portion in which this formant inflexion occurs, though too short to be perceived as of a particular vocoid colour, may contribute to the perception of the contoid. A similar effect, but in reverse, will occur in a sequence [ip], though here the part played by the transitional phase is probably still more important.

7.14.   As long as only analytic methods of phonetic research were available, the phonetician had no means of checking the role of these transitional phenomena in the speech wave. The different synthetic methods now used in some speech laboratories—and particularly the so-called pattern playback of the Haskins Laboratories in New York (Cooper et al., 1952)—have made possible an assessment of the importance of transitions. We now know, thanks to numerous auditory tests of synthetic material in which the stimulus under consideration (in our case the formant inflexion) is isolated, that these transitions alone are capable of producing the auditory effect of certain contoids (especially plosives and nasals, but to a certain extent also liquids, and some fricatives). Experiments of this kind have also shown that the rate of transition alone, from one formant structure to another, may be responsible for the distinction between a diphthongal combination, a sequence fricative —vocoid, and a sequence plosive—vocoid. For example, the passage from an [i]-position to an [a]-position may be heard as [ia] (diphthong), as [ja] (fricative—vocoid), or as [ga] (plosive—vocoid) simply according to the type of change (slow, rapid, or very abrupt and sudden respectively). Functionally speaking, such formant inflexion transitions are subsidiary manifestations of the consonants, manifestations which ordinarily assist in, but sometimes take over the role of primary cues to, the identification of those consonants. Whether, in the latter cases, a given transitional portion in a spectrogram or on a sound-curve is to be looked upon as belonging to the contoid or to the vocoid segment is a matter of linguistic function and of auditory perception, not of acoustic nor articulatory analysis.

These formant inflexions may be considered as the effect of close combinations of a contoid and vocoid in succession and consequently taken to be absent or weaker when the two segments belong to different units (syllables, etc.). We shall revert to this question in the next section.

7.15.   It has also long been well-known that contoids are modified in different ways by adjacent vocoids. The vocoid was looked upon in traditional phonetics as the centre of the syllable, extending its influence to preceding as well as following contoids. On the articulatory level, the contoids were said to be formed within the resonance room shaped by the vocalic position of the tongue, lips, etc. (Forchhammer, 1923, etc.) When a group like [pip] was pronounced, the tongue took its position for [i] at the same time as, or even before, the lip closure started, and remained there till the explosion of the final [p] had taken place. In other instances, the tongue positioning might be somewhat modified by the necessity of articulating lingual contoids, but in general contoids were conceived of as being pronounced more or less simultaneously with the vocoid of the syllable, not before and/or after it.

Experimental evidence on both the articulatory and the acoustic levels has completely confirmed this traditional view (cf. § 4.60 f.). We have already mentioned, in connection with glottal contoids (§ 6.22 f.), that they share the formants of adjacent vocoids. But this is, typically, the case with any contoid. On spectrograms, voiced contoids display formants on the level of adjacent vocoid formants,

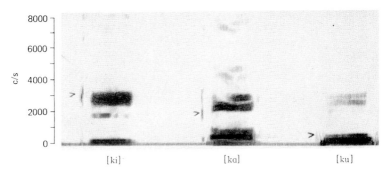

[ki]   [kɑ]   [ku]

Fig. 7.1. Spectrograms of the groups [ki, kɑ, ku]
The arrow-head indicates the position of the explosion noise in each
case. Notice how the frequency of this essential cue to the consonant
varies with the formant structure of the following vowel

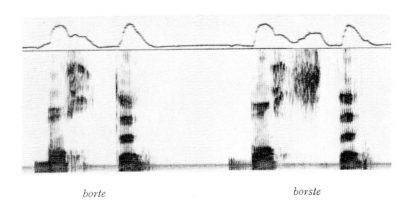

borte   *borste*

Fig. 7.2. Spectrogram of the Swedish words *borte* 'away' and *borste*
'brush', with, above, an overall intensity-curve (a display of the relative
intensity of the sound wave from moment to moment). Notice that
the fricative [s] in *borste* gives rise to an extra peak of intensity, but this
is not in Swedish heard as a syllable: both words have two syllables only.
The fricative [r] in *borte* also produces a slight rise in the curve, but not a
real peak

and the same is to a large extent true also of voiceless contoids, particularly of fricatives. The explosion burst of an aspirated stop (§ 6.28) likewise shows a considerable concentration of acoustic energy at the frequencies of neighbouring vocoid formants. Further, we know from the articulatory description of dorso-velar plosives [k] and [g] that they change their point of articulation according to the surrounding, especially following, vocoids, [ki] having a fronted, [ku] a retracted point of articulation. Now spectrograms show a corresponding dependency of the explosion burst structure on the formant positions of the following vocoid (Fig. 7.1). It remains to be shown whether this colouring influence makes itself felt more strongly if the contoid and vocoid belong to the same syllable than if they are separated by a syllabic boundary. *A priori*, the former seems likely. It is probably supported by the instances of strong vocoid reduction in unstressed positions in which such colouring of a contoid, in the form of palatalization or velarization (cf. § 4.56) takes over the function of the reduced vocoid and serves as the only cue to this. (Examples of this phenomenon occur in Rumanian.)

It is evident that vocoid colouring of contoids as well as transition effects on vocoid formants from neighbouring contoids are consequences of the coarticulation of articules (§ 4.6). A further inference may be drawn. Since the closer the combination of elements, the stronger the coarticulation of them, transitional phenomena may be viewed as potential juncture phenomena on the phonemic level, i.e. phonetic features whose function it is to mark the limits of units by signalling the beginnings and ends of phonetic groups (§ 7.9) or words.[1]

7.16. So far, mainly plosives and nasals—and also to a certain extent liquids—have been examined with regard to transition phenomena. And there seems to be no doubt that their importance is greatest for these contoids, although combinations of fricatives and vocoids are also, as mentioned above, characterized by specific transitions. Thus it seems as if most contoids can be identified either through their inherent acoustic properties or through the

---

[1] Though the 'word' is a concept on the content level of language, there is in most languages a tendency—though of varying strength—to make content units such as words (at least those which are full lexical items) and word groups correspond to phonetically delimited units of expression, i.e. to make the words, or at any rate the principal words of a sentence, phonetic as well as semantic segments.

transitions between them and adjacent vocoids. Recent work has also shown the existence of transitions in sequences of fricative and plosive contoids, [-sp-, -st-, -sk-], etc., and auditory tests have shown the possibility of identifying contoids by means of these noise transitions (Carney, 1966; E. Uldall, 1964a).

7.2. Transitions as Cues

7.20. Since experiments with synthetic speech and auditory tests have demonstrated that transitions may serve alone as cues to the consonant phonemes in question, there need be little doubt that they play a part in communication and help in the identification of contoids when other cues (explosion noise, etc.) are weak or lacking (e.g. in unexploded plosives). They are of extreme importance for the hard-of-hearing who do not perceive the high frequency noise of contoids but are able to react to changes of vocalic colour in the low frequency range where the essential vocoid formants are to be found. The informative value of transitions is also the physical background to the ear training of partially deaf children.

7.3. Glides between Articules

7.30. As described in Chapter IV above, the process of articulation is a continually changing series of coarticulated movements of the speech apparatus, and each of the apparently static settings of the vocal tract described in Chapter VI is primarily a positioning of the articulatory organs at some characterized moment (or sequence of moments) during the central portion, the hold, of the articule. But between any two successive holds of articules are a release and an approach (§ 5.25), and these movements, normally coarticulated in the stream of speech, constitute the glide between the two articules. These glides are the counterparts of the transitions at the acoustic level, but because of the difficulties of segmentation at either level, precise correspondence between the two is difficult to establish.

A few examples of coarticulation were given (in § 7.13) to explain the origin of formant inflexions in vocoids. Evidence from X-ray pictures and sound films, those made by Truby, by Cooper & Lotz, and by Strenger, for example, has fully confirmed the traditional coarticulation theory. There are no steady-state phases to be seen on such films. All organs involved move continuously from one position to another without remaining at any of them. During the hold phase of a plosive the tongue or the lips move to the next position, and during the formation of an intervocalic consonant the passage from the preceding to the following vocoid gradually takes place. (We can also see these passages in the changing formant structure of many voiced intervocalic contoids.)

7.4. Assimilation

7.40. The glides and passages between articules of similar phonetic structure in the stream of speech may vary to some extent, most clearly in the phasing and synchronizing of the different coarticulated movements. Such variations may, of course, be simply individual and cluster around a norm for the dialect or language; but these norms, which are themselves likely to differ, contribute to the totality of features characteristic of that dialect or language. The fully idiomatic pronunciation of an acquired language thus may, and to some extent certainly will, involve the acquisition of new habits of phasing articulatory movements in glides between articules.

This point may be illustrated by considering an example or two of the effect of variation in the phasing of coarticulated movements. In the glide from a vocoid to a nasal contoid, as in [ɑːm], one articulatory movement is the closing of the lips to block the air passage through the mouth used in [ɑː], and a second is the lowering of the velum to open the air passage through the nasal cavities for [m]. These two movements may be well synchronized, with one positioning of the supraglottal apparatus being smoothly reformed into another and the airflow transferred unchecked from the oral to the nasal tract. But they may not be. If the labial blockage precedes the velar lowering, then, in the intervening period, the setting of the vocal tract is as that for the hold of the contoid [b], and the sequence might be represented in fine analysis as [aːᵇm]. On the other hand, if the velar lowering precedes the labial blockage, the articulatory setting in the intervening period is that of the nasalized vocoid [ɑ̃], and the sequence might be represented in detail as [ɑːᵃm]. Similarly, in a sequence [mt], four articulatory movements are involved: cessation of voice, closure of velum, release of labial occlusion, formation of alveolar or dental occlusion—and differences in the phasing of these movements will result in a variety of possible glides, [mₒ̃t], [mᵇt], [mᵖt], for instance, and even more complex cases as [mₒ̃ᵖt], and [mᵇᵖt].

7.41. The transition and glide phenomena so far discussed may be regarded as mutual modifications between successive sounds in the chain of speech: the ending of one sound is modified by being adapted to the beginning of the next, and this beginning is also modified by being adapted to that ending.

The general term for adaptive modifications of a sound in the chain by a neighbouring—and not necessarily immediately neighbouring—sound is *assimilation*. The term suggests one of the traits usually discernible in such modification, namely, the tendency of one or more features of one sound to be modified by being made like a feature or features of the other. For example, the transition in the case analysed above, [ɑːᵇm], represents assimilation of the open articulation feature of [ɑː] to the closure of [m], and at the same time the assimilation of the lowered velum feature of [m] to the raised velum feature of [ɑː].

A distinction is often made between assimilation affecting features of a succeeding sound, and assimilation affecting features of a preceding sound. The former is termed *progressive* assimilation, and the latter *regressive* assimilation. Thus in the example in the paragraph above the first assimilation described is regressive and the second progressive.

7.42. Given the coarticulated nature of the speech chain some degree of assimilation between closely neighbouring sounds is probably always present. In some cases, however, the extent of assimilation between neighbouring sounds may be such that one or more features of the affected sound is replaced by a feature or features of the inducing sound. Consider the English word *triumph*. In careful pronunciation this is [traɪəmf] but in ordinary pronunciation is commonly [traɪəɱf]. This is regressive assimilation: the labio-dental feature of the following [f] has modified—by replacement—the bilabial feature of [m]. Similar examples are [eɪt̪θ] *eighth*, with apico-dental blockage in the plosive instead of the more usual lamino- or apico-alveolar, [hçuː] *hue* with voiceless [ç] instead of the usual voiced [j], and [rɪdᴸɬ] *riddle* in which the usual central release of the plosive is replaced by lateral release.

In each of the above cases the result of the assimilation is a sound which occurs only in certain specifiable phonetic environments and may be interpreted as a *variant* of the more usual sound, a variant which occurs or may occur in those environments. Assimilation may,

132

however, be of such a nature that its effect is to produce a sound which occurs elsewhere in the language. For example, in the word *happen* progressive assimilation between the last two sounds commonly results in a pronunciation [hæpm], in *income* regressive assimilation commonly results in the pronunciation [ɪŋkʌm], and so on.

7.43. In our first examples the contextual change concerned only certain irrelevant features of the units modified. A laterally exploded [d] for instance still belongs to the [d]-class. The same is true of the partly nasalized [ɑ], etc. Under such conditions the assimilation does not introduce any modification of the set of functional or distinctive sound units, the phonemes, of the language. Theoretically the number of such contextual variants is as great as the number of possible combinations of one element with all the others.

In examples of the type *happen* with [m] we have to do with a more far-reaching change. Here the contoid [n] is replaced by a sound belonging to a different class or type (an allophone of another phoneme of the language), namely [m], which in other positions is distinct from [n]. This implies that in the position in question there is *free variation* between the two types (depending on the rate of speech, the style, individual habits, etc.). Closely related, but a sort of further stage, is *syncretism* or *neutralization*, either term being used to denote a phenomenon which gives the appearance of a systematized assimilation: the possible occurrence of only one of two or more otherwise distinct units in a particular environment. For example, in English [ŋ] is the only possible nasal contoid before [k] within the syllable—[θɪŋk] *think*, [læŋk] *lank*, [sʌŋk] *sunk*, etc., but no [-mk] or [-nk]—and the nasal contoids are thus said to be neutralized in this position. In both free variation and neutralization a reduction is entailed in the possibilities of distinction within the system of the language, and assimilation in this more explicit sense always implies such reduction (see further Chapter X).

7.44. Many instances of sound shifts and changes in the history of languages may be regarded as assimilation phenomena which, from being accidental or facultative, have become standard. Thus Latin *affĕro, attŭli, allātum* from earlier *ad-fĕro, ad-tŭli, ad-lātum; collĭgo* from *con-lĭgo;* Italian *fatto* from Latin *făctu-, rotto* from *rŭptu;* etc., are well-known examples. It should be stressed, however, that to apply to such cases the label *assimilation* does not explain the

133

change in any sense; it simply classes it with other cases on the grounds of similarity in the processes involved. The problem as to why such assimilations develop and sometimes become part of the usual pronunciation must be solved otherwise.

7.45. Of a slightly different kind are the assimilatory phenomena which take place at a distance. In certain languages, for example, a tendency exists to let the vowel of one syllable of a word (commonly the first, or stressed syllable) determine partly or fully the quality of other vowels. This phenomenon is termed *vowel harmony*. It is clearly exemplified in Finnish and Turkish, where the vowels of derivational and inflexional syllables are partly determined by the vowel of the stem. Thus Finnish inessive case *talo-ssa* 'in the house' but *metsä-ssä* 'in the wood,' Turkish plural *at-lar* 'horses' but *gül-ler* 'roses,' and so on. Traces of vowel harmony are discernible in French, in the more open quality of the first vowel in *était* before half-open [ɛ] of the second syllable and the more close quality of the first vowel in *été* before the half-close [e] of this second syllable.

Historically, the numerous examples of *metaphony* or *umlaut* in the Old Germanic languages—of which traces remain in English *man—men, goose—geese*, German *bruder—brüder, ich halte—du hältst*, etc.—are likewise to be classed as distance assimilations.

7.46. A comparable phenomenon, *consonant harmony*, is of much rarer occurrence. An example often quoted is French *chercher* from an original **cercher*. Examples are more common in children's speech and are therefore often met in nursery words like *Dad, Mum*, or in pet-names like English *Bob* (for *Robert*), Spanish *Pepe* (for *Josepe*), etc.

7.5. Dissimilation

7.50. The converse of assimilation is *dissimilation*, the modification of a sound in the chain of speech by a neighbouring sound, but a modification which is the opposite of adaptive, and results in an increase of the extent of difference between the sounds concerned. The term *differentiation* is sometimes used, especially when the dissimilation affects immediately neighbouring sounds.

Examples of dissimilation in consonants are Spanish *arbol* in which final [l] is the result of a dissimilation of the earlier [r] which appears in Latin *arbor*. Similarly, English *marble* and *pilgrim* both show [l] from dissimilation of earlier [r], as in French *marbre* and Latin *peregrinus*. English *heaven* and German *himmel* may be the result of dissimilation of the one and the other of the two nasal consonants in an earlier form **hem(e)n*. Latin *anima* has developed into Spanish *alma*. As suggested by this collection of examples, nasal and resonant consonants such as [m, n, r] are especially likely to be involved in dissimilation. Other classes of consonant are more rarely so involved.

But Sanscrit and Greek show a dissimilation of aspiration, in that in words with two aspirated plosives, the first became replaced by a non-aspirate: Sanscrit *dádhāmi* 'I do' from a stem **dhadhā-*; Greek nominative *thríx* 'hair' but genitive *trikhós*; and so on.

Dissimilation of the vowel in one syllable under the influence of a neighbouring vowel occurs very rarely in any systematic way, and in this respect differs from assimilation and vowel harmony. A number of cases do, however, occur in Old English, where there was a tendency for the first of two unaccented back vowels in successive syllables to become centred or fronted. Examples in traditional spelling are *fugelas*, plural of *fugol* 'bird,' *eafera* beside *eafora* 'offspring,' *nafela* beside *nafola* 'navel,' etc. Spanish *hermoso* from Latin *formosus* is another example.

7.51. Dissimilation or differentiation is not infrequent between the beginning and final segments of a diphthong. Thus the common, partly dialectal pronunciations of English [weɪ] *way* as [wɛɪ], [wæɪ], [waɪ], may be the result of dissimilation of the two segments of the diphthong by increase of the difference of tongue height between them. Even the diphthongization of simple vowels may be interpreted as a process of differentiation of the segments of the vowel. In English, for example, the long vowel [iː] of *see* is often, perhaps regularly, diphthongized to [ɪi] and occasionally to [ɨi] or [əi].

7.52. Historical cases of such dissimilation in vowels and diphthongs abound. The Primitive Germanic [iː] and [uː] have been diphthongized to [ai] and [au] in German, to [ɛi] and [œy] in Dutch, and to [aɪ] and [aɵ] in English. Low Latin [e] in open stressed position became diphthongized to [ei] in Old French. The dissimilation of the initial and final segments with regard to tongue height continued to a stage approaching [ai], when a further dissimilation with regard to lip-rounding developed, resulting in [oi], a stage reflected in the present day spelling *trois*, *roi*, etc.

7.6. Metathesis

7.60. It sometimes happens that neighbouring speech sounds change places in the chain of speech. The phenomenon is usually called *metathesis*, but sometimes *interversion* when the sounds concerned are in contact with one another. Examples are the common pronunciation of English [enmɪtɪ] *enmity* as [emnɪţɪ], the vulgar pronunciations of French [lyks] *luxe* and [fiks] *fixe* as [lysk] and [fisk] and of [magazɛ̃] *magazin* as [mazagɛ̃], Swedish dialectal [pɛrsa] for [prɛsa] 'to press'; and so on. Interversions are very common in children's speech.

7.61. Numerous historical examples of metathesis are discernible. Italian *Orlando* derives from a Germanic source with [ro-] as in French *Roland*, while French *fromage* has undergone metathesis in its descent from Latin *formaticum* (cf. Italian *formaggio*), Rumanian *frumos* from Latin *formōsus*. Dutch *naald* shows metathesis of [l] and [d] in comparison with English *needle*, etc.

Careful recording and analysis of liquids as [r] (voiced and trilled) or [l] preceded or followed by other contoids often shows the presence of a vocoid element between the two units, a transition of a strictly vocalic character, which in narrow phonetic transcription might be written as [tᵉr-] or [-lᵉk-]. Normally this element forms part of the phonetic substance of the liquid and is not perceived as independent by the ear. On the other hand its length and intensity somtimes seem to be so important that the ear hesitates how to interpret it and therefore may take it as the expression of an independent vowel (cf. Chapter IX). Such hesitation may explain some of the phenomena just referred to. Spanish and Ibero-romance sound history offers numerous examples of this kind; thus Spanish *crónica* is often written *corónica* in early Spanish texts. The transitional vocoid element between [k] and [r] has been heard as a vowel. So listeners may hesitate if a sequence [kᵒron-] is to be interpreted [koron-], [kron-] or perhaps as [korn-]. Spectrographic analysis of these transitional vocoids shows that they have the same formant structure as the neighbouring vowels. Similar hesitation may also concern the number of syllables of a sequence. Compare, perhaps, the Spanish form *berebere* with English *Berber*, French *berbère*, etc.

7.62. Not all the phenomena labelled metathesis are necessarily the result of the same complex of factors. The common occurrence of metathesis of [r] and [l] with an adjacent vowel suggests that these contoids are, from some features of sound or articulation, particularly susceptible to the process. In some cases, but by no means in all, the result of metathesis is a sequence of sounds which is more in accordance with a permitted or a numerically dominant pattern in the language, which suggests that in these cases at least the phonological structure of the language, particularly its distributional patterns (§§ 7.72, 10.20, 11.1), may be a factor. In very many cases, however, the factors and causes involved in the process are still obscure.

7.7. Elision

7.70. A careful investigation of a full recording of a stretch of speech to determine what has actually been articulated often reveals that a number of features or segments of the chain which the speaker believes he has pronounced are missing. This phenomenon is termed *elision*, and a missing feature or segment is said to be *elided*.

For example, English [kɑːnt] *can't* is frequently pronounced as [kɑːn] in such phrases as [kɑːndu] *can't do*, the [t] being elided. [ɑːst] with elided [k] is probably the usual pronunciation of *asked*. Elision of a vowel is also common—[spəǫz] and [fæktrι] are very common pronunciations of *suppose* and *factory* (cf. also § 7.61).

Historical examples of elision are common. English [nɔː] *gnaw* and German [naːgən] *nagen* show elision of the original initial [g], retained as [k] in Dutch [knaːyən] *knagen*. In English *wrong, write*, etc., the *w* is no longer sounded. The vowel of the definite article in French is always elided before a following vowel: *l'enfant, l'ami*, etc. All such cases must be supposed to have started as occasional simplifications in current speech. Why some of them have been generalised is one of the unsolved problems of diachronic phonetics.

7.71. Elision phenomena vary in extent and in frequency of occurrence in differing contexts. They are likely to be minimal in slow, careful pronunciation and maximal in rapid, relaxed colloquial forms of speech. They are also, in a language such as English in which there are considerable variations of stress among syllables (§ 8.33), much more common and extensive in syllables with little or no stress.

7.72. The causes of elision are no doubt to be sought primarily in the human tendency to minimize expenditure of energy. Its widespread occurrence in speech is, however, both possible and facilitated through the *redundancy* of the speech signal (§ 9.57): in ordinary circumstances more information is conveyed by the signal than is necessary for the interpretation of the message. One form of this redundancy is the patterning of the speech sounds, both with regard to their phonetic form—certain phonetic features occur clustered together, others do not—and with regard to their sequence —certain sequences of sounds occur and certain sequences do not occur in any particular language. Here is perhaps the explanation for the interesting fact that in normal circumstances, neither the speaker nor the hearer is aware of the elisions occurring in the chain of speech. The native or practised user of a language appears to use his knowledge of these patterns, however unconscious this knowledge may be, both in the interpretation and control of his own speech and in his interpretation of that of others. He may, accordingly, interpret the heard signal in terms of known clusters and sequences, supplying, so to speak, from his own language storehouse quite unawares a missing feature or segment (cf. also § 9.83).

7.73. A phenomenon which appears to show similarity to elision is that termed *haplology*: the omission in pronunciation of one or two closely neighbouring occurrences of a sound or sequence of sounds within a word. Examples are the common English pronunciations of [regjələlɪ, sɪmɪləlɪ] *regularly, similarly* as [regjəlɪ, sɪmɪlɪ], [laɪbrərɪ] *library* as [laɪbrɪ], and so on. Again, historical examples are not uncommon: *tragi-comic* from *tragico-comic*, Latin *stipendium* from *stipipendium*, Greek *amphoreus* 'amphora' from *amphiphoreus*; England from *Englaland*, etc. The English adverbs of the type *probably* (for *probable-ly*) are also explained as due to haplology.

7.8. Sandhi

7.80. When words or parts of words such as affixes are combined in larger linguistic forms in the chain of speech, various phonetic phenomena may appear at the points of junction. These are traditionally termed *sandhi*, the term being a Sanscrit word meaning 'putting together, joining,' and its use in phonetics is due to the early Indian grammarians.

7.81. Languages vary in the extent and the nature of the sandhi-phenomena occurring in them. In some, relatively little is discernible, in others considerable sandhi appears, sometimes confined or largely confined to word boundaries, sometimes occurring also at morpheme boundaries within the word. Sandhi-phenomena may, in some cases, serve as phonetic markers of word endings and beginnings, and in other cases obscure them. This difference may be illustrated by comparison of German [dər-ʔaːl-tə] *der Alte* with French [le-zɑ̃-fɑ̃] *les enfants*. (The hyphens in the phonetic transcription separate the syllables.) In the German example, [r] belongs to the first syllable, while the initial vocoid of the words *Alte*, and hence the word boundary, is marked by the appearance of a preceding glottal stop. In the French example, a common pattern of syllable structure is imposed on the final contoid of *les* and the initial vocoid of *enfants*. The word boundary thus falls inside the syllable, and is obscured.

7.82. English has preserved from loss a final [r] when the next word in the chain begins with a vocoid, [ðərɪz] *there is*, [kɛərəv] *care of*, etc., being examples. This *sandhi*-[r] separates what would otherwise be two vocoids in succession, and by analogy is often extended to other word boundaries where two vocoids occur in succession. Thus [aɪdɪərəv] *idea of*, [lɔːrəndɔːdə] *law and order*, etc.

7.83. Assimilation phenomena are very common in sandhi. In Spanish any final nasal consonant is automatically assimilated, with regard to its place of articulation, to the initial consonant of a following word (*están blancos* with [m]: [esˈtam-ˈblaŋkos], *están grandes* with [ŋ]: [esˈtaŋ-ˈgrandes], *están llenos* with [ɲ]: [esˈtaɲ-ˈʎenos], etc. In the same way a final *s* is automatically voiced by the initial voiced consonant of a following word: *más grande* [mazˈgrande]. Lack of assimilation marks a boundary of higher level than the word between the units concerned.

7.9. Phonetic Groups

7.90. In all languages the sounds occurring in the chain of speech show a tendency to cluster or group themselves in such a way that the transitions between members of such groups are distinguishable, usually in their greater degree of closeness or tightness of combination, from the transitions between members of different groups. Such clusters or groups may be termed *phonetic groups*. The most important and widespread are the syllable, the stress group, the tone group, and the breath group.

The smallest phonetic group, and that with the closest transitions between its component sounds, is the *syllable*.

In the construction of their syllables, all languages appear to show a tendency to use some of their speech sounds centrally and others more marginally. The former are usually sounds produced by open articulations (§ 5.41) or characterized acoustically as resonants (§ 5.50). Such sounds are vocoids or vocoid-like. The marginally-used sounds, on the other hand, are normally those produced by closing articulations or characterized acoustically as semi- or non-resonants. Such sounds are contoids or contoid-like. It is these physical and functional differences between speech sounds which are clearly the basis for the traditional and widespread classification of sounds as vowels and consonants. The idea of vocoids as "opening sounds," contoids as "closing sounds" is quite old (Menzerath, 1941, etc.). Recently the theory has been put forward that, when strengthened under emphasis, vocoids become more open than before, contoids more closed (Straka, 1963). In fact, the fundamental difference between these two categories, on both levels (i.e. as vocoids-contoids or as vowels-consonants), has to be defined in close connexion with the definition of the syllable.

The syllable, however, is by no means a simple concept. Within the one language a child can usually count on its fingers the number of syllables in a sequence, but no phonetician has succeeded so far in giving an exhaustive and adequate description of what the syllable is. The difficulties seem to arise from the various possibilities of approach to the unit.

7.91. At the phonetic level there is both the articulatory syllable formed by the minimum groupings of articules and the acoustic syllable formed by the minimum groupings of phones. At the phonemic level there is the phonemic or structural syllable formed by certain selections and combinations of phonemes. The units isolated as syllables by criteria valid at one of these levels do not necessarily or always correspond exactly with the units isolated at any other level. Nor, of course, does the syllable at any level in one language agree with its correspondent in another. And as a further complication, there appears to be at least one language, Bella Coola of the Pacific Coast of North America, in which a unit corresponding to traditional conceptions of the syllable hardly exists (Newman, 1947).[1]

7.92. A syllable theory which goes back to Jespersen and de Saussure is based on the concept of sonority. Jespersen established a ranking of speech sounds according to sonority. This starts with the open vocoids as the most sonorous, continues, in order, through the close vocoids, the liquids and nasals, the voiced fricatives, the voiced plosives, the voiceless fricatives and ends with the voiceless plosives as the least sonorous. In any sequence, the more sonorous phones tend to form the centres of syllables and the less sonorous the marginal units. Thus in a word such as English [plɑːnt] *plant*, the sequence passes from minimally sonorous [p] through [l] with a medium degree of sonority to the maximally sonorous [ɑː]. It

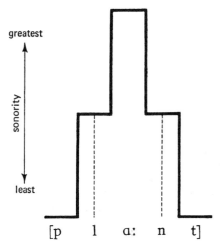

Fig. 7.3. The word *plant* according to Jespersen's theory of the relative sonority of sounds

[1] When such information is found in descriptions of languages, it is often difficult to know, unless expressly stated, what level is referred to. Within his glossematic theory Hjelmslev (1939, 1943, 1961, etc.) defined the syllable as a unit capable of carrying an accent (in turn a concept which has to be defined from some starting point). With this definition, a language like French which has no phonemic accent (on the level of word phonology, since the accent is automatically on the last syllable on the word) has no syllables either, only "pseudo-syllables" on the purely phonetic level.

141

continues, with decreasing sonority through [n] to a second minimum with [t].

It is true that this principle seems to be very general but there are, on the other hand, syllables in many languages which contradict it. In terms of sonority variation, a sequence such as English [stɒps] *stops* should have three syllables instead of its actual one. Further, the concept 'sonority' with which the theory operates is not very clearly defined. It is usually conceived as being some quality of the sound which determines the range of its audibility, given a certain level of intensity, but it will be observed that Jespersen's rank-ordering of the speech sounds is based primarily on their voicedness or voicelessness and, secondarily, on the degree of opening of the vocal tract in their articulation. The theory seems to give a good description of some ideal acoustic syllable, perhaps even an ideal to which many languages tend, but one which is inevitably disturbed by other factors. If there is any distinctive characteristic of the syllable, it does not seem to be this pattern of sonority.

7.93. Other phoneticians have tried to define the syllable in articulatory terms. Grammont and Fouché developed a theory of the syllable as a peak in the continual fluctuation of tension in the articulatory musculature; and Stetson conceived of syllables as basically the result of a ballistic-type periodicity of movement in the expiratory muscles, so that each syllable was "a puff of air from the chest." His theory has not been confirmed by recent findings of Ladefoged, Draper & Whitteridge (1958). Work by Strenger (1959) has shown that subglottal air pressure, which doubtless reflects in sensitive fashion the extent of muscular activity in the lungs and larynx, varies with the syllabation of the speech chain. Menzerath's idea (1941) that the downward-upward movement of the lower jaw characterizes the syllable may be the result of a correct observation, since the mandible normally moves in a pattern corresponding to that of opening and closing articulation (§§ 3.46, 5.41), but such movement does not define the syllable, since, as can be easily shown, it is not at all necessary for syllabation. No physiological theory of the syllable so far developed seems to be sufficiently well founded instrumentally to be acceptable as definitive and exhaustive.

7.94. On the other hand, there seems to be a striking correspondence between the variation with time of the overall intensity of the chain of speech sounds and the units conventionally considered as syllables. The syllabic centre is an intensity maximum and the syllabic boundaries intensity minima (as has been shown by Zwirner and others). This variation of the intensity seems to be a natural correspondence on the acoustic level to the varying muscular tension on the physiological. Yet the strong intensity in fricatives may disturb very considerably the otherwise smooth curve form of the over-all intensity variation of the syllable (see Fig. 7.2, facing p. 129).

7.95. On a basis of the spectrographic evidence referred to in § 7.15—the colouring of contoids by surrounding vocoids on the one hand, and the modification of vocoid formant structures by contoids on the other—it seems to be possible to look upon the syllable to a certain extent as an acoustic unit determined by the degree of interdependence between central and marginal elements (Skaličková, 1958). Experiments have been carried out with synthetic combinations of two vocoids and an intervening contoid, contrasting the effect of transitions only in the initial part of the second vocoid with that of transitions only in the final part of the first vocoid. Listeners hear the former type as if the consonant belonged to the same syllable as the second vocoid, and the latter as if it belonged to the same syllable as the first vocoid (Malmberg, 1955) (see Fig. 7.4). The much discussed syllabic boundary—the linguistic function of which is not doubted (English *a name* [ə-neɪm] — *an aim* [ən-eɪm]) may consequently be looked upon as physically founded in a difference of transition and connexion between contoids and vocoids. More instrumental evidence is needed, however, before this can be regarded as established.

7.96. In many cases the phonetically very subtle syllabic boundary is reinforced or replaced by other phenomena of a more audible character. Jones (1956, etc.) has mentioned a whole series of differences between syllable-initial and syllable-final consonants in English. In [naɪ-t'ɹeɪt] (sc. *nitrate*) the [t] is aspirated and the [r] (by assimilation to the initial [t]) more or less voiceless. In [naɪt-reɪt] (sc. *night-rate*) the [t] is final, unaspirated and the initial [r] fully voiced. Swedish experiments recently carried out have shown a strong tendency among listeners to identify syllabic boundaries as junctures between words when aspiration—versus lack of aspiration —of stops is among the cues to the distinction. A similar tendency occurs when the glottal stop is among such cues (cf. § 7.81). Evidently, different cues may work together in marking syllabic boundaries. These boundaries, like the syllables themselves, are potentially distinctive prosodic features (Sommerfelt, 1936, Gårding, 1967), even though they may often be obscured in the actual stream of speech.

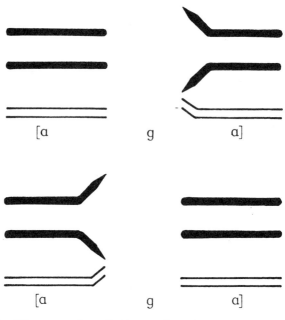

Fig. 7.4. Diagrams of synthetic speech patterns to reproduce [aga] with transitions in the initial part of the second vocoid (above) and with transitions in the final part of the first vocoid (below). The former is heard syllabically as [a-ga] and the latter as [ag-a]. (Essentially similar results are obtained over the range of 20 to 200 milliseconds for the duration of the hold segment of the contoid pattern) (after Malmberg)

7.97. Syllables in their turn are grouped into larger units, but the nature of the unit next larger to the syllable appears to be differently characterized in different languages. There seems little hope of setting up a simple type of such unit which would be as generally valid or useful as the syllable.

In languages with a stress type of accent (§ 8.30 f.) a convenient unit is often the *stress group* or *phonetic foot*. This consists basically of a stressed syllable together with any unstressed and/or semi-stressed syllables which are grouped with it, and in the phonetic structure of the utterance are subordinated to it. In English the stressed syllable normally comes first in the foot and subordinates any and all syllables until the beginning of the next foot. Unstressed syllables before the first stressed syllable are best treated as anacrusis.

| 'When will | 'Jim be | 'home? ‖
(He) | 'promised to be | 'back about | 'six ‖ (so
there's) | 'still | 'plenty of | 'time ‖

In this example stressed syllables are marked by preceding ' and the feet separated by |. Anacrustic syllables are in parentheses, and the ‖ marks the end of a larger unit, the tone group.

It will be noted that feet vary in length from one to four syllables —the limit is probably about six—but one of the features of English is that the more syllables there are in a foot the shorter each is, with the result that each foot in the next larger unit, the tone group, tends to have an approximately equal duration. Thus the foot | 'promised to be | with one stressed and three unstressed syllables has similar duration to the foot | 'back about | with one stressed and two unstressed and | 'six | with one stressed syllable only. Languages in which groups or sequences of phonetic feet show this feature are termed *stress-timed*.

In French, the stressed syllable usually falls at the end of the foot.

'Quand | est-ce que 'Jacques | sera de re'tour ‖
Il a 'dit | qu'il serait de re'tour | vers six 'heures ‖
Il 'reste | tou'jours | beaucoup de 'temps ‖

Again the feet vary in size from one syllable | *quand* | [kɑ̃] to several syllables, but in French each syllable tends to be of approximately equal duration, though the stressed syllable is often slightly longer than the unstressed. Accordingly the length of a foot is closely dependent on the number of syllables in that foot. Languages with this feature in sequences of phonetic feet are termed *syllable-timed*.

A second type of unit larger than the syllable is the *tone group*, described in § 8.27.

7.98. The third unit larger than the syllable, and the largest which is normally considered in phonetics, is the *breath group*. This is the sequence of syllables, of phonetic feet, or of tone groups which occurs between any two successive intakes of breath on the part of the speaker. Physiological phenomena connected with respiration put an upper limit to the possible length of the breath group; its minimum length in voluntary speech is a single syllable.

There are cases or instances in which the ingressive air stream of the breath intake is utilized for speech production, alternating with the egressive, so that there is no practical pause or break in the process of phonation and articulation. An example of this frequently occurs in English during rapid counting. In practically all other cases, however, inspiration introduces a break in the process of speaking and successive inspirations thus segment the flow of speech into naturally occurring segments, the breath groups.

Breath groups, which are, of course, units of expression, need not correlate very highly with units of content, but in practice most speakers acquire sufficient control over speech communication that, save in abnormal circumstances, a pause for the intake of breath coincides with the end of a tone group, with the end of a phonetic foot, and with the end of a syllable; and the breath group as a unit corresponds with an internally coherent unit of content, a word, word group, clause, etc. (cf. § 7.15, note).

This patterning in speech is probably general and widespread not only because it is clearly more efficient both to speaker and to hearer than a lack of such coincidence and correspondence, but also because in very many human societies—speech is widely evaluated and assessed as a skilled art—such patterning is regarded as aesthetically satisfying.

7.99. There is little doubt that still further phonetic units of greater inclusiveness exist, perhaps corresponding in some ways to the periods and paragraphs of the written language. When listening, for example, to news broadcasts on the radio, one is usually able to decide at a pause whether the speaker has finished a report or not. It seems that this information is signalled, as far as the expression side of language is concerned, by a complex of factors involving intonation level and rate of fall, loudness and rhythm variation, voice quality, and duration of pause, but further investigation is needed. Important information and a promising method of approach are to be found in Kerstin Hadding-Koch's work on Swedish sentence intonation (1961).

CHAPTER 8

PROSODIC FEATURES

8.1. Introduction

8.10. In most and probably all languages, some at least of the units discussed in the preceding chapter form the carriers of, or are accompanied by, articulatory and sound features which are often of a generally different type from those used in or associated with segmental speech sounds. These features which thus characterize syllables, phonetic groups, tone groups, and so on, may be termed *suprasegmental* or *prosodic*.[1]

The prosodic features of a language mark off or contribute to the marking off of the phonetic groups in the chain of speech. They do so, it seems, in two distinguishably different ways. One is by increasing the contrast between successive or neighbouring units, the other by signalling the boundaries of such units.

8.11. The prosodic features so used in languages are most commonly expressed in the acoustic stage of the phonetic substance in the form of variation in fundamental frequency, in intensity, or in duration, that is, in variation of the basic attributes of the acoustic substance. Variation of other, less basic, qualities of this substance, for example, the addition or subtraction of the acoustic correlates of nasalization, of palatalization, or of other features of formant structure, of voice quality, or even of voice itself, is not unknown as the expression substance of prosodic features, but is very rare. A third possibility, also relatively uncommon, is a prosodic feature expressed as some form of interruption in the continuity of one or other of the qualities of the acoustic substance, so that a syllable or word with such interruption is contrasted with syllables or words without such interruption.

---

[1] The terms *accent* and *accentual system*, which were formerly used to refer to such features, have become less common in recent years, partly, no doubt, to avoid the use of *accent* both as a general term for any prosodic feature and as a term for a specific type of such feature, the type here termed *stress*.

8. PROSODIC FEATURES

8.2. Intonation: The Use of Pitch

8.20. Variation of the fundamental frequency of the vibration of the vocal cords, and thus of the pitch of the voice (§ 2.30) is widely used for the expression of prosodic features. Such use is generally termed (*speech*) *melody, intonation,* or *musical accent.* There is no confirmed report of a language system in which melodic distinctions are completely lacking. The average tone register in speech varies normally within one octave, or less, but may be extended in abnormal cases. The possible maximal range for untrained voices hardly exceeds two octaves, but the whole of this range is never used in speech. A man's normal speech register varies roughly between 100 and 200 c/s, a woman's between 200 and 400 c/s. The average register is probably a little different for different languages and dialects. Spanish, for example, is said to be pronounced on a somewhat lower average frequency level than French.

8.21. Three main functions of intonation or musical accent may be clearly isolated. The first is that of distinguishing between words.[1] The prosodic features so used are termed *tones* or *word tones,* and the languages using word tones are termed *tone languages.* These are to be found in many parts of the world, though they are particularly numerous in the Far East and in Africa. In Europe, word tones are used only in Norwegian and Swedish, in Lithuanian, and in Serbo-Croatian.

In such languages, the tone is usually associated with the syllable, the number of tones thus corresponding with the number of syllables in the word, or with a given sequence of syllables. The tone or sequence of tones—the tone pattern—is in such cases part of the word's inherent phonetic structure.

The tones themselves may be expressed in the acoustic substance either as stretches of *level* pitch or as stretches of *changing* pitch. Those tonal systems in which the tones are definable in terms of levels of pitch are termed by Pike (1948) *register* systems and those in which the tones are definable in terms of changes of pitch are termed *contour* systems. In practice, however, a very large number of tone systems seem to combine both level and changing tones. It seems to be quite common also that, in languages with many

---

[1] Cf. hereto what was said above (§ 7.15 note) about the concept of word in this context.

tone distinctions, at least one or two of these distinctions are not purely tonal, but involve in addition a feature of voice quality or of interruption.

8.22. The following examples illustrate the use of tones. In the Mandarin Chinese dialect of Peking, according to Karlgren (1948), there are four different tones described as (1) even, (2) rising, (3) broken, and (4) falling. The relative level of, and the changes in, the pitch of the voice in these tones may be suggested by lines as

No. 1 —   No. 2 /
No. 3 √   No. 4 \

The sound sequence [tʃu], romanized as *chu*, with tone No. 1 has the meaning "pig," with No. 2 "bamboo," with No. 3 "master, sir," and with No. 4 "to live."

In Ibo, of West Africa, according to Ward, the sequence [akwa] with low tone on both syllables signifies "bridge," with low tone on the first syllable and high tone on the second "egg," and with high tone on the first syllable and low tone on the second "cloth."

The Scandinavian word tones have a slightly different character since the relevant prosodic feature in both Norwegian and Swedish distinguishes a sequence of syllables, not single syllables as in Chinese or Yoruba, from another group otherwise identical. Thus, in Swedish, the word *komma* 'comma' is distinguished from the word *komma* 'come' by a difference in tones, accent I and accent II respectively. Similarly, *buren* 'the cage' (from *bur* 'cage') with accent I is distinguished from *buren* 'carried' or 'born' (from the verb *bära*) with accent II, *tanken* 'the tank' (from *tank*) with accent I from *tanken* 'the thought' (from *tanke*) with accent II, and so on.

These word tones have usually been looked upon as essentially tonal in substance though other opinions have been expressed. Recently instrumental research and experimentation with synthetic speech (§ 1.32), partly by one of the authors of this book (Malmberg, 1953, 1959, 1962a, etc.) has confirmed that the differences of pitch are to be regarded as distinctive and other variables, stress, length, etc., as redundant. (This seems to be true also for Norwegian.) The differences in pitch movement between the two accents in dissyllabic words in the Swedish of Stockholm is represented in the diagrams of Fig. 8.1.

149

The manifestation of these word tones presupposes a sequence of at least two syllables, of which the first is stressed: ' – – (– –). If the last syllable is stressed (– ' –), which may occur in certain types of words, mostly loanwords, no distinction is possible. As suggested by the examples, the most common type of word with accent I is a monosyllabic noun followed by the postposed definite article. Longer words, mostly compounds, may have either accent, though in compounds accent II predominates. In many cases of compounds, names, and foreign words there is free or, sometimes, regional variation between the two accent types. After an un stressed prefix, accent I is regular, with a few loanwords as excep· tions, e.g. *beställa* 'order' with accent I on *-ställa* but the simplex *ställa* 'put' with accent II.

All Swedish dialects except those of Finland, and all Norwegian dialects except some of the Northern ones, have such an accent distinction, but the distribution of the accents in the vocabulary shows important regional and social variations.

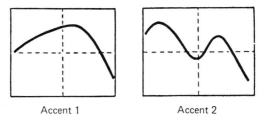

Accent 1   Accent 2

Fig. 8.1. The pattern of pitch movement in Accent 1 and Accent 2 respectively in the Swedish of Stockholm, according to E. A. Meyer

8.23. The previous examples have shown tones functioning as inherent parts of the structures of different words and thus contributing to the distinguishing of those words as simple lexical units. In many tone languages, however, tones appear with grammatical function, that is, their occurrences and uses in a language are related to the morphological and/or syntactical systems of that language, and they distinguish words as belonging to different grammatical classes.

In Ogoni, an African language of Southern Nigeria, for instance, the personal pronouns as subjects to verbs occur in a paradigm of four different forms, two long and two short, each with its own tone pattern[1]. Each form carries grammatical information as to the aspect and/or tense of the action denoted by the following verb. Verbs occur also in paradigms of forms, in which tone is the main differentiating inflexion. There are a number of such paradigms. In the following examples the three tones of the language, high, mid, low are marked by ´, ¯, ˋ, respectively.

(i) *I*: m̀ 'incompleted   m̄ 'simple or completed
he: à   action'   ā   action'
     m̀ḿ 'action not   m̄m̀ 'action completed
     àí   begun'   ā̀ì   in past'

(ii) with *kē bùrà* 'to think' and *kē bɔví* 'to tie,' verbs of different paradigms:

m̀ būrà	I am thinking	m̄ bùrà	I think
m̀ bɔ̀vì	I am tying	m̄ bɔ́ví	I tie
m̀ḿ bùrà	I shall think	m̄m̀ bùrà	I had thought
m̀ḿ bɔ́ví	I shall tie	m̄m̀ bɔ̄ví	I had tied.

Again, in Kikuyu of East Africa a kind of tone reversal is used in negation (Harries, 1952). For example, a high tone in a verb base in the affirmative becomes a mid tone in the negative. A similar process extends over the basic tones of governed forms following in the clause. Thus the affirmative *twàtòmíré mágùtá ténē*, "we sent oil long ago," becomes *tōtīātómīrē māgùtā tēnē* in the negative. Tone markings are used as in the previous example. The verb base is *-tom-*: its high tone in the affirmative, and its mid tone in the negative, occurs, by a separate tone-shift process, on the vowel of the immediately following syllable. Note also the tonal changes in the words *mágùtá* "oil" and *ténē* "previously" following the negatived verbal: in so far as this set of tone changes affects a word group or phrase rather than a single word, it approaches the second type of use of pitch, intonation (§ 8.25).

8.24.   The tones of a tonal system are not, of course, at fixed points or ranges on the frequency scale. They vary in absolute frequency from speaker to speaker, each having his own customary frequencies. Thus a child or a woman, who normally uses a higher fundamental frequency, will have higher pitched tones than a man, who uses a lower fundamental frequency. Tones are also likely to vary in absolute frequency according to the speaker's situation—a speaker's

---

[1] This material from the Gokana dialect of Ogoni is from unpublished notes of Brosnahan.

tone frequencies may change somewhat with change in his emotional state.

The tones, however, do maintain their relative status in the utterance. In a common type of tonal system with tones at three levels, high, mid and low, a high tone in an utterance will be of higher frequency than a neighbouring mid tone and this latter of higher frequency than a neighbouring low tone. The restriction 'neighbouring' is necessary here since in some tone languages intonation is also employed, though usually in very restricted ways, at the level of the word group, as discussed below. The frequencies of the tones within the word are then affected by the position of that word within the intonation pattern of the word group of which it is part. Thus, in such languages, there may be a general downward drift or curve of the pitch during the course of the utterance or of the breath group. In these cases, though the pitch relations between closely neighbouring tones are maintained, the absolute frequency of a high tone late in the utterance may be comparable to or lower than the absolute frequency of a low tone early in that utterance.

The relative status of the different tones may, however, be maintained, at least partly, in a different way. In the type of tone language which has been termed "terraced level" (Welmers, 1959), one or more of the tones in the system have pitch levels which are related to the level of a preceding tone. The reference level of pitch for a particular tone may thus vary from syllable to syllable in the course of the utterance. As an example of this type, Shitswa, a Southern Bantu language, has three tones, a low tone which has always low level pitch, and two non-low tones, one with the same pitch as the last preceding non-low tone, and the other with a lower pitch than the last preceding non-low tone. The three tones are thus consistently distinguished through an utterance, though the pitches on which the non-low tones occur may overlap.

8.25.   The second widespread use of intonation is at the level of the word group or phrase. In numerous languages an utterance may be marked as one or other of the categories or types of word group in the particular language concerned—statement, question, report, non-completed phrase, etc.—solely or partly by means of intonation. The forms which intonation may take in such use are fundamentally two. The first is the use of different levels of pitch. For example, in English an utterance such as 'The house, it seemed to him, was smaller than before' is often pronounced with two basic levels of intonation. One, normal level, extends over *the house* and *was smaller than before*; the other, low level, extends over *it seemed to him*. The former contributes to marking the word group which it accompanies as 'ordinary statement,' the latter to marking the word group it accompanies as 'parenthetic statement.'

8.26. The second form which intonation may take is change of pitch over the word group. The pattern of such change is usually termed an *intonation tune* or *curve* or *contour*.

Intonation contours are widely used in languages to mark or assist in marking different categories of word group. Thus in French in the initial lines of the fable:

Maître Corbeau, sur un arbre perché,

Tenait en son bec un fromage;

the first three word groups *Maître Corbeau, sur un arbre perché* and *Tenait en son bec* are accompanied by an intonation contour of level pitch until the last syllable and of higher pitch on this syllable (- - - ¯, etc.). The last group has on its first syllable the same level as in the former groups, then the second syllable rises to a high pitch and the last falls to a low one (- ¯ _). The first type of contour assists in marking the word group which it accompanies as non-final and subordinate within a more inclusive word group; the second type assists in marking the word group which it accompanies as final in the sentence.

In many languages, the two forms which intonation may take are associated, so that the intonation of a word group or of a category of word group is characterized by both difference in level of pitch and difference in contour. In Spanish, for example, the word sequences *mi padre viene* or *viene mi padre* accompanied by intonation of lower pitch and falling contour are both statements, and accompanied by intonation of higher pitch and rising contour are both questions.

8.27. The use of intonation at the level of the word group leads to the establishment of the *tone group*, that is, the sequence of words with which a unit of the intonation system of the language co-occurs. Thus in the examples above the tone groups are

the house ‖ it seemed to him ‖ was smaller than before ‖

and

Maître Corbeau ‖ sur un arbre perché ‖
Tenait en son bec ‖ un fromage ‖

Such tone groups may vary considerably in length, from a word with a single syllable to a sequence of words with a few dozen syllables, but the longer tone groups occur only in more rapid utterance. The beginnings and endings of tone groups may be marked by various phonetic means, by pausation, by lengthening or shortening of final syllables, by terminal-marking pitch movements, by cessation of voice, and so on.

8.28. Finally, intonation is widely used for stylistic and extra-linguistic purposes, that is, to give various secondary values to utterances. In conjunction with features of loudness and of speed of utterance, intonation may be used to convey a speaker's attitude to what he is saying—surprise, doubt, certainty, and so on.

Within a linguistic community, there are general patterns in the way in which pitch and other prosodic and prosodic-like features —loudness, speed and rhythm—are used for the signalling of such attitudes and emotions. It has, indeed, been suggested that such patterns are of the nature of gestures and basically are analogous to the patterns of gesture with hand, arm, facial expression, etc., which occur within a community.

Our knowledge of these patterns is, however, still very defective. The considerable body of work which has been devoted to the investigation of intonation in English and similar languages has resulted in a general recognition of the existence and the importance of this function of intonation but no consensus of opinion as to its relationship with the more central functions of language. Nor is there full agreement concerning the description and interpretation of these patterns (as levels, as contours or curve forms, as changes, etc.). Differences in these matters may be partly due to the degree of abstraction aimed at by the investigator (Malmberg, 1962, etc.). One view, probably the more traditional, is that the attitudinal and emotional meanings conveyed by intonation are of fundamentally different nature from the lexical and grammatical meanings conveyed by the words and constructions in a language, and that accordingly this function of intonation is best regarded as extra-linguistic, and its analysis as hardly part of language study. Sentence intonation is looked upon as continuous, not as built up of discrete units (Martinet, 1960). The other view is that since the uses of intonation in this function reveal conventional patterns differing from language to language, and since the meanings so conveyed are, in many cases, impossible to separate from meanings conveyed by other means, the attitude- and emotion-signalling function of intonation is integral to language, and its description validly part of the task of the linguist. There is little doubt that this latter view is the more realistic one. The hesitation of some linguists to accept it may be to a confusion of levels. If an English *Yes!* is pronounced with an affirmative concluding intonation (falling, tune 1) and at the same time with a strong emphasis we have to do with two levels and with two linguistic functions: the falling tune 1 is opposed to a rising tune 2 (*Yes?* etc.), and the strong emphatic falling is opposed to a normal, non-emphatic falling. These two functions are manifested physically as one strongly falling intonation.

We may reasonably assume that improved methods for dealing with these phenomena, and deepening experience and understanding of the more properly linguistic functions of intonation, will both clarify the distinction between these functions and other uses of prosodic-like features and suggest linguistic methods of approach to the latter. Valuable work in the investigation of the attitudes and emotions conveyed by intonation has been done by E. Uldall (1960, 1964) and noteworthy attempts to correlate the situations in which intonation patterns occur and the significance of these patterns in such situations are those of O'Connor and Arnold (1961) for British English, and of Hadding-Koch (1961) for Swedish.

8.3. Stress and Loudness

8.30. Variation of the intensity of the vibration of the vocal cords, and thus mainly of the loudness of the heard sound, is also widely used for the expression of prosodic features.

The feature of loudness has long been looked upon as the perceptual counterpart of the linguistic phenomenon termed *stress*, this being conceived as the degree of muscular effort exerted in the production of a sound or of the sounds of a syllable. Languages using stress in their prosodic system are said to have a *stress accent*. Older terms are *dynamic* or *expiratory accent*.

Stress, however, is a more complex phenomenon; recent work has shown clearly that stressed syllables are not differentiated from

155

unstressed ones solely by physical intensity. Other features are always involved: thus, other things being equal, a longer syllable tends to be heard as stressed in comparison with a shorter syllable, a syllable with higher pitch likewise, in comparison with one with lower pitch, and in English at any rate, a syllable with rapid change of pitch in comparison with one with steady or slow change of pitch. It is probable also that in many languages, English, German, Swedish, and Russian, for example, vocoid quality is also a cue to the hearer with regard to stress, since certain distinctions of vocoid colour and length are reduced or lacking in unstressed syllables. Fry's experiments (1958) have shown in fact that, in English, variations of intensity, pitch, length, and vowel colour—all other conditions being equal—are capable of yielding the impression of stress variations. The linguistic feature of stress clearly involves more than the single dimension of perceived loudness; though loudness may be its most important component in the majority of cases, a number of other cues are probably also present, in varying proportions, in current speech.

8.31. Two main functions of stress may be distinguished. The first is the more strictly linguistic use at the word and word-group level. In this use, stress takes the form of a small number of discrete degrees or levels of loudness plus associated physical features, and one of these occurs with each syllable. Such degrees or levels of stress are not located at fixed points along an extralinguistic dimension of stress but are differences in stress relative one to the other, and to some general situational or contextual level of stress in the speaker's voice.

The number of linguistically relevant or significant levels of stress used probably varies a little—perhaps between two and four—from language to language. In a system with two such levels, these may be termed *stress* and *unstress*, in one with three, *primary stress*, *secondary stress* and *unstress*, and so on.

Reliable studies of stress systems are few, but the evidence available suggests strongly that stress is nowhere used so extensively or so significantly at the word level, as is intonation. No language is known in which differences in stress pattern are used to distinguish words of similar phonemic structure to an extent comparable with that in which differences in tone pattern distinguish such words in languages as Chinese or Ibo (§ 8.22).

8.32. The traditional classification of languages using stress is into those with a fixed stress and those with a free stress. In the former the occurrence of the primary stress is limited to a particular syllable in multisyllabic words. Simple cases are French, in which this stress is on the last syllable of the word, and Czech and Finnish, in which it is on the first. Sometimes the location of the primary stress is dependent or partly dependent on other phonemic or prosodic features: in Classical Latin, for example, this stress was on the penultimate in dissyllabic words and in multisyllable words in which either or both of the last two syllables were of the class of long syllables (§ 8.40). In other multisyllabic words the primary stress occurred on the antepenultimate syllable. Stress and word tone may be interrelated in different ways. In Swedish a stress on the final syllable of a word (as in the example, [jɑ'pɑːn], below) excludes the use of the (tonal) word accent distinction (§ 8.22).

8.33. In languages with a free stress the occurrence of the primary stress is not confined in any predictable way to a specific position in the word. In one word it may occur on the first syllable, in another on the second, in a third on the last, and so on. This situation is exemplified in the English words—we adopt the convention of marking the stressed syllable by a raised vertical line preceding that syllable—['lʌvlɪnɪs] *loveliness*, ['fəʊtəgrɑːf] *photograph*, with the stress on the first syllable; [fə'gɪvnɪs] *forgiveness*, [fə'tɔgrəfɪ] *photography*, with the stress on the second syllable; [əʊvə'tɜːn] *overturn* and [fəʊtə'græfɪk] *photographic*, with the stress on the third syllable. Similarly, the Russian ['pravdə] 'truth,' ['zolətə] 'gold' with stress on the first syllable, [da'rogə] 'road' with the stress on the second syllable, [səma'var] 'samovar,' with the stress on the third; and so on.

In such languages the position of the primary stress may be used to differentiate words of the same structure of segmental phonemes. Thus, in English ['trænspɔːt] *transport* (noun) is distinguished from [træns'pɔːt] *transport* (verb), ['bɪləʊ] *billow* from [bɪ'ləʊ] *below*, etc., essentially by the position of this stress. In Spanish ['tɛrmino] 'term, end' is distinguished from [tɛr'mino] 'I finish,' and both of these from [tɛrmi'no] 'he finished,' by the position of the stress. In Swedish, ['jɑːpan] 'Japan' is opposed to [ja'pɑːn] 'Japanese.'

8.34. As was the case with tone, however, (§ 8.23), stress may also be used with grammatical function, though this is relatively uncommon, and, in the cases known, fairly restricted in range. An example of unusually extended use of grammatical stress occurs in Terena, an Indian language of southwest Brazil. Here, contrast in the position of the stress is used to distinguish the subject from the object in a verb in an independent clause as *kúti otopíko* 'who chopped?' but *kúti otópiko* 'what did he chop?'; to mark certain sequences of independent clauses in co-ordinative relationship as *tokopónu namukónu* 'he found me, took me' in comparison with *tokóponu namúkonu* 'he found and took me'; to mark the verb introduced by a sequence particle as *ína aunkópovo* 'then I returned home' in comparison with *aúnkopovo* 'I returned home'; and so on (Bendor-Samuel, 1962).

8.35. The second main function of stress (§ 8.31 above) is rather extralinguistic. The substance of that complex of physical features along which the various levels of stress are differentiated is of a continuous nature rather than a series of discrete steps, and it projects beyond the normal range of differentiation of stressed from unstressed syllables in both directions, towards greater loudness and towards less loudness. The range of stress in these projections may then be exploited, by addition of further levels of stress, for example, by increase of the differentiation between the usual levels, or, while maintaining the normal differentiation, by moving the whole range of the levels of stress towards greater loudness or towards less loudness; and such exploitation may be used for the communication or expression of information other than that conveyed by the more central systems of the language.

In English, for instance, extra loudness in the stressing of a command such as *Come here!* conveys an extra degree of imperativeness and of associated emotion; a less-than-usual loudness in the same command may convey the necessity for quietness in the situation, and so on. But the difficulties of contrasting abnormal levels of stress and of correlating their occurrence with emotional and other accompaniments to linguistic communication have hindered up to the present a satisfactory description of these phenomena.

There is, however, one area in which an extra loud level of stress, often termed *emphatic stress*, is quite regularly used in English. This is for purposes of contrast. As examples (the syllable bearing emphatic stress being marked by a preceding double upright):

158

I said "fifteen, not "sixteen; he lives in "South Carolina, not "North Carolina; and with the contrasting form inferable from the situation: *John "walked there?* (the contrast being with the speaker's expectation that John would not have walked); *the light was "out* (the contrast being with the speaker's expectation of the light's being on); etc.

8.4. Duration

8.40.   It has already been mentioned (§ 8.11) that other phenomena of the phonetic substance may manifest physically suprasegmental or prosodic features. We should note firstly the use of duration. Some languages distinguish two classes of syllables usually termed long and short—the length or shortness being a structural characteristic of the syllable as a whole, and in most cases manifested by more features than the simple length of the speech sounds making up that syllable. The distinction of long and short syllables may be primarily a device contributing to the marking off of syllables as such (§ 8.10) or may be further involved in the prosodic system of the language concerned (§ 8.32). In Classical Latin, for example, a long syllable was one with either a long vocoid or diphthong or, in general, a short vocoid followed by a contoid in the same syllable.[1]

8.5. Interruption

8.50.   The use of an interruption in the phonetic substance (§ 8.11) as a prosodic feature is exemplified in Danish. Some syllables in this language are marked by the occurrence in them of the *Stød*, a sudden and short-lasting disturbance of the vibration of the vocal cords, with or without a complete closure of the glottis. Thus [sto'l] *stol* 'chair,' [man'] *mand* 'man,' [muː'r] *mord* 'murder,' (cf. [muːr] *mor* 'mother'), [hu'n] *hund* 'dog,' (cf. [hun] *hun* 'she'), etc.

---

[1] Latin distinguished two classes of segmental vocoids traditionally also termed *long* and *short*. To avoid this source of confusion Allen (1964) suggests the use of the terms *heavy* and *light* for the classes of the syllable.

CHAPTER 9

HEARING AND PERCEPTION OF SPEECH

9.1. Introduction

9.10. Most of this book is concerned with the production and properties of the sounds of speech and the various ways in which they are combined. The next set of stages in the sequence of happenings which we know as a speech event are those that take place in the listener, the *perception* of the sound wave disturbances in the atmosphere, the *identification* of these disturbances and the *interpretation* of them. In the following pages we shall discuss briefly the mechanism of hearing, of which we have a reasonable, though by no means complete, understanding; some results of experimental work on the perception of speech; and some possible ways in which the brain might identify and interpret speech sounds. These last stages of the process are peculiarly inaccessible to experimental investigation, and our knowledge of them at the present time is still very speculative.

9.11. The discussion of hearing here follows mainly the excellent surveys of hearing and perception of speech in Stevens (1951) and Fletcher (1953), in both of which numerous references can be found. A newer, introductory account, also excellent, is van Bergeijk, Pierce & David (1960).

9.2. The Peripheral Auditory System

9.20. The outer or external ear consists of a convoluted fold, the *pinna*, surrounding a hollow cylindrical tube about 2·5 cm long, the *external auditory meatus*, which is terminated at its inner end by a slightly conical membrane, the ear drum or *tympanum* (Fig. 9.1). This has an area of about 0·75 cm², and a thickness of about 0·01 cm.

Though many animals have the ability to turn the pinna through a considerable range, an ability probably of importance in the localisation of the source of a sound, man is unable to do so. The pinna remains stationary, and its effect on concentrating incident sound waves into the external auditory meatus is probably negligible. The meatus, however, being air-filled, functions as resonator, with a natural frequency about 3,000 c/s, and the ear is very sensitive to sounds about this frequency.

The tympanum is set into vibration by pressure waves impinging upon it. It is extremely sensitive to pressure variations in the air a variation of one ten thousand-millionth of the atmospheric pressure being detectable if the frequency of the variation is about 3,000 c/s.

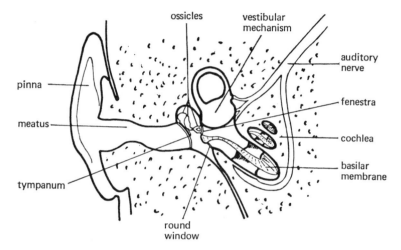

Fig. 9.1. Cross-section of the peripheral auditory system

9.21. On the other side of the tympanum is the air-filled middle ear of about 2 cc volume. In this are three tiny ossicles, the *malleus* (hammer), *incus* (anvil), and *stapes* (stirrup). The handle of the malleus is connected to the tympanum in such a way that the two vibrate together. The movement of the malleus—provided that this is not excessive, in which case a protective release mechanism comes into operation—is communicated through the incus to the stapes. The ossicles act as a set of levers, and in their action the amplitude of the movement is decreased and the pressure considerably increased.

In the transmission of movement exceeding a critical amplitude from the tympanum to the stapes a certain amount of distortion is introduced. This appears to arise mainly from two sources, the unbalanced effect of the tensioning muscles of the tympanum, and the non-mechanical action of the muscular ligaments binding the ossicles in place. The reaction of the middle ear to incident sound waves is thus in technical terms *non-linear*. This phenomenon in the ear, sometimes known as *rectification*, seems to be reponsible for the ear's capacity to create even and odd numbered harmonics from pure tones, and difference and summation tones from two or more pure tone stimuli.

For example, if two pure tones of frequencies 500 and 800 c/s and of sufficient amplitude are sounded together, harmonics 2, 3, 4, etc., of each, i.e. tones at 1,000, 1,500, 2,000 c/s, etc., and at 1,600, 2,400, 3,200 c/s, etc., will be heard, and in addition difference tones, e.g. at $(800 - 500 =)$ 300, $(2 \times 800 - 500 =)$ 1,100, $(2 \times 500 - 800 =)$ 200 c/s, etc., and summation tones, e.g. at $(800 + 500 =)$ 1,300, $(2 \times 800 + 500 =)$ 2,100, $(2 \times 500 + 800 =)$ 1,800 c/s, etc. It is clear that the picture passed to the brain may be very complex when such sounds strike the eardrum.

9.22. The base or footplate of the stapes is ligamented into an oval window, the *fenestra vestibuli*, which gives entrance to the internal ear. This consists of a complex structure of tubes and passages within the temporal bone of the skull, the *bony labyrinth*, which is filled with a fluid, *perilymph*, and totally encloses a system of membranous tubes, the *membranous labyrinth*, filled with a fluid, *endolymph*. The mechanisms of the inner ear can be divided into two, the *vestibular mechanism* which is concerned with the orientation of the organism with regard to gravity and acceleration, and the *cochlea* which is the essential organ of hearing.

As its name implies, the cochlea is a spiralled tube, the cochlear canal, about 35 mm in length winding upwards for two and a half turns around a bony centre, the *modiolus*, so that the whole structure closely resembles a snail's shell. Inside the tube, projecting laterally from the modiolus, is a small bony shelf, and from the edge of this, extending to the other side of the tube, are two membranes, the *basilar* and *Reissner's* or the *vestibular membranes*, so that the whole tube of the cochlea is divided into three sections, the *scala vestibuli*, the *ductus cochlearis*, and the *scala tympani* (Fig. 9.2). The scalae are filled with perilymph, the duct, as part of the membranous labyrinth, with endolymph. Near the apex of the cochlea, the

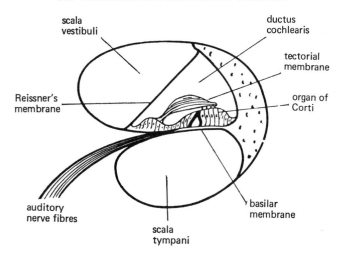

scala
vestibuli

ductus
cochlearis

tectorial
membrane

Reissner's
membrane

organ of
Corti

auditory
nerve fibres

basilar
membrane

scala
tympani

Fig. 9.2.   Cross-section of the cochlear canal

basilar and vestibular membranes fuse together, closing off the cochlear duct, and an opening through the basilar membrane, the *helicotrema*, allows the perilymph to flow from one scala to the other. At the base end of the scala tympani is a small membrane-covered opening, the round window, which prevents the perilymph from escaping into the middle ear.

The basilar membrane, which increases in width from the base to the apex of the cochlea, is composed of layers of fibres both transverse and longitudinal and sealed from beneath with a gelatinous substance. On the upper surface of this membrane, inside the cochlear duct thus, is the *organ of Corti*, a very complex structure extending the whole length of the basilar membrane, and containing several rows of very fine hair cells, about 20,000 in all. The hairs protrude through the upper surface of Corti's organ and terminate in an overlapping cover to it, the *tectorial membrane*. These hair cells are the end-organs of the auditory nerve which runs up the centre of the modiolus of the cochlea and radiates fibres out through the bony shelf, each fibre making connection with several cells.

When an incident sound wave impinges on the tympanum and sets this into vibration, the motion is transmitted by means of the ossicles to the footplate of the stapes at the oval window. Movement of the footplate sets up a pressure disturbance in the perilymph of the scala vestibuli. The disturbance appears to be transmitted through Reissner's membrane to the endolymph of the cochlear duct and to cause a displacement downward of the basilar membrane, and thus of the tectorial membrane and the organ of Corti. Slight differences occur in the direction and extent of movement of these latter structures, which bend and disturb the hair cells in the immediate vicinity of the displacement.

9.23. A full understanding of the action of the cochlea has not yet been reached. What has been clearly established, however, is that there is a position of maximum displacement of the basilar membrane for each pure tone, and that the position of this displacement varies according to the frequency of the stimulating sound wave. Sound waves of high frequency cause maximum displacement of the basilar membrane near the oval window in the base of the cochlea, and those of low frequency cause maximum displacement near the helicotrema at the apex. When the cochlea is disturbed by the vibrations of a complex sound wave, the basilar membrane becomes displaced at points corresponding to the frequencies of its components, and at each point of displacement hair cells of Corti's organ are disturbed.

This frequency analysis appears to be of varying accuracy in different regions of the frequency scale. Békésy's work on the mechanical properties of the ear indicates that the resolving power of the cochlea is relatively poor for frequencies below about 300 c/s but increases rapidly to a peak at about 1,000 c/s, and from here up to about 3,000 c/s remains relatively high; above this frequency, measurement becomes impracticable.

There is strong evidence, however, that this cochlear analysis of frequency, the so-called *place* theory of hearing, is by no means the whole story. Difference and summation tones are difficult to account for in terms of disturbance of cochlear hair cells, since there is no acoustic power at their frequencies in the incoming sound wave. And the measured sensitivity of human hearing to frequency change—a change of 3 c/s is just perceptible at 1,000 c/s—is much greater than can be explained in terms of fluid motion displacement of the basilar membrane.

Little reliable information is available about the reaction of the cochlea to the different intensities of stimulating sound waves.

The simplest view is that the extent of the displacement of the basilar membrane, and hence the extent of the disturbance of the hair cells, at any point is a measure of the power in the wave causing that displacement, but whether this is the complete explanation is very doubtful. Whatever the mechanism and process in the cochlea may be, however, investigation into the activity of the auditory nerve indicates that at each frequency, at any rate up to about 1,500 c/s, differences in the frequency pattern of nerve impulses can be detected, and that in a general way a greater number and rate of impulses corresponds to a higher intensity of the incoming sound wave.

The cochlea thus performs, by means which are not well understood, a harmonic analysis of an incident sound wave. This analysis involves disturbance of the hair cells of the organ of Corti at a different place for each detected frequency and to a different extent at each place according to the power present at each frequency. These hair cells are the end organs of the fibres of the auditory nerve and their disturbance stimulates this nerve into activity, thus effectively transferring the results of the cochlear analysis to the nervous system.

9.3. The Internal Auditory System

9.30. The section of the auditory nerve leaving the modiolus of the cochlea consists of about 30,000 nerve cells or neurons. These are of similar construction to other neurons in the body and appear to function in the same way. Under a stimulus of an intensity above its threshold value, a neuron responds by firing, that is, by transmitting along its fibrous process a series of impulses or waves of activity of electro-chemical nature. Normally a stimulus activates a number of neurons and the responses in these set up similar responses in other neurons across regions of contact known as *synapses*, and so on.

From the cochlear modiolus the auditory nerve enters through the medulla into the hindbrain, passes thence to the midbrain, and finally radiates out to a special area, the auditory projection area, on the temporal lobe of the cerebral cortex. At several places in this course are nuclei, masses of neurons which not only form the body of the auditory nerve, but also branch out to connect it with other brain nuclei not directly concerned with the process of hearing, but with unconscious and reflex adjustments of the organism to

165

sounds. At these nuclei also, neurons connect the auditory nerves from the two ears so that apparently information about the sound waves reaching both cochleae is available to each side of the cortex.

9.31. In general terms, present theory, for which some confirmation is available in experimental work, is that the bending and disturbance of different hair cells on the basilar membrane, by sound waves of different frequencies, results in stimulation of different fibres of the auditory nerve at all its stages, and finally projection to different points of the auditory area in the cortex. This auditory area may thus be considered as a topographical representation of the basilar membrane of the cochlea. There is also some evidence that this cortical map of the basilar membrane, a membrane which is essentially a narrow strip or line of nerve endings, likewise approximates to a line. Lower frequencies tend to be represented by neurons terminating near the posterior or rear end of this line-map, and higher frequencies toward the anterior end.

This is, however, by no means the whole story. One difficulty arises in regard to the cortical representation of the fundamental frequency in cases such as were discussed in § 2.30. If there is no power present at the fundamental frequency, how are the ends of the auditory nerve fibres disturbed at the point on the basilar membrane corresponding to that frequency? Non-linear distortion in the peripheral auditory apparatus may shift some of the power from higher frequencies (§ 9.21), but information about the fundamental seems to be passed to the brain even in ranges of quite low intensity where little or no non-linear distortion can be expected. Several theories have been proposed but the point remains obscure. There is also the possibility (Joos, 1948) that the fundamental is derived in the brain from the higher harmonics, and is not represented in the cochlea output at all.

A further difficulty is that the most careful investigations and experiments of Békésy into the operation of the cochlea lead to the conclusion that this apparatus is physically incapable, as we understand its mechanism today, of performing a frequency analysis to the degree of fineness and accuracy necessary to account for the known sensitivity of the auditory system as a whole to frequency. There must be further, still undiscerned processes by which the sense of hearing perceives the frequencies of sound wave stimuli to the ear.

166

9.3. INTERNAL AUDITORY SYSTEM

The power in each of the components of a sound wave, which appears to determine the degree of disturbance of the hair cells in the organ of Corti, is also represented in the cortex. An increase in the intensity of a stimulus to a sense organ is normally represented in the nervous system first by an increase in the number of impulses passing along the nerve fibres in a given unit of time, and, secondly, by an increase in the number of nerve fibres stimulated to activity. This being so, information about the power or intensity of the components in a complex wave should be available to the cortex in the extent of nerve impulse activity at the points of the auditory projection area corresponding to the frequencies of those components.

There are, however, indications of greater complexity. Galambos and Davis have shown that different nerve fibres carrying or sensitive to the same frequency have considerably different thresholds, i.e. they require considerably different intensities of stimulation before beginning to respond. Further, there is a good deal of evidence that auditory nerve fibres are inhibited from responding by a sound wave of frequency close to that to which they do respond. We have obviously still much to learn about the way in which the auditory sytem deals with the power of incoming sound waves.

The time elapsing between variations in the stimulus is, of course, also represented in the cortex by the time elapsing between the changes in the cortical activity corresponding to those variations. It is probable, however, that there is not an exact correspondence between the two lapses of time, since delays in time arise in the action of the cochlea—probably differing slightly for different frequencies—and in the process of stimulation of nerve endings across the synapses in the nerve pathways to the cortex.

9.32. The result of the operation of the auditory apparatus as just described is that running information about any acoustic stimulus to the ear is passed to the brain. This information may be regarded as being in the form of an approximation to the spectrum of the pressure wave stimulus from moment to moment. The approximation derives partly from weakness or complexity of the components of the stimulus and partly from inaccuracies and limitations in the process of hearing itself. It affects the three main dimensions of sound.

The uncertainty in the dimension of frequency is very small.

At normal loudness the sense of hearing can detect variations in the frequency of a pure tone of under 4 c/s up to a frequency of about 2,500 c/s. Above this level the variation required for detection rises steadily, being about 18 c/s at 8,000 c/s. Though in a rapidly fluctuating complex of sound waves as obtains in speech this uncertainty will be much greater than under experimental conditions it seems unlikely that it is of any great importance in this activity.

The uncertainty in intensity is also apparently of relatively little importance from the point of view of speech. Within the range of frequency where most speech sounds fall, i.e. from 300 to 8,000 c/s, a difference of about half a decibel is usually detectable in sounds of moderate loudness under laboratory conditions.

The uncertainty in the time dimension is much more difficult to calculate, but there are some indications that it may be of considerable importance in speech. The blurring in the cortex of the time relationships between the physical stimuli presented to the ear results mainly from differences in the time required to process stimuli of differing composition in the cochlea and from variations in the period taken by impulses to reach the cortex along different neurons and across synapses. But in most methods of measurement of temporal discrimination a further uncertainty is probably introduced in the process of recognition of the cortical stimuli.

From a consideration of several sources of evidence Joos (1948) concludes that there is a phonetically effective time indeterminacy in the perception of speech of a magnitude of 5 to 6 centiseconds, a figure which is, as he says "astonishingly large—practically the duration of one phone in rapid conversation!"

This does not mean, as he is careful to point out, that sounds of shorter duration are not perceived at all, but only that the brain is uncertain as to the time relationship between phenomena of lesser duration within the period of uncertainty. For example, any abrupt change in the spectrum of the incident wave can be located in time only as somewhere within this period. Thus, in fact, the brain is effectively averaging all the sound energy striking the ear over each period of 6 centiseconds, and any transient sound will contribute to the total perceived impression of every six-centisecond period in which it occurs.

9.33. Within the limits of these uncertainties, a phone in a steady state, such as a prolonged vocoid or contoid, will be represented on the line-like map of the basilar membrane in the cortex as a spatially distributed series of points of activity, each point corresponding to a component of the complex sound wave constituting this phone. The intensity of each component will be represented by the extent of the activity at each point, i.e. by the number of impulses conducted to that point.

If the sound is one whose spectrum approximates to a line spectrum (§ 2.50), we may picture its representation in the cortex as a series of separated points of activity along the cochlea projection area. If it is a speech sound having well-defined formants these will be represented by small clusters of adjacent points manifesting relatively high activity separated from each other by stretches in which relatively low activity is manifested at any point. If, on the other hand, the sound is one whose spectrum shows a random distribution of acoustic power over a range of frequency, its representation will be a series of points of activity located with a corresponding randomness along this cortical map of frequencies.

A change in the frequency of a component in a sound wave stimulus to the ear will be represented by a shift in the cortical locus of the point of activity corresponding to this component, and a change in the intensity of that component will be represented by a change in the extent of the activity at that point. Thus, if the incident sound wave represents a complex of components varying in frequency and intensity, as is the case in a musical tune, a bird's twittering, the clanging of a pneumatic drill, or a succession of speech sounds, its representation in the projection area will be a series of peaks of activity moving backwards or forwards with the changes in frequency and manifesting greater or less nervous activity with the changes in intensity.

9.34. From this brief review it appears that, though the details in many cases are not clear, the operation of the auditory mechanism may be interpreted in a general way from the point where an incident sound wave enters the external auditory meatus until it is represented as a pattern of nervous activity in the cortex. In contrast, however, what happens subsequently is still very obscure. We know that besides the primary auditory projection area, certain other regions of the cortex seem to be closely connected with the sense of hearing. These are the auditory association areas, differing from the projection area in that they have apparently no direct nerve connexions with the midbrain or other parts of the nervous system. They are stimulated to activity during the operation of hearing, presumably as a result of their connexions with the auditory projection area, but "although we can record their activity it cannot be said that we can tell what they are doing" (Adrian, 1947, 35). Further progress in the study of hearing seems thus to require a clearer understanding of the functioning of the cerebral cortex.

9.4. The Limits of Hearing

9.40.   The sense of hearing is able to perceive sounds over considerable ranges of frequency and intensity. The frequency range for audible sounds is from about 20 c/s to 20,000 c/s for a young person with good hearing. With age the ear becomes increasingly insensitive to higher frequencies and above 60 years the limit of audibility is seldom higher than about 12,000 c/s. Maximum sensitivity is for sounds of about 3,000 c/s.

The range of intensity with which the auditory mechanism can cope is remarkable. At about 3,000 c/s the intensity of a just detectable sound can be increased by a factor of over 1,000,000,000,000 before the upper threshold of hearing, a threshold where pain begins, is reached.

These data are set out in Fig. 9.3, which shows the thresholds of hearing and of feeling as functions of frequency and intensity. Sounds falling within the enclosed area are perceptible to the normal human ear.

Not all this range is used for speech. A very low bass speaker may on occasions drop as low as 80 c/s in the fundamental, but few speakers have a normal pitch lower than about 125 c/s. On the other hand, components with frequencies up to and even above 8,000 c/s have been detected in speech. But experimental work in filtering out different ranges of frequency and in synthesizing speech shows that perfectly intelligible and not unnatural sounding speech can be transmitted using frequencies from about 200 to 4,000 c/s. Less is, of course, necessary for intelligibility; an average telephone system, for example, uses only the frequencies between about 400 and 2,400 c/s. Most of the energy in any reasonably lengthy sample of speech is in the frequencies below 1,000 c/s, but since this is not the best range of frequency analysis in man (§ 9.23), it seems unlikely that it is the most important for speech.

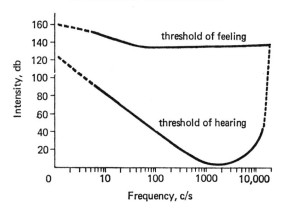

Fig. 9.3. The limits of hearing
Sounds which fall within the enclosed range of frequency and intensity
are perceptible to normal hearing

9.5. Experimental Work on Speech Perception

9.50. How the nervous activity in the auditory projection and association areas in the cortex generates those sensations which we know subjectively as sounds, and how the brain is able to recognize or identify those sounds and relate them to the sections of past experience with which they are associated, or to file them away as new experience for future reference, is still mysterious. We may, from the fact that we are able to recognize a tune on different pitches, infer that the temporal and spatial patterning of the peaks of activity in the auditory projection area is more important than the stimulation of particular points, but we are still left with the problem of the generation of the sensation of the tune and the recognition of it from shifting and changing patterns. Similar problems arise, of course, in other forms of sensory perception; visual sensations and the recognition of the *gestalt* of a square, for example, are also derived from patterns of nervous activity in the visual projection area, but though vision has in many respects been much more intensively studied than hearing, no clear indication toward the solution of such problems has yet appeared.

Speculation, however, suggests that auditory perception and especially the perception of speech offer a very promising line of inquiry. Man does not produce light waves to be seen, but he does

171

produce sounds to be heard. This being the case, there must be speech concepts at some level of the brain's functioning which are approachable from two pathways, one sensory through the mechanism of hearing, and one motor through the mechanism of speech, or, putting this in other words, a set of neural patterns at some level of language are both auditory and muscular. This duplex feature widens the possible field of investigation, and at the same time offers much better conditions of experimental control than any feature in other forms of sensory perception.

9.51. A good deal of recent experimental work in the field of speech perception has been concentrated along two separate approaches. The first is exploration of the effect of interference with the unanalysed speech-carrying wave on what is heard by the listener. The second approach is through an analysis of the speech-carrying wave into components and distinguishable features, and is directed to investigation of the perceptual effects of such components and features separately and in various combinations and contrasts. This work is of interest broadly to two groups of people, engineers in many forms of speech-transmitting communication who are interested in finding out what features of the wave are essential or carry essential clues for the interpretation of speech, and psychologists who are interested in the reactions of the listeners and the light that such work throws on the mechanism of perception.

9.52. One of the commonest forms of interference with speech is that of extraneous sound. Pressure waves from the source of this sound will mingle with those carrying the speech, and to understand the latter the brain has to unscramble the two by means of its ability for selective attention. In the process the perception of the speech is often hindered and the speech wave is said to be *masked* by the other sound.

The extent of the masking depends on the intensity and on the nature of the masking sound. If this is a pure tone the masking effect at ordinary intensities is concentrated into a small range of frequency about its own, and the perception of speech is relatively little affected. If, on the other hand, the masking sound is of a noise type with a continuous spectrum over a large range of the frequencies used for speech, its masking effect can be considerable. In general in such cases, the intelligibility of the speech depends on the ratio of the intensities of the speech wave and the masking sound; the higher this is, the more intelligible the speech. One of the most effective masking sounds for speech is a wave carrying other speech; it appears difficult for the brain to distinguish one set of speech signals from another presented at the same time. This difficulty is no doubt at the base of the common experience of trying to listen to two people speaking at once and failing to understand either.

9.53. Variation of intensity may also be used to study the perception of speech. If we reduce the intensity of a speech wave below the range found in, say, normal conversation, the intelligibility of the speech begins to fall. At 40 decibels above threshold, for example, only about 65 per cent of monosyllabic words are recognized, and at 20 decibels above threshold fewer than 20 per cent. Similar tests on single speech sounds show that vowels are distinguishable at lower intensities than consonants, and that some consonants, e.g. [p, f, θ] require considerable intensity before they are clearly perceptible.

9.54. Another possible distortion of the speech wave is that of amplitude selectivity. The speech wave can be passed through a device which clips off all the peaks beyond any desired limit and passes these to the listener, or, conversely, passes the remainder (Fig. 9.4). The results are quite different in the two cases. Peak clipping has little effect on the intelligibility of normal speech, even when practised to a considerable degree. Centre clipping on the other hand is disastrous, and rapidly deprives the wave of all intelligibility. The reason for the different effects in the two cases seems to lie in the nature of speech and in the differences between vocoids and contoids. From a physical point of view, speech is a succession of sounds of varying amounts of energy. Most of the energy comes in the vocoids, so that these are well above the threshold of perception. Clipping of the peaks, therefore, affects the vocoids most, but very extensive clipping is necessary before they are reduced below the threshold value for perception. On the other hand, the relatively weak contoids have small peaks clustered around the centre line of the wave, and quite small centre clipping will remove them almost entirely, so that continuity is lost and speech becomes a series of interspersed bursts of unintelligible noise.

9.55. Very interesting results have been obtained in experiments on the effect of filtering out different ranges of frequency in speech.

A The complete wave

B Peak clipping

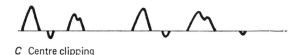

C Centre clipping

Fig. 9.4. Peak and centre clipping (after Licklider)

In Fig. 9.5 are given the results of filtering out both high and low frequencies in a series of nonsense syllables (French & Steinberg, 1947). Filtering out all frequencies below 1,000 c/s leaves a score of about 90 per cent correct, while filtering out all frequencies below 3,000 c/s reduces this to about 30 per cent. On the other hand, filtering out the high frequencies above 3,000 c/s makes relatively little difference to the intelligibility, but if only the frequencies below 1,000 c/s are left intelligibility is a mere 20 per cent.

The two curves cross at 1,900 c/s. Either the range of frequencies above 1,900 or those below 1,900 will give us the same score, i.e. about 67 per cent correct responses. Now, as Miller (1951) points out, conditions giving such a score in nonsense syllables permit easily intelligible conversation or discourse. Thus it would appear that there is no range of frequency which is completely indispensable to the perception of speech.

174

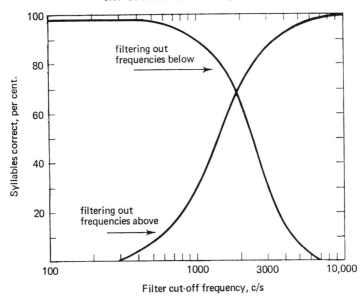

Fig. 9.5. The effect of limiting frequency range on intelligibility (see text p. 174; after French & Steinberg)

9.56. The effect of interrupting the speech wave has also been investigated. If the wave is fed through a device which switches it on and off so that the listener hears speech only half the time and silence the other half, the intelligibility of the speech varies with the number of times the switching takes place each second. If this is once a second, about 40 per cent of monosyllabic words are perceived correctly, but if the frequency of the interruption is increased, the intelligibility of the speech as so measured also increases, though not steadily, until the rate of interruption nears 10,000 per second, when the intelligibility approaches 100 per cent. Moreover, even when the speech is on a mere sixteenth of the time, an interruption rate of the same order will still give almost full intelligibility.

The high intelligibility of speech when the interruption rate is high is doubtless closely connected with the temporal uncertainty in the auditory mechanism. The uncertainty results in a certain degree of blurring in the time dimension (§ 9.32), and if the periods between the fractions of speech contain nothing but silence, some of the speech in these fractions will be, so to speak, smeared into

175

the periods of silence, and the brain will hardly notice the difference, providing, of course, that the periods of silence are short enough.

9.57. The general conclusion to be drawn from these and many similar experimental results is that speech is very resistant to distortion. Most of the interferences discussed modify considerably the listener's total impression of the speech—interruptions, for example, cause the speech to sound as if the speaker were suffering from some phonatory disorder producing hoarse or husky speech but nevertheless appear to have relatively little effect on what is presumably the central characteristic of speech, its intelligibility. It would seem that the temporal and spatial pattern of peaks of activity projected on to the auditory cortex need not be complete for the interpretative faculty of the brain to be able to recognize the sequence of words involved.

This feature of speech can be discussed from another viewpoint. If speech is intelligible in spite of considerable interference, there must be more evidence in a sequence of speech sounds than is necessary for the recognition of that sequence, since we may reasonably assume that some clues are destroyed by the interference. If, for example, both frequencies above 1,900 c/s and those below 1,900 c/s each contain sufficient evidence to permit normal conversation, it is clear that the two ranges taken together carry more evidence than is strictly necessary for intelligibility. Speech, in other words, is characterized by a certain measure of *redundancy*, and in this redundancy lies the explanation of the resistance of speech to distortion and interference. Because of this redundancy we can use speech communication successfully over the radio, through a telephone or against the heterogeneous background of sounds accompanying normal existence.

Redundancy may be of different kinds. It may be purely *phonetic*; for example, when a feature of one phone signals the presence of another, as the colouring of a contoid may signal the following vocoid or the formant transitions of a vocoid signal the adjacent contoid (§ 7.14 f.). It may be *phonemic*, the system of the language limiting the possibilities of interpretation—a phoneme may be interpreted correctly only because there is no other possible choice for the native speaker (§ 10.10 f.). It may be *distributional*, the rules for phoneme combinations, for instance, admitting only a limited number of alternatives, as an English nasal before tautosyllabic

/k/ is heard as [ŋ] because this is the only possible nasal contoid in that position (§ 7.43); or as a bilabial plosive in *spy* is heard as /p/ and not as /b/ because the latter phoneme does not occur after /s/ in the same syllable. It may also be *grammatical*, the /d/ in "he called me" being 'heard,' for instance, even if obscured or missing in the sound chain, since the grammatical structure, *he call*, hardly occurs. It may, of course, finally be *semantic* or even *extra-linguistic*, the meaning of the utterance as a whole, or the situation in which it is uttered being sufficiently clear to permit a certain predictability of the words uttered and to preclude misunderstanding.

9.6. Experimental Work on Synthetic Speech

9.60. Investigation of the nature of the clues provided for the recognition of a sequence of phones has stimulated the analytical approach to speech perception (§ 9.51). This has been very greatly facilitated in the last fifteen years or so by the development of synthetic speech.

Once an exhaustive acoustic analysis of a speech sound has been carried out, it is possible to produce a synthetic replica by generating artificially the various components with correct frequencies and amplitudes and combining them into a pattern corresponding to that of the original speech sound. Various techniques and devices for doing this exist, each with its own advantages and disadvantages, but all of them enable experimental investigation into sound perception. Thus the perception of different features and patterns of the sound complex of a phone, or of the transition between two phones, can be studied, both in isolation and in any desired combination. In the following paragraphs are some indications of the sort of work which has so far been carried out in this field.

9.61. In the vocoids, analysis and synthesis have confirmed the importance which has long been attributed to the formants in perception, but at the same time have thrown much light on the effect of varying the frequencies, the frequency-widths and the intensities of such formants.

A vocoid is generally characterized by three formants (§ 4.44), and the perceptual distinction between vocoids depends primarily on the pattern of frequencies and amplitudes of these formants. Such a pattern is fairly constant for each individual speaker, and for homogeneous groups, as, e.g. adult males, speaking the same

177

dialect, but the whole pattern is differently located in the frequency scale in the higher-pitched voices of women and children. This, together with the results of much experimental investigation, indicates that it is rather the relations between the frequencies of the formants than their absolute position on the frequency scale, which is significant in vocoid recognition.

The ear, it may be noted, is very sensitive to the frequency of a vocoid formant, a difference of the order of 15 c/s in the centre frequency of a formant about 300 c/s being generally perceptible.

9.62. The features contributing to the recognition of contoids vary with the type of contoid. In the resonant and semi-resonant contoids the pattern of formant frequencies and intensities appears to act as the major clue to identification; in other contoids the pattern of the position and spread in frequency of the noise components, together with their relative and total intensities, becomes more important.

Plosive contoids and semi-resonants as [j, w] are generally further characterized by abrupt changes in, and relatively brief duration of, their acoustic components. There is, indeed, some evidence that any phone with such features tends to be interpreted as a contoid.

With all contoids, the nature of the transitions to adjoining vocoids (§ 7.15 f.) provides important cues to identification.

9.63. The cues to the identification of a contoid need not, however, be the same in all its occurrences; they may vary from context to context. Some indication of the complexity of the matter is given by the following experiments.

Observation suggested that the three voiceless plosives [p, t, k] of English might be distinguished in perception largely by the frequency of the burst of noise arising from the release of the blocked air. To examine this, a series of bursts of noise with different centre frequencies was synthetically produced and followed by a series of synthetic cardinal vocoids. The results were of considerable interest. If the frequency of the noise burst was high, i.e. over about 3,000 c/s, the listeners, a group of college students, heard the sound as [t], if it was close to the frequency of formant 2 of the following vocoid, they heard it as [k], while in practically all other cases they heard it as [p] (Liberman, Delattre & Cooper, 1952).

Confirmation of some of these results has been published by Schatz (1954), who found that [sk] cut out of a magnetic tape recording of the word *ski* and fixed before the combination [uːl] from the word *school* was perceived in the great majority of cases (87 per cent) as [sp] and in only a few cases (6 per cent) as [sk].

In general, these results seem to show that [k] differs considerably in its acoustic make-up before different vocoids, and to indicate clearly that an identical burst of noise may be identified as different voiceless plosives before different vocoids: what constitutes [k] before one vocoid may be identified as [t] before another, and so on. There appears no simple relationship between these variations; the contoid [t], in contrast, seems to be fairly consistently the same both acoustically and perceptually, whereas Schatz found ambiguous results in experimentation with [p]. As he summarizes, the 'context of an initial voiceless stop is an important factor in its perception.'

Though this is surely correct in a general way, it may be argued that in these investigations, insufficient attention has been paid to the variations in a contoid articule before different vocoids as a result of the phenomenon of coarticulation (§ 4.6). Thus, [k] in a sequence [skiː] is not only fronted on the velum, but is also articulated with spread lips and with the front of the tongue raised towards the hard palate in anticipation of [iː]. All these articulatory features will tend to raise the frequency location of formant 2 in the resultant phone. On the other hand [k] in a sequence [skuːl] will, in English, generally be articulated medially on the velum, with well-rounded lips, and with no raising of the front of the tongue, a combination of features resulting in a much lower frequency location of formant 2. To substitute in a sequence the acoustic substance of one of these for that of the other inevitably results in a sequence which does not occur in normal speech and in which the perceptual processes of the speakers are inexperienced.

9.64. The important role of context in the perception of contoids is also indicated by the results of investigation into the transitions between contoid and vocoid. A slight rise in the frequency of formant 1 at the beginning of an isolated synthetic vocoid [a], for example, gives the impression that it is preceded by a voiced plosive contoid, while a more level beginning suggests a voiceless plosive. Different beginnings to formant 2, rise, small fall, and large fall in frequency, contribute to the distinction between [b, p], [d, t], and [g, k], respectively. See Fig. 9.6. But the relationship between these modifications of the formants and the contoids suggested is not a simple one, and different modifications seem necessary for similar impressions with other vocoids (see also § 7.13 f.).

In this, and similar experiments on the perception of synthetic speech, the role of the phonemic patterning of the listener's own language must be considered. If an English-speaking listener interprets acoustically different stimuli before different vocoids as [k], the reason may be at least partly that he has, so to speak, no other alternative. Any voiceless plosive which is not [p] or [t] must be [k] since the repertory of English phonemes has only three voiceless plosive phonemes. The testing would probably give different results with speakers of a language which made a phonemic distinction, say, between a voiceless palatal [c] and a voiceless velar [k] (see further, Chapter X).

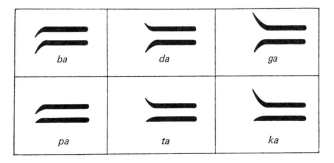

Fig. 9.6. The effect of vocalic transitions on contoid interpretation in synthetic speech patterns (see text p. 179)

That variation of the beginning of the lower two formants of a vowel can by itself give a clear impression of a preceding consonant and considerable indication of its nature, may seem strange, but Joos (1948, 122) had already been led to suggest that "identification of consonants by their effects upon contiguous resonants is apparently depended upon by listeners to a far greater extent than commonly supposed." This spreading of acoustic clues in contiguous resonants obviates the necessity of the conclusion, urged frequently, for example, by Forchhammer, that, since the silences in the holds of all voiceless plosives are identical, the acoustic aspect of speech is unsuitable as a basis for the analysis of speech.

9.65. It may be tentatively concluded that at least as far as the plosives are concerned more than one cue to the perceptual recognition of the consonants is given in any succession of speech sounds. It is not necessary, of course, that each of these should be of equal value for recognition; it is possible, for example, that in different contexts different cues are of more importance, but the significance of a rank-ordering of the discernible cues in terms of their relative contributions to intelligibility has already been foreseen.

In this multiplicity of cues we may also see redundancy (§ 9.57) contributing to the resistance of speech to distortion and interference. Thus, quite simply, if the burst of noise resulting from the release of a plosive consonant should be inaudible either because of a simultaneous interruption in the speech wave or because of the presence of a high-frequency masking sound, sufficient evidence for the recognition of this plosive may still be available from the movements of the formants in a lower frequency range at the beginning of a following vowel.

It may be noted, too, that the continual flow of multiple cues to the identity of the successive phones is a fortunate circumstance for those with hearing deficiencies of certain types. Persons, for example, who are unable to hear sounds at frequencies above 3,000 c/s, and thus miss the high-frequency noise cues in plosives and fricatives, may still be able to identify a contoid by the nature of transitions to adjoining vocoids.

Further, from these investigations into synthetic speech, comes strong evidence as to the importance of context. If an acoustically identical stimulus gives the impression of different consonants before different vowels, or if, as Schatz (1954) has shown, a consonantal segment from one context may give a different impression in another, it would appear that there is a lower limit to segmentation in the acoustic aspect, and this limit is not at the level of the discrete speech sound or phone. Is it, then, at some higher level? Some investigators have spoken tentatively of an acoustic unit having the approximate dimensions of a syllable or half-syllable. We shall return to the problems of segmentation below (§§ 9.81, 11.4); in the meantime we shall, however, observe that the interdependence of consonant and vowel seems to be further confirmation of the importance, at the level of speech sound identification, of the temporal patterning of the peaks of nervous activity in the auditory projection area of the cortex. For the pattern formed by stimulation of one particular set of nerve endings may be identified at one moment with one consonant and at another with a different one depending upon the patterns preceding and following on each occasion.

All in all, the work with synthetic speech has opened up a fascinating new field of investigation which has already provided important contributions to our knowledge of the mechanism of speech perception.

9.7. Articulation and Perception

9.70. The relationship of motor patterns of muscular movement in articulation to the perception of speech should throw light on the latter, but the main difficulty at present seems to be that of devising experiments to reveal the nature of the relationship. Some general considerations may, however, be touched on.

9.71. It is probable, for example, that each speaker monitors and adjusts his articulatory movements by means of some *feed-back control* in the general manner being currently investigated in the science of cybernetics. In speech there are two sources of this proprioceptive feed-back, the first kinesthetic, i.e. the speaker's feeling for the setting and the movement of his articulatory muscles (§ 3.50), and the second auditory from the speaker's perception of the sounds produced by his articulation. The relative importance of these two is, however, not easily discerned.

The role of the auditory control is clearly revealed by the difficulty with which congenitally deaf children learn to speak, by the ill-defined formants frequently found in individuals with hearing defects (illustrations in Potter, Kopp & Green, 1948, p. 330 ff.), and probably also by the articulatory abnormalities characteristic of the speech of the deaf (Brannon, 1966). It has been observed also that there is frequently a rapid deterioration of speech in persons who become hard of hearing. The actual muscular adjustment under auditory control is presumably carried out by the cerebellum as the main organ of unconscious muscular co-ordination, but the nature and details of the process are still very obscure.

The role of kinesthetic perception in the monitoring control is more difficult to specify, but it is clearly suggested in the idea of the primacy of articulation over sounds in the construction of speech (§ 5.70). If speech is "a set of movements made audible" it is conceivable, and perhaps even probable, that kinesthetic perception is the basic means of control. This view has frequently been expressed in recent years, but it is by no means clearly established.

9.72. The existence of an auditory feed-back is of further interest in that it establishes a close connexion between the motor and sensory patterns of speech sounds. Such a connexion would strengthen the possibility of viewing speech as basically a set of motor patterns at some high level of the brain, higher than that referred to in § 9.50. In this would lie an explanation of the widely current view that a listener tends to interpret sounds heard in terms of his own speech, i.e. in terms of his own motor patterns. (Recent investigation of this matter is recounted in Liberman, Cooper, Harris, & MacNeilage, 1963). It would also throw light on the difficulty involved in segmenting and identifying the sounds or other phonological features of a language for which one does not have a well-practised set of motor patterns (§ 11.5). But it must be admitted that the nature of speech at the higher levels of functioning in the brain is extremely obscure, and at the present open only to speculation (for the motor theory, see also § 5.70).

9.8. Discussion

9.80. The temporal and spatial patterning of nerve impulses in the cochlear projection area in the cortex, which results from the auditory processing of a speech-carrying sound wave, contains, encoded, so to speak, in itself, a considerable amount of information. The brain can decipher this code, in a process which we may view as involving several stages: decomposition of the total pattern into subpatterns of articulation, accentuation, intonation, and vocal gestures; segmentation of each of these subpatterns into appropriate units; identification of these units; and finally interpretation of the meaning being conveyed.

We may reasonably assume that the mechanism of speech perception has available the memory of a great number of similar decodings of cortical patternings and also information from the motor patterns of the individual's own speech. Hence it is very probable that the action of this mechanism varies not only during the period of its development as the individual acquires his faculty of speech, but also, at any time, with the nature of the material presented, for example, whether it is a relatively familiar or unfamiliar patterning, and with the degree to which segments of the pattern flow are predictable, by means of statistical or structural features of the language, from preceding segments.

A further and more important result of the availability of information other than that in the cortical patterning is that there is *not a direct cause-to-effect development between the patterning as input and the finally identified forms as output*. The operations of speech perception and interpretation are, at least in part, imposed on the material and influence the results. What these operations are, how they process the incoming material, and to what extent they influence the results, we are as yet not at all sure, since different theories of speech and language postulate different requirements from the operation of the speech perception mechanism. We have already tacitly accepted one common theory in the statement that the brain can recognize the articulation, the accentuation, etc., of the speaker, and shall now briefly speculate as to the nature of a set of possible operations which could give these results.

9.81. The first stages are those of decomposition and segmentation of the incoming patterns of nerve impulses in the auditory projection area. Decomposition will result in the continuous breaking down of this changing pattern into a series of simultaneous smaller patterns, one carrying information about the articulation, one about the accentuation, and so on. Each of these smaller patterns, we may imagine, is then led away into a different channel or layer of nerve cells. Segmentation, taking place in each layer separately, breaks down these continuously changing patterns of nerve impulses into sequences of discrete units, each a spatially and temporally bounded cluster of nerve impulses.

The methods by which such decomposition and segmentation of the incoming pattern are performed are quite obscure. As to the units resulting from their operation, however, though their spatial size will depend merely on characteristics of the nervous system, their temporal extension in each layer will vary according to the presupposed theory of speech perception. In the articulatory layer it is commonest to assume that these units are more or less co-extensive in time with the phonetician's articules, but other possibilities exist. For example, they might be considered to correspond to syllables; the ease with which syllables are perceived by the phonetically naïve, and the difficulty of defining them on articulatory or acoustic data (§ 7.90 f.) are perhaps indications that syllables are basically perceptual, rather than phonetic or linguistic units. Whatever the units, however, it appears probable that some sort of segmentation does occur in the perceptual aspect.

9.82. The next stage is the identification of these units, again a process taking place separately in each layer. Licklider (1952) has discussed the relative merits of two possible means of identification, filtering and correlation. For the former he assumes a battery of filters in each layer, one for each possible class of units in that layer, and so designed that it will accept or react to member-units of that class only. Each incoming unit is fed along the battery until it reaches the one which accepts it; this acceptance identifies it as a member of that class of units for which the filter was designed. For correlation he assumes a mechanism which draws standard models of each class of unit from memory storage, compares them with the incoming units, and identifies the latter by correspondence with the former. The structure and functioning of the nerve cells in the cortex, Licklider considers, would be quite suited for the operation of either of these methods, but he suggests that the more passive nature of the identification of such units perhaps indicates that the method of filtering is more likely.

A slightly different mechanism in the second stage would be required under the theory, currently being developed by Jakobson and his co-workers (§ 10.6), that the ultimate distinctive entities of language are the distinctive features, i.e. the choice between two polar qualities of the same category or between the presence or absence of a certain quality, and that varying combinations of these distinctive features are bundled together more or less simultaneously to form the different phonemes. In the appropriate layer a system of filters at successive points, each tuned to accept or reject an incoming pattern on the grounds of its having or not having a particular distinctive feature, would allow each different bundle of distinctive features to take a different route through the system to a different end point. Since the maximum number of distinctive units so far found in any language is eleven (Russian: Cherry, Halle, & Jakobson, 1953), this method would require fewer filters than the former method. A possible further advantage might be the elimination of the segmentation in the second stage. Since the distinctive features come in bundles, the flow of nerve impulses in the articulatory channel could be fed into the filtering system continuously, but segments of incomplete or irregular patterning in the flow of nerve impulses, such as may appear in transitions, would not reach the normal end points of the system. Hence the output could consist of a sequence of discrete, identified units.

In both of the suggestions above, however, the process of identification is based on the characteristic or typical structure of a unit. Obviously this structure is likely to be most clearly represented in the central portion of the unit concerned, and present only partially or in disturbed form before and after this portion. There seems thus in them no adequate accounting for the apparent importance of the transitions between sounds in the recognition of the units concerned (§ 7.1 f.). We are clearly still a long way from any adequate hypothesis of the nature of this process.

9.83. The last stage in the perception of speech is the comprehension of meaning. This probably requires the synthesizing of the identified units of each layer into a total pattern, and the identification of the latter. Licklider suggests that correlation is possibly the better model for this stage, since it is a more active process than filtering and allowing perhaps greater capacity for the storage of standard patterns. These features correspond to our impression of the active nature of the process of comprehension, and of the great number of standard patterns necessary to cover all the speech events in a language. Among these, however, the choice of standard patterns for comparison is probably facilitated by the expectation of the listener from situation, context, and meaning.

A more recent, and a more intuitively satisfying, suggestion is that the hearer's brain, using its understanding of context and situation and aided by cues from the incoming stream of sound, generates high-level internal forms of speech which appear to match the input. If this match is satisfactory, meaning is assigned to the input in terms of the grammatical and lexical rules needed by the brain's own language-producing mechanism to produce the internal signal (Halle & Stevens, 1962; Miller & Chomsky, 1963).

This conception accords with the tendency in current thinking to assign a considerable role in speech perception to active processes in the hearer. It also seems to offer the beginning of an explanation as to why speech is so resistant to distortion and interference—the hearer's brain supplies the interpretation on the evidence available to it, filling in any gaps—and why misinterpretations of speech are so often explicable in terms of the psychological *set* of the hearer, the complex of feelings, attitudes and ideas which influence the individual in any activity and thus in his selection of rules to produce a match to the input. It is also able to account for the established experimental results that meaningful material is much more easily and accurately perceived than non-meaningful sequences of sounds: the brain has no set of rules for generating nonsense, and therefore is unable to interpret it in terms of such rules.

9.84. This stage of speech perception is the boundary area where phonetics shades into linguistics: 'to study the co-ordination of certain sounds with certain meanings is to study language' (Bloomfield, 1933). We have already noticed how our discussion of the earlier stages of perception has been influenced by linguistic theory; the final stages are almost impossible to discuss without taking into consideration a great amount of data from linguistics and from psychological studies of sensory perception in general. This seems, therefore, a convenient point to terminate the discussion in a book on phonetics.

CHAPTER 10

THE FUNCTIONING OF SOUNDS IN LANGUAGE

10.1. Sound and Phoneme

10.10. In speech, few if any sequences of sounds can be regarded as identical in their acoustic content. It is true that the human ear and mechanism of hearing, with their perceptual uncertainties and limits of definition, will not appreciate all acoustic differences in two occurrences of a sequence of speech sounds which recording equipment with finer limits of definition may reveal, but nevertheless, in many cases, clearly perceptible acoustic differences occurring in such a sequence may be ignored by members of a speech community.

As a first example, let us consider two occurrences of the sound sequence [pæk] spoken by different persons using the same form of English. To members of this speech community, these two sequences constitute the 'same' word, and the linguist is able to test this belief by observing the response of the community in both cases. Yet the actual acoustic differences between the two occurrences may be of sufficient magnitude to enable the identity of the speakers to be established. The explanation of this paradox appears to be that members of a speech community habitually ignore personally introduced acoustic qualities in the identification of linguistic elements. For this reason such qualities are normally assumed to be abstracted in phonetical studies (cf. § 5.11).

But even after such personal voice qualities have been abstracted, an English-speaking community will accept as the same [k] the final segments of the two segments [pæk] and [siːk] or as the same [iː] the middle segments of [biːd] and [biːt], though in these cases the acoustic differences between members of these pairs of segments are considerable, and discernible by the attentive listener.

Further, we may note that acoustic differences which are normally ignored in one community may not be so in others. For example, the differences between the first and last segments of the word [lʊtɬ] are seldom noticed by a member of an English-speaking community, but are sufficient for the segments to be heard as quite different sounds by a unilingual speaker of Polish. And again a Spaniard may pronounce what is to him the 'same' word as [dia] or [ðia] without noticing a difference which is very obvious to a native English speaker.

10.11. The question which arises from these considerations is why communities often ignore the phonetic differences between certain occurrences of sound segments and attach the label 'same' to them (cf. § 5.23). The reason is clearly not that the perceptual uncertainties of a speaker prevent him from discerning the differences, though it does, in fact, seem that the phonetically naïve seldom observe differences in the actual qualities of different occurrences of such a segment. Likewise, the reason cannot be sought in the totality of phonetic features of the segment in question, since this varies considerably with different occurrences.

The answer appears to be, partly if not entirely, since with a written language and literate speakers the influence of a particular orthography cannot be ruled out, in the functioning of such segments in the language concerned. Segments which have similar functions in the language system tend to be considered the 'same' by the community using that language, while those which have different functions tend to be classed as 'different.' Our next step is, therefore, to consider the idea of linguistic functioning in a little more detail.

In linguistics, function is usually understood to mean discriminatory function, that is, the role of the various elements of the language in the distinguishing of one sequence of sounds, such as a word or a sequence of words, from another of different meaning. It is not part of our task here to attempt to define differences of meaning; we must content ourselves by describing such differences as those leading to different responses by members of the speech community. On this understanding, a number of methods have been developed by which we may use meaning as a control in order to ascertain which segments of a sequence of sounds have a discriminatory function in the language.

10.12. The first step is to determine the minimum recurrent segments in an adequate sample of the language. To do this the investigator gathers a large number of sound sequences with different meanings in the language under investigation and compares them. For example, in English, comparison of [stɪk] and [stæk] reveals

189

the segments [ɪ, æ], comparison of [stɪk] with [spɪk] the segments [st, sp], and further comparison of these two with [tɪk, pæk] and [sɪk, sæk] splits these segments into smaller segments [s, t, p], and so on. Eventually the investigator arrives at a number of segments, the phones, which he is unable to split into smaller segments. The number of these segments will depend in theory on the discriminatory limits of the investigator's ear, or of the recording equipment he is using. Since at this initial stage the investigator does not know which phonetic features in any phone are used in the language to carry differences in meaning and which are ignored, his only sure method is to record as a different phone each minimum recurrent segment which he can discern as acoustically different from all others.

10.13. The next step in the procedure is the arranging of the phones into functionally similar groups, i.e. groups of phones in which the members of each group are not opposed to one another, but are opposable to members of any other group to distinguish different meanings in otherwise similar sound sequences. Each of such groups of phones can be viewed as a group of varying realizations in speech of one minimum distinctive unit of the language. Such a distinctive unit is termed a *phoneme*, and its various realizations on the phonetic level are termed *allophones*.[1]

For example, if two sequences of different meaning in a language are differentiated in their phonetic form solely by the fact that

[1] Up to this point, we have confined ourselves to acoustic phonetic differences, and hence the allophones as defined are strictly realizations in the acoustic layer. But, in view of the lack of any convenient and generally accepted description of features of this layer, it is normal practice for phoneticians and linguists to describe allophones in articulatory terms, thus (usually tacitly) assuming that different articulations result in different acoustic complexes. This assumption is theoretically a little shaky (§ 10.50f. below), but works very well in practice. There has been, it is true, considerable progress in the discernment and description of the acoustic features distinguishing phones from one another but it has not reached the stage where descriptions in terms of articulatory features can be replaced. Nor is it perhaps yet desirable to do so in an introductory text. We therefore continue, in this chapter and elsewhere, to describe allophones in articulatory terms, even though we determine them and distinguish them in the acoustic layer. The same problem arises with regard to the phoneme, but since this is a linguistic entity and by definition thus distinct in both the articulatory and the acoustic layers, we can view it as being abstracted from either layer, just as convenient.

each has a different phone in a corresponding position, as, for instance, English [stɪk] and [stæk], the two phones [ɪ] and [æ] being thus functionally opposed to one another—in technical terms being in *phonemic opposition* to one another—can be classed as allophones of different phonemes, say /ɪ/ and /æ/, where the symbols / / are used to indicate a phoneme. Similarly, the word sequences [stɑːk, stɒk, stɔːk, stʌk, stɒk] enable the phones [ɑː, ɒ, ɔː, ʌ, ɒ] to be classed as allophones of different phonemes; the word sequences [sɪt, sɪp, sɪb, sɪn, sɪŋ, sɪɫ] enable the segments [t, p, b, n, ŋ, ɫ] to be classed as allophones of different phonemes; and so on.

10.2. Distribution and Phonetic Similarity

10.20. The criterion of phonemic opposability for the determination of phonemes is, however, complicated in every known language by distributional characteristics. The investigator may expect to find in any language that certain phones do not occur in certain positions, and/or that no two words are differentiated in meaning solely by the opposition of particular phones. For example, in Modern German and Dutch no [b, d, g, z, v], etc., i.e. no voiced plosive or fricative, occurs as the final segment of a word,[1] and hence an investigator will not find in his material two linguistically complete sequences of sound with a phonemic opposition in their final segments between such a voiced phone and any voiceless one. Similarly, in English no two words are differentiated solely by the fact that [h] is opposed to [ŋ] in the same position, since [h] occurs only initially or before a vowel and [ŋ] only medially or finally after a vowel.

10.21. Such presumably universal characteristics permit a method of identification of phonemes on the grounds of complementary distribution. For example, if a phone occurs only in certain phonetic environments, and another occurs only in different environments, no two words of the language can be distinguished solely by means of an opposition between these two. Hence the two sets of phonetic environments can be considered as complementing one another, and the two phones classed as allophones of the same phoneme. Thus, in English, in the position before a stressed vowel, [tʻ], an aspirated alveolar plosive, occurs, but in the position between [s]

---

[1] This is a case of neutralization (§ 7.43).

and a stressed vowel, [t], an unaspirated alveolar plosive occurs. Therefore, neither when preceded by [s] nor when not so preceded, can [tʻ] be opposed to [t] and these two may for this reason be classed as allophones of the same phoneme, /t/. This procedure can be continued. For example, in English a voiceless dental plosive occurs before [θ], e.g. in [eɪt̪θ]. Since no voiceless alveolar plosive occurs in this environment, and hence no phonemic opposition between the two is possible, the dental [t] may also be added to the group of allophones of the phoneme /t/ of English.

It will be observed that, in this procedure, the phonetic form, acoustic or articulatory, of the speech sound need not be used as a criterion by which that phone is assigned to a particular phoneme. For instance, since, as pointed out above, the environments of [h] and [ŋ] are not the same in English, these environments may be classed as complementary, in the same manner as those of [tʻ] and [t] above, and a single phoneme set up with allophones [h] in certain environments and [ŋ] in others.

This procedure of setting up phonemes by grouping phones together on the basis of complementary distribution is a methodologically rigorous technique developed in contemporary linguistics, but the results of its application, however important they may be for our understanding of the structure of a language, have not yet been shown to be of much value in the study of phonetics.

10.22. As a sort of compromise the identification of phonemes on grounds of complementary distribution is sometimes modified by the addition of a criterion of phonetic similarity. In this case, phones in complementary distribution are grouped as allophones of one phoneme only if they are similar in phonetic form. In the examples we have discussed in the previous paragraphs the application of this criterion would doubtless invalidate the grouping of [h] and [ŋ] as allophones of the same phoneme, but permit the grouping of [tʻ, t, t̪] into the phoneme /t/.

The criterion of phonetic similarity seems to work well enough in practice in the case of any particular language, but suffers from the methodological disadvantage that the determination of the degree or extent of phonetic similarity permissible in the allophones of any phoneme must be left to the discretion of the individual investigator, since no generally applicable theory has yet been

proposed (Jones, 1962a, § 32). For example, let us assume that in
a particular language a voiceless velar fricative [x] occurs only
after back vowels, e.g. [zuxt], and a voiceless palatal fricative only
after front vowels, e.g. [ziçt]. (This is a somewhat simplified version
of the state of affairs in Modern German.) Since the environments
are complementary the two phones [x] and [ç] could be classed as
allophones of the same phoneme, but the application of the criterion
of phonetic similarity does not lead to a conclusive solution. The
two phones are similar in that they are both voiceless fricatives;
they are dissimilar in that one is velar and the other palatal.
Whether this phonetic difference is of sufficient extent to justify
the setting up of two phonemes, /x/ and /ç/, or not, must be decided
by the investigator by means of still further criteria.

10.23. One criterion which may be applied in cases of this nature
is that of the use or non-use elsewhere in the system of the phonetic
feature or features of difference between two phones. If we find,
for example, that the phonetic feature or features of difference
between two phones *a* and *b* occur elsewhere differentiating allophones *c* and *d* of different phonemes, we may reasonably consider
this phonetic difference as performing a phoneme-differentiating role
in the system and accordingly class the phones *a* and *b* as allophones
of different phonemes. Thus in the case of [h] and [ŋ] the contrast
between the fricative feature of the former and the nasal feature
of the latter recurs in the contrasts between [s] and [n], [f] or [v]
and [m], all of which are allophones of different phonemes. The
phonetic contrast, fricative—nasal, may then be regarded as part
of the system in the language and phones showing it as allophones
or different phonemes, though no phonemic opposition occur between
them.
   This criterion, however, is not always useful: there may be no
other case in the language of two phones in phonemic opposition
being distinguished by the phonetic feature or features in dispute.
Thus if there is in the language concerned in the example above, no
cases of velar-palatal contrast distinguishing allophones of different
phonemes, the problem of [x] and [ç] is not elucidated.

10.3. The Commutation Test

10.30. A second method of classifying phones into allophones of
phonemes is by the systematic substitution of one phone for another

in order to ascertain in which cases, where the environment remains constant, such substitution leads to a change of meaning. This procedure is usually referred to as the *commutation test*. As an example, let us assume that an investigator of a particular language has by recording and analysis, arrived at the phones [b, p', t+, t'+, t−, t'−].[1] He now takes some such sequence as [bɪg] and substitutes the phone [p'] for the phone [b] of the sequence. He observes that this leads to a change of meaning, and infers that [b] and [p'] are in phonemic opposition to one another, and hence allophones of different phonemes. He continues to substitute in the environment [−ɪg] the phones [t+, t'+, t−, t'−], and finds that while each of these phones is in phonemic opposition to both [b] and [p'] they are not opposed among themselves, since [t+ɪg, t'+ɪg, t−ɪg, t'−ɪg] are all taken to have the same meaning by the speakers of this language. On this basis, the investigator is able to set up three phonemes and classify the phone [b] as an allophone of the first, the phone [p'] as an allophone of the second, and the phones [t+, t'+, t−, t'−] as all allophones of the third.

10.31.   Neither the theory nor the use of the commutation test, however, is without its problems. The difficulty arises basically from the fact that the theory is framed as if the phones in any sequence of speech sounds were a succession of discrete, replaceable units, and it pays insufficient heed to the coarticulated nature of a sequence of speech sounds and to the closely related phenomenon of positional variants. These two features detract from the rigorousness of any test based on actual commutation of two phones.

For example, in the environment [−ɪn] Standard English has a phone [k'+] and in the environment [s−ɪn] a phone [k+]. If we provisionally adopt the hypothesis that all the [−ɪn] segments can be equated, the substitution of the former in the place of the latter, [sk'+ɪn], gives a sequence which does not normally occur in this dialect. The phonetic difference is, it is true, relatively small, and the response of the community may be the same as to [sk+ɪn]. But in the environment [−uːl] this form of English has a phone [k'−], and commutation of this phone with [k+] in our example

---

[1] The diacritics + and − are used to indicate advanced and retracted varieties of the articules concerned. Thus the closure in [t+] is in the front part of the alveolar area, that in [t−] is in the rear part of this area, and so on. (See Appendix I.)

gives [sk'−ɩn], a sequence in which the phonetic difference from [sk+ɩn] is so marked that it may well not be taken to be the same word by the community (cf. § 9.63). In such a case the investigator would conclude that [k+] and [k'−] are allophones of different phonemes, a conclusion which would add unnecessary complication to his final result. And when in their turn he comes to the commutation of the phones in the [ɩn] segments he may find similar differences and be forced to conclude that his provisional hypothesis was also faulty.

Of course an investigator may neglect certain phonetic features of a phone which he expects or assumes to be conditioned by each of its particular environments, but in so doing he comes up against a similar difficulty as appears with the use of the criterion of phonetic similarity, namely the degree or extent of phonetic difference which can be neglected as merely positional or coarticulatory. Hence in our example the investigator applying the commutation test is faced with the choice of neglecting the phonetic differences between [k+, k'+, k−, k'−] as merely positional or coarticulatory, which makes a mockery of the commutation test, or of maintaining those differences and running the risk of having such forms as [sk'−ɩn, sk'−uːl, k+ɩn] rejected by the community as not being the 'same' sequences as [sk+ɩn, sk−uːl, k'+ɩn], etc., which leads to an uneconomic proliferation of phonemes.

10.4. The Phonetic Features of a Phoneme

10.40.   A third method of classifying phones into allophones of phonemes is based on the assumption that in a phonemic opposition the phonetic form of the two allophones is different. Analysis of the phonetic forms of allophones in phonemic opposition will therefore show what phonetic features are functionally distinctive or relevant in these oppositions, and phones can be classified as allophones of different phonemes on the grounds of their possessing these features. We shall outline this method of approach first with reference to the articulatory layer alone.

Thus in English the phonemic opposition [p' : b] in the sequences [p'æn : bæn] is manifested phonetically by the voiceless, fortis, aspirated quality of [p'] opposed to the voiced, lenis, non-aspirated quality of [b]. These are, then, the relevant phonetic features in this oppositition. Other phonetic features which these two sounds have in common, such as their egressive, labial, plosive nature, do not function in, and are thus irrelevant in this particular opposition. But in the oppositions [p' : t' : k'] in the sequences [p'æn : t'æn : k'æn], the relevant phonetic feature of [p'] is labiality, which is opposed to the alveolarity and the velarity of [t'] and [k'] respectively, and in the pair [p'æn : mæn] and [p'æn : fæn] other relevant features of the allophone [p'] appear, namely its oral and plosive qualities. The investigator then proceeds to an investigation of the [p'] in the oppositions [p'ɔːn : bɔːn : t'ɔːn : k'ɔːn], etc., and finds that this allophone is also characterized by the relevant phonetic features: voiceless, fortis, aspirated, labial, oral and plosive. After a number of similar investigations, he is able to set up a provisional phoneme /p'/ characterized by this specific cluster or bundle of relevant phonetic features, and classifies all the phones in the language which show these phonetic features as allophones of that phoneme.

10.41. From such oppositions as [spaʟ : staʟ : slaʟ] by a similar procedure he sets up a provisional phoneme /p/ with allophones showing the phonetic features: voiceless, fortis, oral, labial, plosive; and groups all the phones in the language which show these phonetic features as allophones of that phoneme. In a similar way he sets up other provisional phonemes, /b/ with allophones all characterized by the phonetic features: voiced, lax, non-aspirated, oral, labial, plosive; /u/ with allophones characterized by the phonetic features: close, back, tense, long, rounded; and so on.

10.42. But after an exhaustive analysis of all the types of phonemic opposition in the language, it will be observable to the investigator that no allophone of the provisional phoneme /p'/ is ever in phonemic opposition with an allophone of the provisional phoneme /p/ and that the relevant phonetic features which allophones of the two provisional phonemes have in common are sufficient to distinguish them from allophones of all other phonemes. He therefore concludes that there is in fact only one phoneme and that the phonetic differences between the allophones of the two provisional phonemes are connected with the operation of some other factor or factors, such as different neighbouring sounds, accentuation, etc., and he can systematically test each of these possibilities during his further analysis of the language. In our particular example, he will discover that the allophones preceded by [s] are regularly non-aspirated and that those final in a sequence are facultatively non-aspirated. It is, then, clear that the features, aspirated or non-aspirated, are not functionally relevant to the phoneme /p/ in English. He may further find that some phonetic features always or regularly occur together. For example, after an exhaustive analysis of the phonemic oppositions in English he will observe that the feature fortis occurs only together with the feature voiceless, and in this case he need accept only one of these features as relevant to the phoneme, and subsume the other as a concomitant to it. Similarly he will observe that the feature plosive is always accompanied by the feature oral, that the feature nasal is always accompanied by the feature contoid, and so on.

Through these procedures of analysis, classification, grouping and simplification, the investigator arrives at an identification of the phonemes of the language in the form of a description of the permanent bundle of relevant phonetic features which characterize all the allophones of each phoneme.

10.43. This method of classifying the minimum recurrent phones of a language into allophones of its phonemes has the advantage, from the viewpoint of phonetics, of working with phonetic data and yet not suffering from the drawbacks of the commutation method. It appears basically sound and workable, though additional considerations of a linguistic nature—pattern congruity, morphological convenience, etc.—will doubtless be influential at some points of the investigation, at least in the analysis of some languages.

10.5. The Acoustic Correlates of Articulatory Features

10.50. The assumption that in a phonemic opposition the phonetic form of the two allophones is different can also be used to establish what features are relevant in such oppositions in the acoustic layer. This can be done in two ways. Either we can seek in this layer the acoustic correspondences or correlates of the relevant features of the articulatory level, or we can start afresh on the acoustic level and proceed to compare and contrast the acoustic complexes of allophones in phonemic opposition to find the features which are used for differentiating purposes.

The former method assumes that the results or effects of the relevant articulatory features are encoded in the total sound wave output of the speaker, and that an investigator can or should be able to decipher the code. Thus the sound of the initial segment of the English word [bæn] may be analysed to find the acoustic correlates of its articulatory relevant features, its voiced, labial, oral, and plosive qualities. In this particular case we may deduce that the voicedness of the sound is conveyed by the presence of a periodic wave structure emanating from the action of the vocal cords, the orality by the specific quality of the resonance resulting from the use of the throat and mouth tract, but not the nasal cavity, as a resonator, the labiality from the peculiar modification of this resonance resulting from the use of the lips as a modifier of the throat and mouth tract, and the plosiveness by the rapid changes in the sound structure as the lips close and open.

10.51. Though this is the obvious method of approach, there has not been, so far as we are aware, any thorough-going investigation into the acoustic correlates of the articulatory relevant features of the phonemes of a language. The reasons are probably partly practical and partly theoretical. The practical difficulty has been in analysing the acoustic effects or correlates of articulations which show a wide range of continuous variation, particularly when the effect of such articulation is essentially a resonance one. For example, in vowels it is customary to set up a range of tongue movement from open to close, and to allocate, as required in each language, distinct positions or sections of this range to different vowels as relevant features. But the variations in the spectra of vowels resulting from different tongue positions result essentially from differences in resonance, and have until recently been difficult to determine. Hence phoneticians have generally had to be content to work with the particular acoustic quality of each vowel as a whole. In modern acoustic phonetics, however, it is possible to analyse quickly and easily the spectra of vowels, and an investigation into the acoustic correlates of specific tongue positions and other articulations has become realisable. Though a beginning has been made, e.g. by Delattre, and by Jakobson, Fant, and Halle, and though there are many isolated observations in phonetic literature no systematic survey of the topic has yet appeared.

The theoretical difficulties are twofold. In the first place there is not a one-to-one correspondence between articulatory features and their acoustic results. A specific articulation may well have

10.6. THE DISTINCTIVE FEATURES

a fairly constant effect on the spectrum of the phone being produced, but this effect need not be unique to that articulation nor of a simple nature in itself. Thus, rounding of the lips may always produce a fall in the frequency of formant 2, but such a fall may also result from other, entirely different articulations, from the displacement of a linguo-palatal constriction to the rear, for example (cf. § 4.52). And the effect of the lip rounding will not be confined to lowering the frequency of formant 2; it will extend, to some degree, through its effect on the resonance properties of the vocal tract, to the frequencies of all the components of the spectrum of the phone being produced. Secondly, and more important, is the difficulty of attributing individual component parts of an acoustic spectrum subjected to resonance in the whole or part of the vocal tract to the action of specific articulatory features in subsections of that tract (§§ 4.50, 4.6).

It would appear from these considerations that the complex relationship between the articulation and the acoustic result seems to preclude any simple decoding of the speech wave in the laboratory to ascertain the reflexes of the relevant phonetic features in the articulatory layer.[1]

10.6. The Distinctive Features

10.60. The second approach to the determination of those features which are relevant in distinguishing phonemes is through the acoustic substance alone. This avoids the drawbacks of any attempt to correlate relevant articulatory features with components of the acoustic spectrum. It implies that the function of articulation is to produce allophones with different acoustic structures in phonemic oppositions, and that the listener's brain may identify the allophones from their different structures without any attempt to derive articulatory correlates from the whole or part of those structures. For example, a certain vibration in the sound complex [b] need not be interpreted by the brain as resulting from vibration of the vocal cords, but may be merely recognized as a feature which is present in [b], and in [d, g, z], etc., but absent in [p, t, k, s], etc. Or again, the acoustic complexes of two speech sounds may differ in that

---

[1] We may recall that though this may be at present impracticable in the laboratory, there is some evidence and considerable belief that this is what the brain does. (§ 9.72.)

the majority of the acoustic energy is distributed among the higher frequencies in one and among the lower frequencies in another. In this case the listener's brain must choose between one or other of these differing distributions of energy.

Features which in this way permit a choice between two alternatives may be considered to perform on the acoustic plane similar functions in phonemic oppositions as the relevant features on the articulatory plane. In other words, a phonemic opposition between [b] and [p] may be viewed not as based on the articulatory relevant features of voice versus voicelessness but on the—to use Jakobson's term—*distinctive feature* of the presence or absence of periodic vibration in the sound complexes. A distinctive feature is defined as the choice between two polar qualities of the same category or between the presence and absence of a certain quality. This conception of the nature of phonemic oppositions, that the listener is faced with a series of two-choice situations, fits in well with some modern theories of the operation of the mechanism of perception, though investigators are by no means all agreed upon this as a sufficient reason for assuming that phonemic interpretation is necessarily carried out as a series of choices between two, and only two, possibilities. No serious difficulty seems to prevent, for instance, an identification in terms of three alternatives at any point.

10.61. The distinctive features described up to the present are twelve in number, though no single language yet investigated makes use of all twelve. A majority, the *sonority features*, are contrasts mainly in the amount and/or the concentration of acoustic energy from moment to moment during the production of a phoneme, and a minority, the *tonality features*, are contrasts in the distribution of the energy in the frequency spectrum of a phoneme.

The SONORITY FEATURES are:

    I. *Vocalic versus non-vocalic*

        The choice here is between the presence or the absence, respectively, of a sharply defined formant structure.

    II. *Consonantal versus non-consonantal*

        The choice is between the presence of, relatively, little or a large amount of total energy. These two binary choices suffice to classify sounds as vocoids—vocalic and non-consonantal; contoids—non-vocalic and consonantal; liquids [l, r]—vocalic and consonantal; or glides [h, ?]—non-vocalic and non-consonantal.

III. *Compact versus diffuse*

The choice is between the concentration of energy in a relatively narrow central region of the frequency scale and the lack of such concentration. Velar and palatal contoids are compact in comparison with alveolars and labials, and open vocoids in comparison with close.

IV. *Tense versus lax* (cf. § 4.56)

The choice is between a larger total energy with wider spread in frequency and in time and a smaller total energy with less spread.

V. *Voiced versus voiceless*

The choice is between the presence of periodic low-frequency energy from vocal cord vibration and its absence.

VI. *Nasal versus oral*

The choice is between the wider spread of energy in the frequency scale from the presence of additional nasal formants (§ 4.56) and the reverse.

VII. *Discontinuous versus continuant*

The choice is between an abrupt onset and/or abrupt changes in the spread of energy in the frequency scale during the course of the phone and no such abruptness. Plosives and trills are discontinuous in comparison with continuant fricatives.

VIII. *Strident versus mellow*

The choice is between higher intensity with greater randomness of the noise component and lower intensity with less randomness. Affricates tend to be strident in comparison with the mellow plosives; English [s, z] likewise in comparison with [θ, ð], etc.

IX. *Checked versus unchecked*

The choice is between a relatively high rate of energy flow over a shorter period, together with an abrupt decay, the result of compression or closure of the glottis, and a relatively low rate of energy over a longer period, with a smooth decay.

The TONALITY FEATURES are:

X. *Grave versus acute*

The choice is between a predominance of low frequency formants and a predominance of high frequency formants. Back vocoids are grave in relation to front, and velar and labial contoids in relation to palatal and alveolar.

XI. *Flat versus plain*

The choice is between a phone with a lowering or weakening of one or more of the higher frequency formants and one which, in comparison, has no such lowering or weakening. The flattening seems generally produced by increasing the volume or decreasing the area of the orifices to the mouth part of the supraglottal tract.

XII. *Sharp versus plain*

The choice is between a phone with a raising, often resulting from some palatalized articulation, of one or more of the higher frequency formants and one which, in comparison, has no such raising.

10.62. In accordance with this hypothesis a phoneme may be regarded as characterized by a bundle of superposed, more or less concurrent distinctive features which are realized in the acoustic substances of its allophones. For example, the phoneme /b/ of English is characterized by the distinctive features: non-vocalic, consonantal, diffuse, grave, oral, lax, interrupted; and is opposed to /p/ which has a similar set of distinctive features save that the feature of laxness is replaced by a feature of tenseness. Likewise English /u/ is characterized by its vocalic, non-consonantal, diffuse and grave features, and opposed to /i/ which has vocalic, non-consonantal, diffuse, and acute features. Certain simplifications of these bundles are often possible in a similar way to that indicated on the articulatory level (§ 10.42) since in any specific language the presence of some distinctive features in a phoneme may be predictable from the presence of others.

10.6. THE DISTINCTIVE FEATURES

10.63. Though several of the details in this provisional sketch are somewhat dubious, these will doubtless be corrected and improved with further work. Major criticism of the theory should be on the principles on which it is based. Is the postulation of distinctive features the best means of describing the observed differences in the sounds of speech? Are allophones recognized by the listener as the result of a series of two-choice situations?

To the affirmation of the second of these questions is a difficulty: the importance of context in the identification of stop consonants (§ 9.63). The results of Schatz's experiment are particularly interesting in terms of distinctive features, since he was operating with segments recorded in and cut out of the acoustic layer. The recognition of [sk] from the context [-iː] as [st] in the context [-uːl] would seem to be explicable in this theory only if this segment [sk] had the same distinctive features as the segment [st] in [stuːl]. This appears to be a serious difficulty; the orientation of the theory is towards a description of phonemes as discrete bundles of concurrent distinctive features and the segmentation basic to this discreteness is difficult to apply to the acoustic substance of speech which results from and reflects superimposed, interconnected, and coarticulated muscular movements.

10.64. The whole theory, however, is of considerable interest, both in itself and since it predicts a method of operation of the mechanism of speech perception, a particularly obscure field (§ 9.8). It is possible also that attention to the sequential patterns of distinctive features in the stream of speech may enable it to cope with such cases as the above where the correct identification of a segment of the acoustic layer is dependent on its context—the listener's brain apparently does it quite easily.

Nevertheless, the emphasis on the acoustic layer of speech has its disadvantages. It would seem a rather uneconomical use of its resources for the brain to perform an analysis on the stream of sound and so identify the linguistic units without reference to its own motor patterns of articulation. Speech is, at some level of functioning of the brain, both articulatory and acoustic, and the lower this level is, the simpler the explanation of the production and interpretation of the units of speech.[1]

---

[1] One of the authors of this book has recently proposed to reinterpret the features in terms of auditory perception (Malmberg, 1967d).

10.7. Distinctive Features and the Phoneme

10.70. The number of phonemes which we arrive at by classification of the minimum recurrent segments of speech utterances is, in all languages so far analysed, quite limited, not exceeding a few dozen. Each phone of the language is an allophone of one or other phoneme, and is recognizable as such, either on the articulatory level by the presence of a set of relevant organic features, or on the acoustic level by the presence of a set of distinctive sound features. Such a set of features is characteristic of each phoneme and realised phonetically in each of its allophones—with few exceptions.

Exceptions to the presence of all the relevant or distinctive features may occur as a result of distributional characteristics of the type mentioned above (§10.20). Thus in modern Dutch, at the end of a word where no voiced plosive occurs the opposition of the relevant features, voice and voiceless, does not occur: any allophone of the phoneme /b/ in this position lacks the relevant feature of voice. That such an allophone is an allophone of /b/ and not of /p/ may be decided by the response of the community to the form, or on the grounds of linguistic criteria such as pattern congruity.

The set of relevant or distinctive features characteristic of each phoneme is that which distinguishes it from ęach other phoneme and it is upon these distinctions that a language is built up. The discriminatory function of a phoneme is performed in speech by its allophones, and it appears that this function is performed not by each allophone as a whole but by a limited selection of the totality of phonetic features, articulatory or acoustic, constituting it. This combination of similarity in discriminatory functions and of similarity in the set of relevant or distinctive features is doubtless the major factor in the community's classification of some sound segments, namely, the allophones of a phoneme, as the 'same' in its languagǝ (§ 10.10).

In the selection from the totality of phonetic features languages may differ. Features which are relevant in phonemic oppositions in language A need not be so in language B. Thus the feature of plosiveness is opposed to the feature of fricativeness in English [d] and [ð], as in [dɛn : ðɛn], since to the English speaker these are different words, but not in Spanish [d] and [ð], which are both allophones of /d/. The sequence [dia] and [ðia] are merely unimportant variant pronunciations of what is to the Spaniard the 'same' word. It is these non-relevant or non-distinctive features which a community tends to ignore in the hearing of its own language.

10.8. Suprasegmental or Prosodic Phonemes

10.80. The functioning of suprasegmental or prosodic features may be taken to be similar. The tones occurring in the utterance in a tone language for example may be allocated, by a process of comparison and contrast within otherwise similar environments, to groups, the members of each group having the same discriminatory function of contrasting with members of any other group. The members of each such group may be regarded as *allotones* of a *toneme*, a minimum distinctive unit of pitch in that language.

Such a classification is in fact presupposed in the discussion above (§§ 8.21–8.23): each of the four tones in Peking Mandarin is a toneme with an allotone characterized phonetically by specific features of pitch.

In the case of intonation, the linguistic use of pitch in the word group or phrase (§ 8.25 f.), two main possibilities of analysis and description exist. A level of pitch, or a pitch contour which contrasts with other levels or contours, may be classed as an allotone of a pitch-level toneme or a pitch-contour toneme as appropriate. In this case, the toneme will be marked by the phonetic features distinguishing it from other tonemes and its allotones will *inter alia* vary in length according to the length of the word group they accompany. A second approach is to view the pitch level or contour as a more complex unit composed of a sequence of minimal units, the tonemes. Thus a falling intonation contour may be taken to consist of a toneme *high* followed by a toneme *low*, a rising-falling contour of three tonemes *low-high-low*, and so on. An intonation contour will then be formed by a particular selection and order of tonemes, as analogously, a word is formed by a particular selection and order of phonemes.

The analysis and description of stress in its linguistic functioning may be done along similar lines: each significant level of stress in a language may be classed as a suprasegmental or prosodic *phoneme of stress*—the term *stresseme* is hardly used. The phonemes of stress associated with a word or word group then constitute an integral part of the phonemic form of that word or word group.

Other features from the total range of phonetic substance available to human beings may be used for prosodic purposes. We have noted duration and interruption (§§ 8.4, 8.5), but further possibilities, differences in voice quality, for example, are conceivable. The use of any such features in language is based on contrast: the occurrence of a particular feature in association with a linguistic unit is functionally opposed to its non-occurrence or to the occurrence of a different feature in association with that unit or with similar units. The features so opposed constitute terms in a system of contrasts within the language, and such terms may be regarded as suprasegmental phonemes or, to use a general term, *prosodemes* of that system.

To return to the question with which this chapter opened, we may finally answer that the normal use of a language involves the recognition of or response to those features of the utterance which are allophones or allotones of distinctive units of any of the phonological systems of that language. Members of a language community respond with sureness and ease to such features, but tend to ignore or not to perceive other features of the utterance, however audible, as not relevant to the language.

10.9. The Structure of Phonemic Systems

10.90. The different phonemic structures established on the principles discussed in the above paragraphs vary in complexity from language to language. Whereas some languages use only relatively few phonemic units, others have quite complicated systems. There are, for example, languages with only three vocalic phonemes, usually /i/ - /u/ - /a/. A five vowel system, /i/ - /e/ - /u/ - /o/ - /a/, is also widespread among the world's languages. On the other hand, such languages as French, English and Swedish have extremely rich vocalic systems (French with 16 phonemes, Swedish with 18, English with possibly as many as 20 depending on the method of interpretation). A no less striking variation is also observable in consonant systems. Most languages seem to have between 15 and 25 consonants but the range so far established is from 8 for Hawaiian to about 42 for Kwakiutl, an American Indian language.

Different languages consequently make, for their phonemic units, different choices among the very numerous possibilities of sound production offered by the speech organs. The choices, however, are not due simply to chance. There seems, on the contrary, to be a pattern in the way in which the expression system of a language is extended, or reduced. We owe the discovery of this patterning in expression-system development to Roman Jakobson.

In the poorest systems, i.e. those with the fewest phonemes, the phonetic features chosen are always those which are most differentiated from one another, acoustically, physiologically and perceptually. This seems, in turn, to be a general psychological law. If we have to make a communication system of just two units ("yes" or "no") it is quite normal to choose two extremes, and not two nuances which are close to each other (for example, to choose green and red, not two shades of red). This is an expression of the principle of economy. It demands more attention and precision, and thus more energy, to work with subtle differences. No three vowel system known has /i/, /y/, and /e/ as phonemes; such systems almost always have /i/, /u/, and /a/, the extreme, most differentiated types.

This implies that it is possible to set up (with Jakobson, 1941) a number of hierarchial rules for the structure of phonemic systems. Since the front (acute) and rounded (flat) type /y/ falls acoustically between /i/ (extreme acute) and /u/ (extreme grave), no language has rounded front vowels without also having back vowels. The presence of rounded front vowels in a system thus presupposes the presence of back vowels, but not inversely. In the same way, no system has the intermediate /e/ and /ɛ/ types without also having the extreme /a/ type, etc. Similar rules may be stated with regard to the structure of consonant systems. Thus fricatives presuppose plosives (the extreme type among consonants, i.e. the most differentiated from vowels), but not inversely. Voiced consonants presuppose voiceless ones, etc.

It should be emphasized that these structural rules concern distinctive units, not simply sounds with distinguishable phonetic qualities. Poverty of phonemes does not necessarily imply poverty of sounds. On the contrary, if the system is poor in phonemes, a greater range of phonetic substance is available for variation of the contextual realizations, i.e. the allophones, of each phoneme. A system with only three vowel phonemes may have numerous allophones of these phonemes. The smaller the number of distinctions, the freer the variation. In a system with only one series of plosives, both voiced and voiceless allophones of such plosives may occur. The non-use of the presence versus the absence of voice as a distinctive feature in the system of plosives does not necessarily imply the absence of voiced or voiceless plosive contoids, but simply the absence of any phonemic contrast between the two types.

Jakobson's law seems to apply also in the process by which the individual acquires his mother tongue. The first phonemes (not sounds) that the child distinguishes in his speech are the extreme ones, those which are general in human language. From this basis he proceeds to develop the other phonemes of his language in an order which exemplifies the hierarchial structure of the phonemic system. These facts also make a further assumption at least worth considering, namely, that this order has also been that of human language in its development from its most primitive stages in which, as is the case in the child's pre-linguistic and early linguistic stages, a very restricted number of oppositions may have occurred with an extreme richness of sounds.

The same law, finally, seems to apply also to the aphasic phenomena known as central linguistic disturbances, where the patient loses his phonemic distinctions in the inverse order to that in which the child acquires them. The absence of the phonemic approach in earlier descriptions of children's and aphasic speech is no doubt the explanation of the lack of such observations in earlier descriptions of these types of speech. Jakobson's discovery is perhaps the most valuable contribution of modern linguistics to phoniatrics and logopedics.

CHAPTER 11

SYNTAGMATIC STRUCTURES AND SEGMENTATION

11.1. Paradigm and Syntagm

11.10. A *structure* may be defined as a complex of interrelated units. The *form* of the structure is determined by the nature of the units and the relationships between them. Since Ferdinand de Saussure's famous *Cours de linguistique générale* (1916), it has been customary within linguistics to look upon a language as a structure in which relations between the units extend in two dimensions, the *paradigmatic* and the *syntagmatic*. At the phonological level, the paradigm—with an extension of the meaning of the term in school grammar—is the repertory of expression units (phonemes, prosodemes, etc.) usually referred to as the phonemic system of a language. The problem of establishing a paradigm was discussed in Chapter X.

We must now turn our attention to the chains of phonemic units which occur in utterances and which, in turn, suppose the existence of models or patterns of sequence here labelled *syntagms*. The structure of the syntagm consequently is the distribution, that is, the selection and arrangement, of the phonemic units within it. This kind of structure, like the paradigmatic one, has both general and specific aspects. There are certain features of syntagmatic structure which appear to be general in human languages, and which we may thus take as in this sense fundamental to their structure. But any syntagmatic system, as a whole, is characteristic of and specific to a particular language.

11.2. Syllabic Structures

11.20. We have already in Chapter VII, in connection with different syllable theories, given an example of a distributional definition of phonemic units, when we discussed the possibility of setting up two classes of phonemes according to their position in the syllable: *central* and *marginal* units. Vowels, according to this definition, are all the phonemes in a language which may be used as syllabic nuclei in that language, and consonants all those which cannot, and which, consequently, are unable to occur singly or in sequence by themselves as an utterance.

11.21. We may now give a few examples of *syllabic structures*. Languages vary considerably in the numbers and types of combinations of phonemes used as syllables. Syllable structure thus shows a wide range of complexity. The most widespread—and probably the most primitive—syllable is the combination CV (consonant + vowel). Many languages—for example, Japanese, numerous African and American languages—have only this type of syllable. If, in addition to this, the number of phonemes is small (the vowels, for instance, only five, as in Japanese, or even three, as some Indian languages), it is apparent that the number of possible combinations of, say, one or two syllables is extremely restricted and the number of words available to that language may then be increased only by the use of longer sequences of syllables. The advantage of simplicity in the paradigmatic dimension of the phonemic system is offset by the complexity of length in the syntagmatic structures.

It is customary to distinguish between *open* and *closed* syllables. The open syllable, which admits consonant phonemes only in initial position, exists in all languages, closed syllables only in certain languages. No language has closed syllables without having at the same time open ones. The open syllable is the first type to appear in the ontogenetic development of language in the child and the last to disappear in aphasic speech (Jakobson, Malmberg). It may not be too bold to conjecture that the open syllable was also the original type in the phylogenetic development of human language, and the closed syllable a subsequent innovation.

11.22. The number and variety of clusters of consonantal phonemes admissible within a syllable is another factor of variation in syllabic structure. Some languages, as for instance Japanese, admit no consonant clusters within the syllable; others, as Old Church Slavic, permit clusters only in initial position. Still others, notably the Germanic and Slavic languages, show a variety of consonant clusters both initially and finally within the syllable. English easily admits syllable-final groups as /-kt, -pt, -spt, -kst/,

German such as /-lk, -lkt, -tst, -tʃt, -çst, -ltst, -st/, and Swedish groups such as /-ln, -rp, -rsk, -lms, -tskt, -lmskt/.

When a speaker of a language without consonant clusters within the syllable hears such clusters, he is likely to perceive them as sequences of syllables. The habits of perception and segmentation of the chain of speech in his own language lead him to hear a vowel after each consonant in the cluster. This process is often crystallized in the forms of borrowed words: English *club* and *film* have been borrowed into Japanese as *kurabu* and *hirumu* respectively. On the other hand, there are very often vocalic segments in the speech chains of, say, English, German, French, or Spanish, which are just as important physically as many of the actually perceived vowels but which simply remain unnoticed because they have no correspondents in the phonemic pattern.

11.23. The poverty of final consonantism which characterises the syllabic structure of so many languages may also take the form of a reduced number of phonemic distinctions at the end of the syllable. In fact, most languages, even those which admit consonants and consonant clusters at the end of the syllable, have a smaller number of phonemic contrasts there, and often also assimilate those consonantal elements to following initial ones more easily —thus further restricting the distinctive possibilities—than in non-final positions. Spanish is a typical example of a language with a strong tendency to reduce its syllable-final possibilities to a minimum. Some of the phonemes distinguished at the beginning of syllables, the palatals and voiceless plosives, do not occur at all at the end. Nasals do occur but distinction between the three phonemic types contrasted in syllable initial position (i.e. the labial, apico-alveolar, and palatal nasal phonemes) is given up and the quality of the only nasal sound in syllable-final is automatically determined by the place of articulation of the following phoneme: in word-final position [n] or [ŋ], before labials [m], before dentals [n], before palatals [ɲ], before velars [ŋ]. The table in Figure 11.1 illustrates the difference with regard to syllable-final nasals between Spanish and Swedish, in which the nasal phonemes are contrasted both initially and finally in the syllable. In dialectal or vulgar forms of Spanish this simplification goes still further, and tends to reduce the distinction to one between palatal and velar. In this way certain phonemic changes (the simplifications in our example)

211

may reflect general structural tendencies of human language on the syntagmatic level.

11.3. The Order of Phonemes within the Syllable

11.30.   The order in which phonemes, and particularly consonants, may appear in admitted clusters, is also to a large extent due to conventions which vary from language to language, though ease of articulation and of perception may play a part in the establishment of the rules.   In English, a sequence /-kt/ is perfectly possible at the end of a syllable but it is impossible at the beginning, and consequently as word-initial (e.g. act [ækt], walked [wɔːkt], picked [pɪkt]).   In ancient Greek, however, a similar cluster was also word-initial (kteis).   In Swedish /pr-, tr-, kr-/ are only initial, not vice versa.   In English /-pl, -tl, -kl/ are final, /pl-, kl-/ also initial but not /tl-/; /-lp, -lt, -lk/ are final, but not initial.

11.31.   From the existence of general patterns in syllable structure, it may be inferred that certain consonants are more *vowel-adherent* than others.   In consonant clusters, liquids, nasals, and voiced fricatives mostly come closer to the vowel than stops and voiceless fricatives.[1]   For example, in English, /pl-, pr-, kl-, sm-, spl-/ occur prevocalically in the syllable, but not /lp-, rp-, ms-, lps-/, whereas the converse is the case postvocalically in the syllable.   Evidently /p, k, s/ in English are less vowel-adherent than /l, r, m/.   Within a given system of syntagmatic structure it is consequently possible to establish a *rank-order* of consonants according to their vowel adherence (Sigurd, Gårding).

11.4. Structural Features and Segmentation

11.40.   Though their phonetic status varies from one language to another (§ 7.15, note) the words of a language are also subject to structural restrictions concerning their phonemic make-up. Finnish does not admit consonant clusters in word-initial positions but, though the word-end is mostly vocalic, has a considerable number of closed syllables.   A consequence of this is that initial clusters in loan-words have been reduced, in early borrowings (*ranta* < Primitive

---

[1] Cf. "The basic generalization that can be made about consonant clusters is that the more vowel-like consonants are nearer the vowel than are the less vowel-like." Hultzén (1965).

SWEDISH

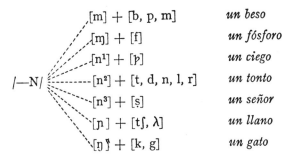

/—m/ ⤳ [m] + all consonants (*omkring, omtala, omsluta*, etc.)
          [ɱ] + [f, v] (*om vi* — —; facultative variant)

          [m] + [p, b] (*en påse;* facultative variant)

/—n/ ⤳ [n] + all consonants[1] (*en mås, ensam, en kung*)
          [ɱ] + [f, v] (*en vas;* facultative variant)

          [ŋ] + [k, g] (*en kung;* facultative variant)

/—ŋ/ --------[ŋ] + all consonants[2]

[1]Not before /k/ within the morpheme.
[2]Only at morpheme boundaries.

SPANISH

          [m] + [b, p, m]   *un beso*

          [ɱ] + [f]   *un fósforo*

          [n[1]] + [þ]   *un ciego*

/—N/ ⤳ [n[2]] + [t, d, n, l, r]   *un tonto*

          [n[3]] + [s̩]   *un señor*

          [ɲ] + [tʃ, λ]   *un llano*

          [ŋ] + [k, g]   *un gato*

[1]interdental nasal
[2]postdental nasal
[3]alveolar nasal

Fig. 11.1. The contrast in the behaviour of nasals in syllable-final position in Swedish and Spanish. The former has three different nasal phonemes with allophones depending on the nature of the following consonant (and partially overlapping); the latter has only one nasal phoneme in this position with a variety of allophones also depending on the nature of the following consonant (after Malmberg)

Germanic **stranda-*) as well as in modern ones (*nivi* < Swed. *kniv*, *Tukholma* < Stockholm, etc.). The phoneme sequences incorporating such conventions of a language may in some cases signal the presence, or conversely the absence, of a word boundary in that language. For example, German does not admit a voiced plosive in word-final position, so that the presence of such a plosive in a sequence excludes the possibility of a word boundary following that plosive. This is the case in *badezimmer* ['baːdə‚tsimər], while in *badanlage* ['baːtʔanlaːgə] the voiceless [t] and the following glottal stop [ʔ] combine to signal the end of the first element and the beginning of the second in the compound.

11.41. In a general way, distributional rules are strong cues to the linguistic segmentation of the speech wave. This is, of course, also true of the distribution of allophonic variants. In languages like English or Swedish, where aspirated and non-aspirated stops appear in complementary distribution, a sequence like [stʻ-] + vowel is a clear indication of a morpheme boundary [s|tʻ-] since within the morpheme the sequence would be [st-] + vowel. In British English, a velarized or 'dark' [ɫ] must be postvocalic; in a position between vowels then it automatically indicates a syllable and morpheme boundary after itself. Many Spanish dialects have a weakened allophone of /s/, the so-called "aspirated" s, in syllable-final position. The quality of the sound thus tells a listener whether it is initial or final. Such phenomena consequently often become strong cues to syllable division. (Cp. Gårding, 1967).

11.42. Certain languages have a tendency to generalize some phonemic feature within a syntagm (a syllable, a word, a word-group, etc.). We have given examples above of distance assimilation (vowel harmony, metaphony, "umlaut," etc. (§ 7.45 f.)). Such phenomena imply in fact a reduction of the distinctive possibilities of the system in the syntagm, since they limit the available range of units. If in a language with vowel harmony the vowel quality of the following syllables depends on that of the first, a choice is possible only in this first syllable. Thus a language which has $A + A$ and $\ddot{A} + \ddot{A}$ (but not $A + \ddot{A}$ nor $\ddot{A} + A$)—where A means any back, $\ddot{A}$ any front vowel—is poorer in distinctive possibilities than a system which admits the four alternatives. Vocal harmony thus also becomes a cue to segmentation since the occurrence of a different vocalic quality in the sequence of phonemes indicates that a different unit in the system has begun. The South-American language Guarani is reported to have a possible distinctive nasality in the vowel of the first syllable in the word. If this feature occurs with the vowel of that syllable, all subsequent syllables in the words become nasalised in a process of nasal harmony. This nasality of the following syllables is thus predictable from that of the first and consequently without any distinctive value of its own. But its cessation may indicate the end of the sequence which is dependent on the first element, and thereby signal a word boundary. It facilitates segmentation.

11.5. Listening and Identifying

11.50. The segmentation of the speech wave into a sequence of linguistic units is not a matter of acoustics, of articulatory patterns or of auditory perception alone. Listening to the stream of speech is *selective listening*. We have already had occasion to point out that the process of listening to speech seems to a very large extent a process of applying a pre-existing pattern to the acoustic continuum, in itself not segmented (§§ 7.11, 7.72, 9.8).

We know from general psychology that any act of perception implies the application of a pattern on a continuum. We perceive anything as one of a number of possible alternatives, taking into consideration certain species-distinctive properties of the item perceived and neglecting others as irrelevant. Perception thus implies interpretation, i.e. in the final instance identification with a pre-existing model. If we perceive a dog as a dog, this means that we have taken into consideration those characteristics which are relevant for that species and have neglected irrelevant features such as the colour, the length of the tail, the shape of the ears, etc. We *identify* the concrete animal with a species or a class, thus opposing it to all others. Any act of perception and interpretation implies in fact *identification* and *opposition*. This is true also of the sounds of language.

If we think of what was said above (§ 7.70 f.) about the defective relationship—or rather the lack of regular correspondence—between the sound-wave and the pattern on which it was built up by the speaker (i.e. roughly the speaker's idea of what he was saying), we are led to describe the interpretation of speech as guess-work, the success of which is to a very large extent dependent on the listener's knowledge of the model[1] (the linguistic system as a whole),

---

[1] No listener has a complete knowledge of any linguistic system in all its aspects (phonemes, forms, syntax, vocabulary, style). The difference between a native speaker and a foreigner is a gradual one. The smaller our knowledge of the language, the greater our need for external context or cues to the identification.

and on his experience and acquaintance with the language in use, with the speaker's personal speaking habits, and with the whole context and situation within which the speech occurs (§ 9.8). In other words, the extent to which we understand a message is related to our faculty of guessing not only at parts actually missing from the message but also at such signals as are received by the brain in defective or unsatisfactory state. We know from our everyday experience that it is much easier to follow a conversation in a foreign language if we are well acquainted with the topic discussed. The fact that a native speaker understands more easily than a foreigner is due to the former's greater facility in guessing what is meant. Both hear physiologically the same sound-wave. But even a native speaker easily misses parts of a conversation dealing with topics he knows little about. Likewise, our ability to understand speech over the telephone (§ 9.40) is to a large extent explained by our ability to guess—hence the difficulties and misunderstandings when, as with names or foreign words, guessing is ineffective. Many laboratory experiments have confirmed these common experiences.

11.51. On the phonemic level such general points of view lead us to the conclusion that a given stimulus in the speech-wave is heard and interpreted by being referred to one of the phonemes in the repertory of the language. To a Frenchman the vocoids [i] and [y] are two different vowel phonemes. The acoustic pattern characteristic of the latter is consequently identified with the phoneme /y/ and opposed to /i/. The listener hears, for example, that the speaker says /vy/, not /vi/. In the same way he hears /ø/ in *feu* as opposed to /e/ in *fée*. An Italian would hear physiologically the same acoustic stimulus but be acquainted with only one type of vocalic distinction within the front (acute) series, i.e. a distinction along the dimension close - open, and consequently have no box to put the [y] in. Thus, since he has no other choice, he interprets [y] and [ø], even if he notices a peculiar quality in them, as allophones of his /i/ and /e/. The Frenchman has since his earliest childhood become accustomed to the distinction between /i/ and /y/, whereas the Italian has not learnt to listen to this difference and consequently is incapable of "hearing" and of reproducing it.

In the same way, a Frenchman, who is extremely sensitive even to very slight shades of musical distinctions on the sentence level and uses in his own language a very subtle system of intonation contours, is normally incapable of hearing the Swedish word-accent distinction, since he has never become accustomed to listen to musical differences on the word level. In the ordinary course of events, the vast majority of people acquire their phonemic habits during their first 10–12 years of age and remain thereafter bound by the limitations of perception and of production imposed on them by their habits. Language learning is a question of acquiring new habits, not simply a matter of listening. In order to arrive at understanding and using a second language we must free ourselves of the tyranny of our own system. We must *learn* to listen to the new language, i.e. we must *learn* to apply another segmentation pattern to the sound-wave perceived.

APPENDIX I:

THE INTERNATIONAL PHONETIC ALPHABET.
(Revised to 1951.)

	Bi-labial	Labio-dental	Dental and Alveolar	Retroflex	Palato-alveolar	Alveolo-palatal	Palatal	Velar	Uvular	Pharyngal	Glottal
CONSONANTS											
Plosive	p b		t d	ʈ ɖ			c ɟ	k g	q ɢ		ʔ
Nasal	m	ɱ	n	ɳ			ɲ	ŋ	N		
Lateral Fricative			ɬ ɮ								
Lateral Non-fricative			l	ɭ			ʎ				
Rolled			r						ʀ		
Flapped			ɾ	ɽ					ʀ		
Fricative	ɸ β	f v	θ ð s z ɹ	ʂ ʐ	ʃ ʒ	ɕ ʑ	ç ʝ	x ɣ	χ ʁ	ħ ʕ	h ɦ
Frictionless Continuants and Semi-vowels	w ɥ	ʋ	ɹ				j (ɥ)	(w)	ʁ		
VOWELS											
Close	(y ʉ u)						Front: i y Central: ɨ ʉ Back: ɯ u				
Half-close	(ø o)						e ø	ɤ o			
Half-open	(œ ɶ)						ɛ œ	ɜ	ʌ ɔ		
Open	(ɒ)						a	æ	ɑ ɒ		

(Secondary articulations are shown by symbols in brackets.)

OTHER SOUNDS.—Palatalized consonants: ţ, ḍ, etc.; palatalized ʃ, ʒ: ɕ, ʑ. Velarized or pharyngalized consonants: ɫ, đ, s, etc. Ejective consonants (with simultaneous glottal stop): p', t', etc. Implosive voiced consonants: ɓ, ɗ, etc. r fricative trill. σ, ς (labialized θ, ð, or s, z). ʓ, ʓ (labialized ʃ, ʒ). ɿ, ʇ, ʅ (clicks, Zulu c, q, x). l (a sound between r and l). ŋ Japanese syllabic nasal. ƕ (combination of x and ʃ). ʍ (voiceless w). ɿ, ʏ, ɐ (lowered varieties of i, y, u). ɜ (a variety of ə). e (a vowel between ø and o).

Affricates are normally represented by groups of two consonants (ts, tʃ, dʒ, etc.), but, when necessary, ligatures are used (ʦ, ʧ, ʤ, etc.), or the marks ‿ or ͡ (ts or ts, etc.). ͡ also denote synchronic articulation (m͡ŋ = simultaneous m and ŋ). c, ɟ may occasionally be used in place of tʃ, dʒ, and ʒ, ʒ for ts, dz. Aspirated plosives: ph, th, etc. r-coloured vowels: ɛɹ, aɹ, ɔɹ, etc., or eɹ, aɹ, oɹ, etc., or ɐ, ɑ, ɔ, etc.; r-coloured ə: əɹ or ɵɹ or ɹ or ɹ ɚ, or ɹ.

LENGTH, STRESS, PITCH.— : (full length). · (half length). ' (stress, placed at beginning of the stressed syllable). ˌ (secondary stress). ⁻ (high level pitch); ˍ (low level); ' (high rising); ˏ (low rising); ` (high falling); ˎ (low falling); ^ (rise-fall); ˇ (fall-rise).

MODIFIERS.— ~ nasality. ₒ breath (ḷ = breathed l). ᵥ voice (ş = z). ' slight aspiration following p, t, etc. ˌ labialization (ṇ = labialized n). ̯ dental articulation (ṭ = dental t). ̣ palatalization (ẓ = ʒ). ̥ specially close vowel (ẹ = a very close e). ̤ specially open vowel (ẹ = a rather open e). ˔ tongue raised (e˔ or ẹ = e). ˕ tongue lowered (e˕ or ẹ = ɛ). ˖ tongue advanced (u˖ or u̟ = an advanced u, ţ = t̞). ˗ or ̠ tongue retracted (i̠ or ɩ̵ = i̵, ţ = alveolar t). ˒ lips more rounded. ˓ lips more spread. Central vowels: ɪ (= ɨ), ʉ (= u̵), ë (= ə̈), ö (= ɵ), ɛ̈, ɔ̈. ᵕ (e.g. n̥) syllabic consonant. ˘ consonantal vowel. ˠ variety of ʃ resembling s, etc.

Reproduced by courtesy of the International Phonetic Association

APPENDIX II: INDEX TO THE PHONETIC
SYMBOLS IN CHAPTER 6

220

FURTHER READING

The purpose of this list of readings is to introduce the student to the commonly used books and a few widely known or important articles in phonetics, additional to those mentioned in the text, and to the main sources of further information in the subject. The list has been kept, with rare exceptions, to works published (or republished) since 1945.

Chapter 1: Introduction

(a) General works and textbooks of phonetics:
Pike, 1943; Stetson, 1945, 1951; Grammont, 1950; Dieth, 1952; von Essen, 1962; Wise, 1958; Heffner, 1960; Laziczius, 1961; Smalley, 1962; Malmberg, 1962d, 1967a, 1967b; Flanagan, 1965; Fischer-Jørgensen, Eli, 1966; Abercrombie, 1967; Malmberg (Ed.), 1968.

(b) The main journals in phonetics are:
Le Maître Phonétique (London).
Zeitschrift für Phonetik (Berlin).
Phonetica (Basel & New York).
Revue de phonétique appliquée (Mons, Belgium).
Most journals in languages and linguistics, and the following from related fields, frequently contain papers of phonetic interest:
Journal of the Acoustical Society of America (New York).
Language and Speech (Teddington, Middlesex).
Journal of Speech and Hearing Research (Washington, D.C.).
Quarterly Journal of Speech (New York).
Folia Phoniatrica (Basel, Switzerland).
Important also are the *Proceedings of the Second, Third, etc. International Congress of Phonetic Sciences*, appearing approximately every four years. (See list of references.)

(c) An annual bibliography of articles and books on phonetics is included in the Linguistic Bibliography (Utrecht-Antwerp, 1949). Another appears twice yearly in the periodical *American Speech*.

(d) The relations between phonetics and phonology or linguistics are discussed in: de Saussure, 1916, 1960; Pike, 1947; Martinet, 1949; Hockett, 1955; Fischer-Jørgensen, 1958; Hjelmslev, 1961, 1966; Trubetzkoy, 1962; Jones, 1962a; Malmberg, 1962c; McIntosh, Halliday & Strevens, 1964.

In addition, almost all introductions to, or textbooks of, the study of language include a survey of phonetics and a discussion of its relationship to linguistics.

(e) For the relations between phonetics and psychology: Gemelli, 1950; Miller, 1951; Stevens, 1951 (several chapters); Saporta, 1961 (97 ff., 331 ff.).

(f) For the relations between phonetics and language teaching: Abercrombie, 1956; McIntosh, Halliday & Strevens, 1964; Mackey, 1965 (extensive bibliography); Valdman, 1966.

Chapter 2: Sound

(a) General works on Acoustics include: Winckel, 1952; Matras, 1960; Denes & Pinson, 1963; (more advanced:) Kinsler, 1950; Wood, 1955; Lafon, 1961. (See also bibliography to Chapter III.)

Chapter 3: The Speech Apparatus

(a) The anatomy and physiology of the organs of speech are described in most textbooks of human anatomy. Some more specialized works are: Garde, 1954; Mörner, 1960; (more advanced:) Negus, 1929; Sicher, 1949; Kaplan, 1960; Terracol & Ardouin, 1963; (with a bias towards Phoniatry:) Aubin & Tarneaud (Eds.), 1953; Luchsinger, 1959; Luchsinger & Arnold, 1965.

(b) Important articles on the vocal cords and their action: Husson, 1951, 1966; Smith, 1954, 1959; van den Berg, 1957a, 1957b; Wustrow, 1957; Sonesson, 1960; Ladefoged, 1963.
Subglottal activity: Ladefoged, 1962b and 1963.
Different types of laryngeal activity: Catford, 1964.

Chapter 4: The Production of Sound in the Vocal Tract

(a) The acoustics of speech and acoustic phonetics are treated in: Potter, Kopp & Green, 1947; Joos, 1948; Chiba & Kajiyama, 1958; Pulgram, 1959; Fant, 1960, 1966; Ladefoged, 1962a; Ungeheuer, 1962.

(b) The classic study of coarticulation is Menzerath & de Lacerda, 1933. See also: Truby, 1959.

(c) The minor articulations are mentioned in Pike, 1943, and most subsequent handbooks. Fortisness and lenisness: Jakobson & Halle, in Jones, 1964.

Chapter 5: The Description and Classification of Speech Sounds

(a) The problem of the decomposition of the expression substance has not received the explicit discussion it deserves. It is touched on by Martinet, 1949 (Chapter I), 1962 (Chapter I), and Joos, 1948 (Chapter II).
Segmentation: Pike, 1943; Joos, 1948.

(b) For the I.P.A., see The Principles of the International Phonetic Association (latest revision), 1949.

(c) Discussions of the classification of speech sounds, and especially of the articulation versus acoustics problem: Malmberg, 1952, 1967c; Fletcher, 1953; Liberman, 1957; Straka, 1963; Peterson & Shoup, 1966; Fry, 1966.

Chapter 6: The Segmental Sounds

(a) Segmental sounds and their articulation are treated in all handbooks of phonetics, usually with a strong bias toward the sounds of the common European languages. The possible range of types is discussed in Pike, 1943, and from about 1930 there has been an increasing number of monographs with reliable descriptions of the phonetics of specific languages or of groups of languages. Among the latter may be mentioned:
Africa: Meinhof, 1932; Westerman & Ward, 1933; Ladefoged, 1964. Arabic languages: Cantineau, 1960. Articles dealing with the phonetics of non-European languages often appear in the *Bulletin of the School of African and Oriental Studies* of the University of London. Further, short descriptions of the phonetics of many languages are included in Meillet & Cohen, 1952.

(b) The acoustic nature of many segmental sounds, as revealed by the Acoustic Spectrograph, is discussed in Potter, Kopp & Green, 1947, and in more theoretical terms in Fant, 1960. Information on the acoustic nature of specific sounds or groups of sounds is scattered in the periodicals, especially the *Journal of the Acoustical Society of America* and *Language and Speech*.

Chapter 7: Combinations of Sounds

(a) Combinations of sounds and the transitions between them are discussed in most handbooks. More specialized are: Menzerath & de Lacerda, 1933; Menzerath, 1941; Gemelli, 1950; Truby, 1959; Delattre, Liberman & Cooper, 1962; Uldall, 1964.

(b) The syllable has given rise to a large literature. Besides the handbooks the following may be referred to: Malmberg, 1955, 1966, 1967 (Chapters III, VII); Jones, 1956; Skaličková, 1958; Ladefoged, Draper & Whitteridge, 1958.

Chapter 8: Prosodic Features

(a) General discussions are usual in the textbooks of phonetics and of linguistics. More specialized: Durand, 1946; Firth, 1948; Pike, 1948; Fry, 1958; Faure, 1962; Elert, 1965; Morton & Jassem, 1965.

Chapter 9: Hearing and Perception of Speech

(a) General works on hearing: Stevens & Davis, 1938; Fletcher, 1953; Tomatis, 1963; Mol, 1963; Lafon, 1961, 1964. An excellent elementary account: van Bergeijk, Pierce & David, 1960. Several chapters in Stevens, 1951, deal with aspects of hearing and the perception of speech. Survey of the field: Diebold, 1965.

(b) Distinctive features: Jakobson, Fant & Halle, 1951; Jakobson & Halle, 1956; Jakobson, 1962.
Bibliography on hearing: Stevens, Loring & Cohen, 1955.

Chapter 10: The Functioning of Sounds in Language

See references to Chapter I (d).

Chapter 11: Syntagmatic Structures and Segmentation

(a) Syllable structures: Jakobson, 1941; Malmberg, 1966a, 1966b.

LIST OF REFERENCES

ABERCROMBIE, D. (1956), *Problems and Principles*. London.

ABERCROMBIE, D. (1967), *Elements of General Phonetics*. Edinburgh.

ADRIAN, E. (1947), *The Physical Background of Perception*. Oxford.

ALBRIGHT, R. W. (1958), The International Phonetic Alphabet: Its Backgrounds and Development, Indiana Research Center in Anthropology, Folklore and Linguistics, Publication Seven (= *International Journal of American Linguistics*, XXIV, No. 1, Part 3).

ALLEN, W. S. (1964), On quantity and quantitative verse. In Jones (1964).

AUBIN, A. & TARNEAUD, J. (Eds.) (1953), *La voix*. Paris.

BÉKÉSY, G. VON (1955), For references see Stevens, Loring & Cohen (1955).

BÉKÉSY, G. VON & ROSENBLITH, S. A. (1951), The mechanical properties of the ear. In Stevens (1951).

BENDOR-SAMUEL, J. T. (1962), Stress in Terena, *Trans. Philological Soc.*, 1962.

BERG, JW. VAN DEN (1957a), Sub-glottal pressure and vibrations of the vocal folds. *Folia Phoniatrica*, IX.

BERG, JW. VAN DEN (1957b), Aspects physiologiques et physiques de la formation de la voix, International Association of Logopedics and Phoniatrics: *Proceedings of the Tenth International Speech and Voice Conference*.

BERG, JW. VAN DEN (1962), Modern research in experimental phoniatrics. *Folia Phoniatrica*, XII.

BERGEIJK, W. VAN, PIERCE, JOHN R. & DAVID, EDWARD E., Jr. (1960), *Waves and the Ear*. New York.

BLOOMFIELD, LEONARD (1933), *Language*. New York.

BRANNON, J. B., Jr. (1966), The speech production and spoken language of the deaf. *Language and Speech*, IX.

BROSNAHAN, L. F. (1961), *The Sounds of Language*. Cambridge.

CANTINEAU, JEAN (1960), *Cours de Phonétique Arabe*. Paris.

CARNEY, EDWARD (1966), The perceptual value of sibilant transitions, *Proceedings of the Fifth International Congress of Phonetic Sciences*, Münster, 1964. Basel/New York.

CATFORD, J. C. (1964), Phonation types: the classification of some laryngeal components of speech production. In Jones (1964).

CHERRY, E. C., HALLE, MORRIS & JAKOBSON, ROMAN (1953), Towards a logical description of languages in their phonemic aspects, *Language*, XXIX.

CHIBA, TSUTOMU & KAJIYAMA, MASATO (1958), *The vowel: Its nature and structure*. Phonetic Society of Japan.

COOPER, FRANKLIN S., DELATTRE, P. C., LIBERMAN, A. M., BORST, J. M. & GERSTMAN, L. J. (1952), Some experiments on the perception of synthetic speech sounds, *Journal of the Acoustical Society of America*, XXIV, No. 6.

DELATTRE, P. C. (1951), The physiological interpretation of sound spectrograms, *Publications Modern Language Association*, LXVI.

DELATTRE, P. C. (1966), *Studies in French and Comparative Phonetics*. The Hague.

DELATTRE, P. C., LIBERMAN, A. M. & COOPER, F. S. (1962), Formant transitions and loci as acoustic correlates of place of articulation in American fricatives, *Studia linguistica*, XVI.

REFERENCES

DENES, PETER B. & PINSON, ELLIOT N. (1963), *The Speech Chain.* Bell Telephone Laboratories. Baltimore.

DIEBOLD, A. R., Jr. (1965), A survey of Psycholinguistic Research, 1954–64. In Osgood, C. E. & Sebeok, T. E., *Psycholinguistics: A Survey of Theory and Research Problems.* Bloomington, Indiana.

DIETH, E. (1952), *Vademekum der Phonetik.* Berne.

DUNN, H. K. (1950), The calculation of vowel resonances and an electrical vocal tract, *Journal of the Acoustical Society of America,* XXII.

DURAND, MARGUERITE (1964), *Voyelles longues et voyelles brèves.* Paris.

ELERT, CLAES-CHRISTIAN (1965), *A phonetic study of quantity in Swedish.* Stockholm.

ESSEN, OTTO VON (1957), *Allgemeine und Angewandte Phonetik,* 2nd ed. Berlin.

FAIRBANKS, GRANT (1966), *Experimental Phonetics.* Urbana/London.

FANT, GUNNAR (1960), *Acoustic Theory of Speech Production.* The Hague.

FANT, GUNNAR (1966), Formants and cavities, *Proceedings of the Fifth International Congress of Phonetic Sciences,* Münster, 1964. Basel/New York.

FAURE, GEORGES (1962), *Recherches sur les caractères et le rôle des élements musicaux dans la prononciation anglaise.* Paris.

FIRTH, J. R. (1948), Sounds and prosodies, *Trans. of the Philological Soc.,* 1948.

FISCHER-JØRGENSEN, ELI (1958), What can the new techniques of acoustic phonetics contribute to linguistics, *Proceedings of the VIII International Congress of Linguists.* Reprinted in Saporta (1961).

FISCHER-JØRGENSEN, ELI (1966), *Almen fonetik,* 3rd ed. Copenhagen.

FLANAGAN, J. L. (1965), *Speech Analysis, Synthesis, and Perception.* (Kommunikation und Kybernetik in Einzeldarstellungen 3.) Berlin/Heidelberg/New York.

FLETCHER, HARVEY (1953), *Speech and Hearing in Communication.* New York.

FORCHHAMMER, J. (1923), *Stimmbildung auf stimm- und sprachphysiologischer Grundlage.* München.

FORCHHAMMER, J. (1951), *Allgemeine Sprechkunde (Laletik).* Heidelberg.

FRENCH, N. R. & STEINBERG, J. C. (1947), Factors governing the intelligibility of speech sounds, *Journal of the Acoustical Society of America,* XIX.

FRY, D. B. (1958), Experiments in the perception of stress, *Language and Speech,* I.

FRY, D. B. (1966), Modes de perception des sons du langage. In Moles, A. & Vallancien, B. (1966).

GALAMBOS, R. & DAVIS, H. (1942), The response of single auditory nerve fibres to acoustic stimulation, *Fed. Proc. of American Society of Experimental Biology,* I.

GARDE, E. (1954), *La voix* ("Que sais-je?"). Paris.

GÅRDING, EVA (1967), Internal Juncture in Swedish. *Travaux de l'Institut de Lund.* Lund.

GÅRDING, LARS (1955), Relations and order, *Studia Linguistica,* IX.

GEMELLI, AGOSTINO (1950), *La strutturazione psicologica del linguaggio studiata mediante l'analisi elettroacustica.* Città del Vaticana.

GRAMMONT, MAURICE (1950), *Traité de Phonétique.* Paris.

GREEN, PETER S. (1959). Consonant-vowel transitions: A spectrographic study, *Travaux de l'Institut de phonétique de Lund 2* (= *Studia Linguistica,* XII, 57–105).

227

REFERENCES

HADDING-KOCH, KERSTIN (1961), Acoustico-phonetic studies in the intonation of Southern Swedish, *Travaux de l'Institut de phonétique de Lund.* Lund.

HALLE, M. & STEVENS, K. N. (1962), Speech Recognition: A model and a program for research, *IRE Transactions on Information Theory.* Vol. IT–8, No. 2.

HARRIES, L. (1952), Some tonal principles of the Kikuyu language, *Word*, VIII.

HEFFNER, R.-M. S. (1960), *General Phonetics*, 3rd ed. Madison, Wisconsin.

HJELMSLEV, LOUIS (1939), The syllable as a structural unit, *Proceedings of the Third International Congress of Phonetic Sciences*, Ghent, 1938. Ghent.

HJELMSLEV, LOUIS (1961), *Prolegomena to a Theory of Language*, 2nd ed. Madison, Wisconsin. (Translation by F. J. Whitfield of the Danish original: *Omkring Sprogteoriens grundlaeggelse*, Copenhagen, 1943.)

HJELMSLEV, LOUIS (1966), *Le langage.* Paris.

HOCKETT, C. F. (1955), *A Manual of Phonology.* Baltimore.

HOCKETT, C. F. (1958). *A Course in Modern Linguistics.* New York.

HULTZÉN, L. (1965), Consonant Clusters in English, *American Speech*, XI.

HUSSON, RAOUL (1936), La phonation: Quelques aspects énergétiques des principaux phénomènes acoustiques et dissipatifs, *Revue française de phoniatrie*, IV.

HUSSON, RAOUL (1950), *Étude des Phénomènes Physiologiques et Acoustiques de la Voix Chantée.* Paris.

HUSSON, RAOUL (1951), Conduction récurrentielle polyphasée pendant la phonation, *Folia phoniatrica*, III.

HUSSON, RAOUL (1960), *La Voix Chantée.* Paris.

HUSSON, RAOUL (1966), Sur le fonctionnement phonatoire du larynx, *Proceedings of the Fifth International Congress of Phonetic Sciences*, Münster, 1964. Basel.

JAKOBSON, ROMAN (1941), *Kindersprache, Aphasie und allgemeine Lautgesetze.* Uppsala. (Also in *Selected Writings*, I. The Hague, 1962.)

JAKOBSON, ROMAN (1962f.), *Selected Writings*, I–IV. The Hague.

JAKOBSON, ROMAN (1956), *In Honour of Roman Jakobson: Essays on the Occasion of his Sixtieth Birthday.* The Hague.

JAKOBSON, ROMAN, FANT, GUNNAR & HALLE, MORRIS (1952), *Preliminaries to Speech Analysis.* M.I.T., Boston, Mass.

JAKOBSON, R. & HALLE, M. (1956), *Fundamentals of Language.* The Hague.

JESPERSEN, OTTO (1926), *Lehrbuch der Phonetik.* Leipzig. (Often reprinted.)

JONES, D. (1956), The hyphen as a phonetic sign, *Zeitschrift für Phonetik*, IX.

JONES, D. (1962), *An Outline of English Phonetics*, 9th ed. Cambridge.

JONES, D. (1962a), *The Phoneme*, 2nd ed. Cambridge.

JONES, D. (1964), *In Honour of Daniel Jones.* Ed. D. Abercrombie *et al.* London.

JOOS, MARTIN (1948), Acoustic phonetics, Supplement to *Language*, XXIV. Baltimore.

KAISER, L. Ed. (1957), *Manual of Phonetics.* Amsterdam.

KAPLAN, H. M. (1960), *Anatomy and Physiology of Speech.* New York/ Toronto/London.

KARLGREN, B. (1948), *Kinesisk elementarbok.* Stockholm.

KINSLER, LAWRENCE E. (1950), *Fundamentals of Acoustics.* New York/ London.

LADEFOGED, PETER (1962a), *Elements of Acoustic Phonetics.* Edinburgh.

LADEFOGED, PETER (1962b), Sub-glottal activity during speech, *Proceedings of the Fourth International Congress of Phonetic Sciences*, Helsinki, 1961. The Hague.

228

REFERENCES

LADEFOGED, PETER (1963), Some physiological parameters in speech, *Language and Speech*, VI.

LADEFOGED, PETER (1964), *A Phonetic Study of West African Languages* (West African Language Monographs, I). Cambridge.

LADEFOGED, P., DRAPER, M. H. & WHITTERIDGE, D. (1958), Syllables and stress. *Miscellanea Phonetica*, III.

LAFON, J. C. (1961), *Message et phonétique*. Paris.

LAFON, J. C. (1964), *Le test phonétique*. Eindhoven.

La voix (Cours international de phonologie et de phoniatrie 2–7 mars 1953. Eds. A. Aubin & J. Tarneaud). Paris.

LAZICZIUS, J. (1961), *Lehrbuch der Phonetik*. Berlin.

LIBERMAN, ALVIN M. (1957), Some results of research in speech perception, *Journal of the Acoustical Society of America*, XXIX. Reprinted in Saporta (1961).

LIBERMAN, A. M., DELATTRE, P. & COOPER, F. S. (1952), The role of selected stimulus-variables in the perception of the unvoiced stop consonants, *American Journal of Psychology*, LXV.

LIBERMAN, A. M., COOPER, F. S., HARRIS, K. S. & MACNEILAGE, P. F. (1963), A motor theory of speech perception, *Proceedings of the Speech Communication Seminar*, Stockholm, 1962. Vol. II. (Royal Institute of Technology, Stockholm.)

LICKLIDER, J. C. R. (1952), On the process of speech perception, *Journal of the Acoustical Society of America*, XXIV.

LUCHSINGER, R. (1959), *Lehrbuch der Stimm- und Sprachheilkunde*, 2nd ed. Vienna.

LUCHSINGER, R. & ARNOLD, G. E. (1965), *Voice, Speech, Language: Clinical Communicology, its Physiology and Pathology*. Belmont, California.

McINTOSH, A., HALLIDAY, M. A. K. & STREVENS, P. D. (1964), *The Linguistic Sciences and Language Teaching*. London.

MACKEY, W. F. (1965), *Language Teaching Analysis*. London.

MALMBERG, BERTIL (1952), Le problème du classement des sons du langage, *Studia Linguistica*, VI.

MALMBERG, BERTIL (1953), *Sydsvensk ordaccent* (South-Swedish word accent). Lund.

MALMBERG, BERTIL (1955), The phonetic basis for syllable division, *Studia Linguistica*, IX.

MALMBERG, BERTIL (1959), Bermerkungen zum schwedischen Wortakzent, *Zeitschrift für Phonetik*, XII.

MALMBERG, BERTIL (1962a), Analyse instrumentale et structurale des faits d'accent, *Proceedings of the Fourth International Congress of Phonetic Sciences*, Helsinki, 1961. The Hague.

MALMBERG, BERTIL (1962b), Levels of abstraction in phonetic and phonemic analysis, *Phonetica*, VIII.

MALMBERG, BERTIL (1962c), Analyse linguistique et interprétation auditive, *Journal français d'oto-rhino-laryngologie*, XI, 6.

MALMBERG, BERTIL (1962d), *Phonetics* (translation of *La phonétique*). New York.

MALMBERG, BERTIL (1966), Stability and instability of syllabic structures, *Proceedings of the Fifth International Congress of Phonetic Sciences*, Münster, 1964. Basel/New York.

MALMBERG, BERTIL (1966a), Primitive syllabic structures, *Proceedings of the Fifth International Congress of Phonetic Sciences*, Münster, 1964. Basel/New York.

REFERENCES

MALMBERG, BERTIL (1966b), Stabilité et instabilité des structures phonologiques, *Phonation et phonétique*, ed. by A. Moles & B. Vallancien, Paris.

MALMBERG, BERTIL (1966c), *Nyare fonetiska rön och andra uppsatser i allmän och svensk fonetik.* Lund.

MALMBERG, BERTIL (1967a), *Lärobok i fonetik.* Lund.

MALMBERG, BERTIL (1967b), *La phonétique* ("Que sais-je?"). Paris.

MALMBERG, BERTIL (1967c), Structural linguistics and human communication, *Kommunikation und Kybernetik in Einzeldarstellungen,* II, 2nd ed. Berlin/Göttingen/Heidelberg.

MALMBERG, BERTIL (1967d), Réflexions sur les traits distinctifs et le classement des phonèmes. *To honour Roman Jakobson II,* The Hague/Paris.

MALMBERG, BERTIL (Ed.) (1968), *Manual of Phonetics.* Amsterdam.

MALMBERG, BERTIL (1968a). *Les nouvelles tendances de la linguistique. 2nd ed. Paris.*

MARTINET, ANDRÉ (1949), *Phonology as Functional Phonetics.* London.

MARTINET, ANDRÉ (1960), *Éléments de Linguistique Générale.*

MARTINET, ANDRÉ (1962), *A Functional View of Language.* Oxford.

MARTINET, ANDRÉ (1964), *Elements of General Linguistics.* (English translation by E. Palmer.) Oxford.

MATRAS, J.-J. (1960), *Le Son* ("Que sais-je?").

MEILLET, A. & COHEN, M. (1952), *Les langues du monde,* 2nd ed. Paris.

MEINHOF, CARL (1932), *Introduction to the Phonology of the Bantu Languages.* (Translation revised and enlarged by N. J. v. Warmelo.) Berlin.

MENZERATH, P. (1941). *Der Diphthong.* Bonn.

MENZERATH, P. & LACERDA, A. DE (1933), *Koartikulation, Steuerung und Lautabgrenzung.* Bonn.

MEYER, E. A. (1937), *Die Intonation im Schwedischen,* I. Stockholm. II, (1954). Stockholm.

MILLER, GEORGE A. (1951), *Language and Communication.* New York/Toronto/London.

MILLER, GEORGE A. & CHOMSKY, N. (1963). Finitary models of language users, in Luce, R. D., Bush, R. R., Galanter, E. (Eds.), *Handbook of Mathematical Psychology.* New York.

MOL, H. (1963), *Fundamentals of Phonetics,* I, *The Organ of Hearing.* The Hague.

MOLES, A. & VALLANCIEN, B. (1966), *Phonétique et phonation.* Paris.

MÖRNER, M. (1960), *The Voice Organs.* 20 illustrations in colour. Stockholm.

MORTON, J. & JASSEM, W. (1965), Acoustic correlates of stress, *Language and Speech,* VIII.

NEGUS, V. E. (1929), *The Mechanism of the Larynx.* London.

NEWMAN, S. (1947), Bella Coola I: Phonology, *International Journal of American Linguistics,* XIII.

O'CONNOR, J. D. & ARNOLD, G. F. (1961), *Intonation of Colloquial English.* Bristol.

PETERSON, GORDON & SHOUP, JUNE E. (1966), A physiological theory of phonetics, *Journal of Speech and Hearing Research,* IX.

PETERSON, GORDON & SHOUP, JUNE E. (1966a), The elements of an acoustic phonetic theory, *Journal of Speech and Hearing Research,* IX.

PIKE, KENNETH (1943), *Phonetics.* Ann Arbor, Mich. (Often reprinted.)

PIKE, KENNETH (1947), *Phonemics. A Technique for Reducing Languages to Writing.* Ann Arbor, Mich.

PIKE, KENNETH (1948), *Tone Languages.* Ann Arbor, Mich.

POTTER, R. K., KOPP, G. A. & GREEN, H. C. (1947), *Visible Speech.* New York. (Reprinted 1966.)

REFERENCES

Proceedings of the First International Congress of Phonetic Sciences (1932). Amsterdam.

Proceedings of the Second International Congress of Phonetic Sciences (1936), Eds. Jones, D. & Fry, D. B. Cambridge.

Proceedings of the Third International Congress of Phonetic Sciences (1939), Eds. Blancquaert, E. & Pée, W. Ghent.

Proceedings of the Fourth International Congress of Phonetic Sciences (1962), Eds. Sovijärvi, A. & Aalto, P. The Hague.

Proceedings of the Fifth International Congress of Phonetic Sciences (1966), Eds. Zwirner, Eberhard & Bethge, Wolfgang. Basel/New York.

PULGRAM, ERNST (1959), *Introduction to the Spectrography of Speech*. The Hague.

SAPORTA, S. (1961), *Psycholinguistics. A Book of Readings*. New York.

SAUSSURE, FERDINAND DE (1916), *Cours de linguistique générale*. Paris. (Often reprinted.)

SAUSSURE, FERDINAND DE (1960), *Course in General Linguistics*. (English translation by Wade Baskin.) London.

SCHATZ, C. D. (1954), The role of context in the perception of stops, *Language*, XXX.

SICHER, HARRY (1949), *Oral Anatomy*. St. Louis.

SIGURD, BENGT (1955), Rank-order of consonants, *Studia linguistica*, IX.

SKALIČKOVÁ, ALENA (1958), A contribution to the problem of the syllable, *Zeitschrift für Phonetik*, XI.

SMALLEY, WILLIAM A. (1962), *Manual of Articulatory Phonetics*. New York.

SMITH, SVEND (1954), Remarks on the physiology of the vibrations of the vocal cords, *Folia Phoniatrica*, VI.

SMITH, SVEND (1959), On pitch variation, *Folia Phoniatrica*, XI.

SOMMERFELT, ALF (1936), Can syllabic division have phonological importance? *Proceedings of the Second International Congress of Phonetic Sciences*. Cambridge.

SONESSON, BERTIL (1959), A method for studying the vibratory movements of the vocal cords, *Journal of Laryngology and Otology*, LXXXIII: 11.

SONESSON, BERTIL (1960), On the anatomy and vibratory pattern of human vocal folds, *Acta oto-laryngologica*, Supplement (1960). Lund.

STETSON, R. H. (1945), *Bases of Phonology*. Oberlin, Ohio.

STETSON, R. H. (1951), *Motor Phonetics*, 2nd ed. Amsterdam.

STEVENS, K. N. & House, A. S. (1955), Development of a quantitative description of vowel articulation, *Journal of the Acoustical Society of America*, XXVII.

STEVENS, S. S. (Ed.) (1951), *Handbook of Experimental Psychology*. New York.

STEVENS, S. S. & DAVIS, H. (1938), *Hearing: Its Psychology and Physiology*. New York.

STEVENS, S. S., LORING, J. G. C. & COHEN, DOROTHY (1955), *Bibliography on Hearing*. Cambridge, Mass.

STRAKA, GEORGES (1963), La division des sons du langage en voyelles et consonnes peut-elle être justifiée? *Travaux de linguistique et de littérature, publiés par le Centre de philologie et de littératures romanes de l'Université de Strasbourg*, I.

STRENGER, FOLKE (1956), Cephalometric X-ray analysis of the position of the mandible in the pronunciation of Swedish vowels, *Odontologisk revy*, VII.

STRENGER, FOLKE (1959), Methods for direct and indirect measurement of the sub-glottic air-pressure in phonation, *Studia linguistica*, XIII: 2.

231

REFERENCES

TERRACOL, J. & ARDOUIN, P. (1963), La morphologie et l'adaptation fonctionnelle du larynx, Supplement to *Journal français d'oto-rhino-laryngologie*, XII.

The Principles of the International Phonetic Association (1959). London (University College).

TOMATIS, ALFRED (1963), *L'oreille et le langage*. Paris.

TRUBETZKOY, N. S. (1962). *Grundzuge der Phonologie*, 3rd ed. Göttingen.

TRUBY, H. M. (1959), Acoustico-cineradiographic analysis with special reference to certain consonantal complexes, *Acta Radiologica*, Supplement 182. Stockholm [thesis, Lund].

ULDALL, ELISABETH T. (1960), Attitudinal meanings conveyed by intonation contours, *Language and Speech*, III.

ULDALL, ELISABETH T. (1964), Dimensions of meaning in intonation. In Jones (1964). London.

ULDALL, ELISABETH T. (1964a). Transitions in fricative noise, *Language and Speech*, VII.

UNGEHEUER, GEROLD (1962), *Elemente einer akustischen Theorie der Vokalartikulation*. Berlin/Göttingen/Heidelberg.

VALDMAN, ALBERT (Ed.) (1966), *Trends in Language Teaching*. New York/ St. Louis/San Francisco/Toronto/London/Sydney.

VALLANCIEN, B. (1960), Cinématique de la glotte en voix chantée, *Current Problems in Phoniatrics and Logopedics*, ed. F. Trojan. Volume I. Basel.

WARD, IDA C. (1936). *An Introduction to the Ibo Language*. Cambridge.

WELMERS, W. E. (1959). Tonemics, morphotonemics, and tonal morphemes, *General Linguistics*, IV.

WESTERMAN, D. & WARD, IDA C. (1933), *Practical Phonetics for Students of African Languages*. London.

WINCKEL, F. (1952), *Klangwelt unter der Lupe*. Berlin.

WISE, C. M. (1957), *Applied Phonetics*. Englewood Cliffs, N.J.

WISE, C. M. (1958), *Introduction to Phonetics*, Englewood Cliffs, N.J.

WOOD, A. B. (1955), *A Textbook of Sound*, 3rd ed. London.

WOOD, ALEXANDER (1940), *Acoustics*. London/Glasgow.

WUSTROW, F. (1957), Zur functionellen anatomie der stimmlippen, International Association of Logopedics and Phoniatrics, *Proceedings of the Tenth International Speech and Voice Conference*, Barcelona, 1956. Barcelona.

ZWIRNER, E. & K. (1933), *Phonometrische Forschungen*, I.

ZWIRNER, E. & EZAWA, K. (1966), Phonometrie I: Grundfragen der Phonometrie, 2nd ed. *Bibliotheca Phonetica*, 3. Basel/New York.

SUBJECT INDEX

English is not indexed, nor are names of languages simply
identifying the sources of words used as examples. References are
to pages; n. draws attention to a footnote.

SUBJECT INDEX

blade of tongue 41 f., 46, 66, 71 f., 94, 103, 110
blockage, as source of sound waves 51 ff., 105 ff., 114 f., 117, 118, 120
Bloomfield 187
borders of sounds; see transitions
Borel-Maisonny 126
boundaries, word, morpheme, etc. 139, 213 f.; of syllable 143 f.; of tone groups 154; signalling of 147
Brannon 182
breath group (∼ phrase) 31, 140, 145 f.
breathing; see respiration
breathy voice 35 f., 99
broad transcription 83
bronchi, bronchioles 30
buccal cavity; see mouth cavity
Bushman 122

Carney 130
cartilages of larynx 31 ff.
Catford 36
cavity resonators 55 f., 60 ff.
central, of vowels 86, 96 ff.
central release of plosive 106
central units/phonemes 209 f.
central vocoids 96 f.
Cherry, Halle & Jakobson 185
Chiba 59
child's learning of phonemes 208
Chinese (Mandarin) 149, 156, 205
clarinet 22 f.
classification of languages re stress 157
classification of speech sounds 74 ff., 140; of [ʔ, h] 83 f.; functional criteria in 84, 126; perceptual impressions in 102, 107 f., 126
click(s) 119, 121 f.; nasal ∼ 123
clipping of speech wave 173
close articulation 83 ff.
close, of vowels, vocoids 85 f., 94 ff.
closing articulation 42, 77, 140
coarticulation 69 ff., 127, 128 ff., 130 ff., 179, 194 f., 203; dialect norms in 131 f.
cochlea 162 ff.; action of 164 ff.
cochlea projection area = auditory projection area
combinations of sounds 125 ff.

communications engineering 10
commutation test 179, 193 ff.
compact, of speech sounds 126, 201
complementary distribution 191 f.
complex speech sounds 108, 110, 115; on pharyngeal airstream 117, 119; on oral airstream 120
complex wave 15 ff., 22
compound speech sounds 108 f., 115; on pharyngeal airstream 117, 119; on oral airstream 120
comprehension, of speech 186 f.
concept 1
configuration of vocal tract and formant frequencies 61 ff.
consonant(s) 83 f., 140; initial/final in syllable 143; and syllable structure 209 ff.; vowel adherence of 212; see also contoid(s)
consonant harmony 134
constriction, of vocal tract 42, 53, 59, 63 ff., 77 ff., 85, 199; in glottis 35; in fricatives 101 ff., 114, 118, 120; and formant frequencies 62 ff.; shape of, length of 102 f.; see also stricture
content 1 f.; correspondence with expression 146
context, in perception 178 ff.
contoid(s) 83 ff.; energy in 173; formants in 128 f.; identification of 129 f., 178 f.; [h] as ∼ 98; in syllables 140, 143; and adjacent vocoids 128 f., 143 f., 212; see also consonant(s)
contour, pitch/intonation 153 f., 205
contour systems, of tones 148
contrast 147; by stress 158 f.
conversion, of kinetic to acoustic energy 47, 49 ff., Chapter 6 *passim*; combinations of methods 91, 99 f., 108, 115; at two points 108 ff.
Cooper & Lotz 130
Cooper *et al.* 127
correlation, in identification 185 f.
Corti's organ 163, 164 ff.
coupling, of resonators 55, 61, 63; of nasal to oral tract 39, 68; of source and transmission line 58
crest of stricture, ∼ segment 77 f.
crico-arytenoid muscles 33 ff.
cricoid cartilage 31 ff.

234

voice quality, 58, 147, 206
voiced, voiceless, of sounds 38, 84, Chapter 6 *passim*, 198, 200 f.; in sonority 142
vowel(s) 57, 83, 140; intensity of 173; and resonance 198; in phoneme systems 206 f.; in syllables 209 ff.; see also vocoid(s)
vowel adherence 212
vowel harmony 134, 214
vowel quadrilateral 85 f.
vowel quality, determination of 39

whisper, glottal setting of 35, 97, 99
Wood 21
word 1 ff., 129 n., 139; and tones 148 ff.; and stress 156 f.; structures of 212 ff.
word group, in intonation 152 ff.

Xhosa (Khosa) 122 f.
X-ray recordings 65, 75, 77

Ward 149
wavelength 13
Welmers 152
Welsh 105
Wheatstone 58

Yoruba 109, 123, 149

Zulu 105, 122, 123

243